Diary of a Soldier

In the Mediterranean.

Diary of a Soldier

Hardy Parkhurst

The Pentland Press Limited
Edinburgh · Cambridge · Durham

First published in 1993 by
The Pentland Press Ltd.
1 Hutton Close
South Church
Bishop Auckland
Durham

ISBN 1 85821 038 0

Typeset by Elite Typesetting Techniques, Southampton.
Printed and bound by Antony Rowe Ltd., Chippenham.

To my dear wife for whom this diary was primarily written, and without whose initiative, determination, and encouragement it would never have seen the light of day; and to all with whom I served in the 2nd Battalion of the Fifth Fusiliers in the Second World War.

IN MEMORIAM
'THEIR NAME LIVETH FOR EVERYMORE'

Fifth Fusiliers – St George's Day greetings to all surviving
Royal Northumberland Fusiliers and in proud memory of
all who wore the red and white rose on this day in or out
of action in over 300 years of dedicated service to Crown
and country. '*Quo Fata Vocant*'.

Blaydon Races

I went to Blaydon Races
Twas on the first of June
Eighteen hundred and sixty four
On a summer's afternoon
I took the bus from Bambrough's
And she was heavy laden
Away we went along Collingwood Street
That's on the road to Blaydon.

Chorus
Oh me lads ye should ha' seen us gannin
Passin the folks upon the road just as they were stannin
There were lots of lad and lasses there
Aal with smilin faces
Gannin along the Scotswood Road
To see the Blaydon Races.

Contents

List of Illustrations

Introduction

I feel I should explain that the 'diary' which commences in March 1941 was, in fact, a resumption of one which I had been keeping for some years, mainly in connection with my bird-watching activities. This promptly ceased on my being called up on the 13th June 1940, for not only was there little opportunity for such private scribbling but I was, to say the least of it, somewhat overwhelmed by the raw military life of a barracks. Nevertheless, looking back, it is a gap in the journal which I very much regret as not only was it such a momentous period in the history of our country but it also covered a very traumatic time in our personal lives. The diary was resumed at Lymington in March 1941, when conditions made this possible, and at first was mainly concerned with bird notes.

Here it would perhaps be as well to say a little about my enforced military 'career'. I was called up to the Royal West Kents at Maidstone Barracks, and after a few weeks of training there was selected to attend 170 (M.G.) O.C.T.U. at Aldershot. I was commissioned into the Royal Northumberland Fusiliers, the Regiment of my choice, on the 11th January 1941. After a short spell at Fenham Barracks, Newcastle, I was posted to their 2nd Battalion at Lymington on the 8th February 1941, and stayed with that unit for the duration of the war.

The Battalion, which had been in France up till Dunkirk, was a Vickers M.G. unit and it subsequently went through two major reorganisations. The first was in the spring of 1943, when it had been left in the United Kingdom for this purpose by the 4th British Division on their proceeding to North Africa in early 1943. The Battalion transformed itself, with additional personnel, into three Support Groups, each consisting of a M.G. Company, a 4.2 Mortar Company and an A/A Company. Before this I had been a platoon commander, and then second-in-command of an

M.G. Company. On the reorganisation I was given the command of the Heavy Mortar Company in 3 Support Group, with the rank of Major.

After the Cassino battle the second reorganisation took place, and, having spent the previous five months as second-in-command of No. 1 Support Group, I was given the command of an enlarged Mortar Company which was divided, and the non-military terminology is hard to believe, into a Right Half and a Left Half, consisting of two platoons each. The Company was used to support Brigades on a Divisional front, and it was this unit I commanded from Cassino to Forli, after which the Battalion was taken out of the line for a rest in Palestine. It was *en route* there that it was diverted to Greece to assist in quelling the civil disturbances. And here, after fifteen months, I finished my war service, being demobilised on the 23rd March 1946.

Prologue

2.6.40   So June has come and I am still a civilian. This weekend has
          therefore been extra, and neither Dulcie nor I thought we
would enjoy it together. The weather has been really beautiful, and the
downs are now garbed with that summery fullness which gives them such
a dreamlike quality. Everywhere you go there is a warm smell of flowers,
clover especially. Hay and other crops are coming quickly now, and
accordingly the 'cornbunting' season is in full swing. I spent the greater
part of last night and today watching these extraordinary birds. But, my
God, it was pleasant to lie back and relax in the long grass and look at the
sky, or, better still, shut your eyes and forget everything. Forget the
nightmare of the Dunkirk evacuation; forget the dead and wounded; forget
that it seems likely that Italy is about to enter the war; in fact, forget the
barbarism of 1940. But not for long do you forget, for the sound of planes
overhead, and the muffled roar of gunfire on the French coast bring you
back to the bitter facts.

And how incredible it all does seem as you lie there in the warm grass
watching the clouds float across the sky. And, as you reflect on the hell-
pot of misery into which the world has been cast, you cannot help thinking .
that man, instead of using his mind to ennoble the race, has indeed abused
it to such an extent as to make us almost sub-normal. What sort of species
is this that uses up all the energy of successive generations in preparing to
destroy itself? For that is what man seems to be doing. That the German
community is responsible for this catastrophe is irrelevant; it is the fact
that in this year of 1940 men still seek to dominate one another. And the
question arises – when will the human race as a whole order itself with the
humility necessary for the continued existence of each separate community within the race?

6.6.40   Well, my number is up, for I was called upon today for
          service with the Territorial Army. I have to report next Thurs-
day, the 13th, to the Infantry Training Centre, Royal West Kent Regiment,
Maidstone. I have got so used to the idea of losing my freedom now that I
have almost given up thinking of the future. After all, Dulcie and I have
been married *over* a year now, and in these days one must consider oneself
lucky to have achieved such a record.

I know only too well when I get there how I shall miss Dulcie and all
that I associate with her. But I have (and she, too) a vast store of memories
to draw from, and although sometimes they are bound to make me sad,
they will, I know, give me strength and hope in the new and very distasteful life ahead. There is consolation, too, in the fact that we are not the only
couple thus separated in the midst of our happiness; indeed, so far our lot
has been extremely fortunate compared with others. But Dulcie in her
heart knows that I would gladly lay down my life, if in so doing I would in
some small measure have helped to rid the world of the threat of brutal
Nazi domination. For life today is not life at all; it is merely a living
death, which is nothing. War has always hit the womenfolk hardest for
they have to wait in dread suspense, while their menfolk act. Action, to a
certain extent, obliterates mental worry, while inaction only accentuates
it. And this last year has taught me that the love of a good wife, such as I
have, brings to man his greatest happiness. I used to think myself lucky in
having a wonderful mother, but never did I dream that one day I would
have as wonderful a wife.

9.6.40   So my last weekend as a civilian has gone by, and it has been a
          beautiful one. I cannot help wondering how long it will be
before I enjoy another in similar circumstances. But the bank have kindly
let me have the next three days off; thus, in reality I have got a short
holiday before joining up.

Since I last wrote I have been pursuing a favourite pastime of mine, i.e.
watching cornbuntings. The weather has been ideal. I could ask for nothing better to do in these last few days of mine than to go on the downs in
the hot sun, sit peacefully in the long grass and watch the bird life around
me. Each hour, each minute, has been so delightful that it has all seemed
like a dream. In such surroundings I have been able to forget the war and
my own immediate future.

10.6.40   So, a new phase in the mad history of 1940 is about to begin.
           Italy has declared that as from tomorrow she will consider
herself to be at war against the Allies. With devilish mathematical cun-
ning she (or was it Germany's decision?) has made this stroke when

France is in the gravest danger. Mr. Duff-Cooper, on the wireless tonight, said that this decision of Italy's would surely go down as the vilest act in history. Somehow this cowardly stab in the back is typical of Italy. Like a vulture hovering over a dying animal, she has bided her time to strike at the moment when the least resistance is likely to be offered.

But there I think Italy will be mistaken, for she will find to her sorrow that the Allies are far from that condition. Nevertheless, the Allied position at the moment is far from being rosy.

12.6.40   For the last time then, God only knows for how long, I sit down at my desk to write up these notes of mine. Time surges on and all human emotion is swept up in the seething foam. Helpless we are flung ever forward into the uncertain future. While I am in the Army I hope to be able to continue some form of diary, though what form it will take depends entirely on circumstances.

These last two days have been very beautiful. Dulcie and I spent the whole time in the country, walking, talking, and sitting in the sun. The hedges and fields are resplendent with summer flowers, the most delightful of all being the dog rose, the pale petals of which seemed to be shining out everywhere. The farmers have started their haymaking, and wherever we went the sweet smell of new-mown hay pervaded the air. The cornbuntings, many of their nests no doubt destroyed, sang continually, and they gave to the countryside an atmosphere of midsummer drowsiness, that intangible quality that belongs so much to this land of ours.

Yesterday we spent most of the day in Hodden valley, near Piddinghoe,* an old childhood haunt of mine; and it has not changed a whit since those carefree days. I remember how proud I was when I found my first magpie's nest there with six eggs.

Today we had a lovely walk from Firle down into Alfriston. While on the ridge I drank deeply of the familiar contours of my native land. I shall never forget these valleys and hills as long as I live. The long, happy days they have given me are too many to count and I cannot be too grateful that I was born amongst them. In Alfriston we had a lovely lunch at 'The Star', afterwards taking the bus to Exeat bridge.

A sentry stopped us going down the Cuckmere, so we decided to go to West Dean. This is a beautiful little village tucked right under the downs; just outside we found a secluded spot where we sunbathed for a while. Cornbuntings seemed very numerous there, and in better days I must

---

*Small village near Newhaven.

certainly pay a visit to this place. We finished up the day by having a good tea at 'The Golden Galleon', a favourite rendezvous of ours.

Well, everything passes, even the best and happiest of days, and now my future, to a great extent, passes out of my control. It will be hard indeed to be separated from Dulcie, but we must, and will, adapt ourselves to the inevitable. To the good old life I must say goodbye, to the new – well, I must just grit my teeth and hope for the best.

First leave after commission, January 1941.

England and Scotland

31.3.41   Decided to resume diary. 5th Corps Conference. Montgomery his usual self.

2.4.41   Demonstration at Larkhill. Co-operation of Infantry, M.G. and Artillery in attack and defence using live rounds. Very instructive but it was bloody cold up there. I was to have gone on leave on Sunday, but Roberts, damn him, told me tonight that I'm on a gas course next week. How uncertain everything is nowadays. Dulcie will be so upset and I know how excited she is even at the thought of my leave; I think the Major could get me off this course if he really tried. I was rather upset when he told me and, to work it off a bit, I went for a walk in the rain. It helped a lot, actually.

3.4.41   A good day – pleasantly spent, and very little work. I had a good walk round the lake, where I watched a male reed bunting quite closely. The reed bunting's snatches of song seem to vary quite considerably. Got back and heard to my delight that I had been struck off the gas course and my leave is still *on*.

4.4.41   Dulcie sounded so excited on the phone last night – I pray that the fates will not upset our plans, but it is difficult to plan more than a day ahead nowadays. Bob Gray was largely responsible for getting me off.

While supervising bayonet practice I had a delightful constrasting experience – for the first time this year I heard the willow warbler in a wood just near us. I felt a great impulse to go out and watch it, and it brought home the futility of war. It was like seeing the blue sky from a prison window. However, I mustn't grumble, these billets are in such beautiful surroundings that even C.B. means nothing.

1

A very new soldier and wife, June 1940.

5.4.41   Leave tomorrow! Had a very unmilitary Saturday; in fact I
           seem to have spent most of it bird watching and walking. It was
a beautiful day.

6.4.41   Home again after three months – it seems unbelievable. On the
           way home I saw some of the terrible bombed area around
Southampton.

7.4.41   How lovely to wake up and feel that there is no necessity to get
           out of bed by any particular time. White sheets after three
months of blankets had the effect of making me even more incapable of
rising than usual. But Dulcie was up and about early, making tea, with
tentative suggestions about getting up and going out into the country
somewhere. It was bright and sunny early but clouded up later, cold and
grey with northeast wind. Eventually, we decided on a walk round
Warningore wood. The warm fire at home after the cold wind sent me to
sleep after tea, but I roused myself and walked down to the village.

11.4.41   Had a grand day with Dulcie at Hook Estate, Chailey. The
           primroses were simply magnificent, and evidently it is a great
year for them. We also found a few cowslips.

15.4.41   My last whole day. What a terrible reflection on our present-
           day existence – or is it? Has it made us realise how precious
and how beautiful life is, has it taught us to live through a day, that to let it
slip by unnoticed, unappreciated and without a feeling of intense gratitude, implies a terrible dull attitude towards the wonder of living? Of
course, leave prompted such a question naturally, but I suppose it should
be thus every day, wherever we are, in Service or not, but it is difficult
sometimes when we are away from our homes and our wives. However,
today Dulcie and I went to our Streat wood to recapture the moods of our
first discovery last year. It was just the same – peaceful and beautiful.
Even the willow tit nesting again in that old oak stump. In the evening
near 'Benallan',* I found a blackbird's nest with three eggs. Oh, Dulcie,
how long will it be before we can always go for a walk in the evening ·
together? – how lonely you must be these dark days.

28.4.41   Started on a wretched gas course, one of the most boring
           subjects I've ever come across. In the evening heard a nightin-
gale in the garden quite near the greenhouses. Blackcaps, I'm sure, will
soon be nesting.

29.4.41   Second day of the terrible gas course. Granny Greaves is going
           through it in miserable parrot fashion. It was a glorious day

---

* Name of home.

and horrible being indoors. However, during the short morning break I did find a chiffchaff's nest half built.

3.5.41   Gas course and exam over, thank goodness. Bird watching all afternoon and evening. Another chiffchaff's nearly built (how late they are this year), and another bullfinch's found. Saw nuthatches displaying and the male was feeding the female.

18.5.41   With Dulcie staying down here with Mrs. Harvey (daughter of Pylewell Estate Game Keeper), my evenings and spare time have been very full. I've managed to get out quite a lot and, except for one night, have also slept out. The weather has been grand and the last few days very hot, although tonight a break seems imminent. We had the General's inspection last Wednesday and the preparation for that took up an incredible amount of time. Next week we have a three-day scheme coming off which is a nuisance as Dulcie is staying on for another fortnight. Already she has found a number of flowers for her annual records. We had a glorious cross-country bike ride from Boldre through Dillon Gardens and Dillon farm to the Brockenhurst wood. Some parts of it reminded me of the Lake District. Today was very lovely and we cycled to Bucklers Hard, then Beaulieu, passing through to Peverley and in the woods around there we spent most of our day. Tree pipits and wood warblers nest in the area and I saw several redstarts.

28.5.41   These last few days have been exciting ones for the Navy, the *Hood* being sunk by a lucky shot (or unlucky) in the magazine. The Navy took swift revenge, however, and yesterday the *Bismarck* was sunk 400 miles off Brest after a terrific chase by naval units, helped to a large extent by the Fleet Air Arm. The position in Crete, however, is desperate and seems a matter of touch and go as to whether we shall be able to hold out much longer.

Dulcie goes back on Saturday and I've managed to get twenty-four hours off. 'Jehu' is taking us in his car, which is a blessing (or is it?)! It has been so good to have her here and to go out together in the evenings and, when possible, cycling.

3.6.41   Well, since I last wrote in these pages I've managed to get home to 'Benallan' for a weekend. 'Jehu' was going down to Hailsham so it was a good opportunity for Dulcie to get back to Lewes without the arduous business of a railway journey, and I went with her. The garden was looking grand and Kingston and the downs looked so green and beautiful – refreshing after the flat country of the forest. It was a lovely evening too and I went for a short stroll along Juggs Hill while Dulcie was cooking the supper. For a brief few moments I felt absolutely out of the atmosphere of the war and military life, reflecting that I was leading a curious unlike-me life. Here in Kingston* and its surrounds I felt as though I was once again in the proper surroundings of my normal life. It was right to be looking at Carr's Farm and Kingston Bottom, at Firle Beacon and Caburn. It was right to be looking at my familiar marshes with the two bumps and the cattle in the deep summer green grass. There would be sedge warblers and reed buntings there, snipe too. God, how I longed to be really free to go down there again in the evenings. Turning back the scene was even richer, the village looking so warm in the evening sun and shades of green in the trees. The old part of the village is hardly visible from here at this time of the year, so thick is the foliage on the trees. You can just see the church nestling securely in the trees and there is something lovely about it. Best of all, though, was to see from the hillside our own small show of flowers and the smoke coming from the chimney, and to know that when I got in I would see Dulcie. Oh God, what is this thing that has so darkened the world and our existence on this potential paradise? Such fleeting happiness is a wonderful and gratifying experience nowadays and one has to store it up to offset the continuous misery and hardships. It's not so much as you yourself experience but rather the unhappiness and misfortunes of others that you hear and read about. In a way, Dulcie was happy to be back. My leave should come along in July, so, all being well, it won't be long before I'm home again.

The withdrawal from Crete and the rationing of clothes were two bad items on Sunday's news. Everything comes to an end, and I was up at 5.00 a.m. Monday morning and off at 6.00 with 'Jehu'. We got back to Lymington just after 9.00 and I was soon on my way to Netheravon with my platoon.

6.6.41   Up till today the weather has been disappointing for June. We've had a lot of rain and the atmosphere has been thundery. Thunder seems quite a strange sound after AA guns and bombs.

How funny to look back on our childhood and think how frightened we were of thunder storms? Today, thought, after a dull start, there has been a clear and nice invigorating air and the sun has shone out of an azure sky.

Yesterday June was back with us in all its glory. In the morning (with the extra hour we see quite clearly these days) everything was soaking with the heavy dew. Then the sun burst through and the dew threw back the light in tiny white sparkles. The warmth drew out the scent of all

---

* Small village near Lewes, East Sussex.

things growing – trees, flowers, shrubs, grasses, weeds – everything, in fact. The chestnuts are at their best at this time of the year, and with the sun lighting up their leaves and chandeliers, they look magnificent. Go into the wood at this time and, if you have not been there for some time, you cannot help being amazed by the riotous uprising of the undergrowth. It is a tangled mass of living green, and it seems to throw back the heat of the sun at you. Garden warblers, whitethroats, nightingales and willow warblers are everywhere revelling in it. The zenith of Spring is here. Come out of the wood again and the hot benevolent sun beats down on your face; you feel it in your hair, warm and friendly. Such has it been today, too good for us warring mankind who don't have time to appreciate it.

After the defeat in Crete reports come in that German infiltration into Syria has begun. They occupy Syrian aerodromes – are we going to watch them consolidate or are we going to take the matter into our own hands, regardless of French caution?

12.6.41   The Range-Finding Course at S.A.S. Netheravon is pleasant, no rushing about, and we have an excellent Instructor in Q.M.S., I. Blake, who is decidedly humorous. It is interesting to watch how he instructs not only by his tongue, but also by his hands. I wonder what it is like to be an Instructor here? I expect one could be very comfortable, but, on the other hand, it could probably become extremely monotonous.

Ever since Hitler conquered Poland he has been massing troops on the Russian frontier. In the last fortnight or so Russo-German tension has increased tenfold, until the last few days, when from various sources the tension has almost reached breaking point. It seems that Hitler has been making fantastic demands on Stalin (at least that is all we can assume) and that worthy gentleman has not come up to scratch. What are Germany's reasons? Is it shortage of raw materials and the longed-for prize of the wheatfields of the Ukraine, or is it to dismember the potential enemy so as to clear his rear, and then throw all his weight against us? Anyway, whatever it is I hear that it was announced on the wireless today that Germany has declared war on Russia. The one o'clock news ought to be interesting. Perhaps his ultimate object of attacking Russia is more subtle, and he may represent himself as being the defender of the world against Bolshevism. What will we do, I wonder, not that we have the resources to do much anyway.

What a swift-changing war this it. Here we are, hardly a year after the collapse of France, fighting Vichy troops in Syria; Germany has conquered Europe, the Balkans, and now she attacks Russia. How will Turkey be affected? What about American reaction? The Hun is gathering a dangerous momentum and somehow, somewhere, he must be stopped.

29.6.41   Another week has gone by and here I am, back at Pylewell. The Course dragged towards the end, as all Courses do, but there is no doubt that this Range-finding Course could be cut down by at least two days. Showing us the indoor apparatus was absolutely absurd in wartime, especially to field units. However, we got out quite a lot and that was compensation to some extent.

It was a long and tedious journey back yesterday as I anticipated. Southampton station is in a terrible mess, having been hit with a land mine and a bomb.

I had hoped for leave shortly, but my hopes were short-lived as I found on my return that C. Coy was moving on the 3rd July to take up defence of aerodromes on Salisbury Plain. I believe we are going under canvas. I shall be sorry to leave the lovely grounds of Pylewell, but I must be grateful to have been here at all.

Russia is putting up a much more gallant fight than many thought her capable; she still has an intact line and has caused heavy losses on the enemy. It is too early yet to forecast how it will end, but another week may well tell.

10.8.41   During a week away with Dulcie, Great Britain and Russia made an 'alliance'; something of great political and military importance always seems to take place when I am on leave. Time seems to be passing at a frenzied rate nowadays. Someone has said that this is a platoon commander's war, and I have discovered that this phrase applies not only to actual fighting but also to soldiering in England. Never before in the history of these Islands have we had so many troops stationed here during war. They are here for two main reasons:-

1. We are still on the defensive.
2. The reorganization and training of such a large civilian army after Dunkirk has taken time and it is a mercy that we have been able to take advantage of it. Production, too, is only now getting into full sway.

The very nature of this second World War would naturally involve keeping more troops stationed here than in previous wars because of the threat of airborne landings. All this presents special psychological and practical problems. The main psychological problem is morale.

Troops get exceedingly 'browned off' when, while they are continually training and rushing about the countryside on schemes, they read of the continual work of the Navy, Air Force and Middle East Armies. To a large extent they feel out of it, and when they feel that they begin to feel bored and lose interest. To keep them interested and happy is one of the main problems. They naturally realise the advantages of being in England, and I think personally they should be allowed, as far as is possible, to reap the benefits of these advantages, because the soldier never knows when he is for other climes. Regular leave, evening passes, concerts, visits to other arms and services, even factories, all help a man to realise what is being done; all this gives variety to his training programme. I do believe that a man can have too much training and that to take him away from it for a while refreshes him and keeps his interest up in his special arm. Under canvas these problems become even more acute, but with a certain amount of good humour (and good weather) they can be overcome by certain easy devices.

26.8.41   I am now on a 'Junior Leader's Course', and my immediate surroundings present rather an extraordinary change after Danebury and its downland. Here at Parkstone I am in a modern beach hotel called 'Sandbanks', and with a hotel mattress, hotel chairs, I am in extreme comfort, a pleasant change from wet camp life, but I miss my M.G. platoon work. The Course, unfortunately, deals chiefly with infantry work, but it will no doubt be of great value to me later. It is Monty's Binge School, full of P.T. and Assault Courses, and in the lecture hall hang all the 5 Corps Crests. I stay here till the 25th September, then soon after comes an Army scheme, then concentrations at Netheravon. But when will I get leave, that is the burning question. It seems ages since I was last home and I'm hoping to go at least after concentrations, if not before. Gilling came back from Battalion Headquarters to take over the platoon and I was glad of that as he seems a conscientious bloke. I think that by the time I get back we ought to be in huts, which will be as well. How long we are staying on attachment, I don't know, but rumour has it that we'll be back at Pylewell on 1st November.

As for greater events, the Russians are still putting up a magnificent resistance to the German onslaught, and losses on both sides must be colossal. I wonder if Hitler is so sure of himself as he was at the outset. He certainly has food for thought. The work of the Russian guerillas must be having a devastating effect on German morale, as indeed must general conditions of ground, the 'scorched earth' policy, etc.

Churchill and Roosevelt have met at sea, and rough and ready peace aims laid down in a declaration. Other practical points, too, must have been decided in the Staff Conference. Yesterday came the news that British and Russian troops had crossed the frontier into Iran. How now the Turkish enigma?

10.10.41   The Course ended on 19th September, much to everyone's relief, and I got home for a long weekend. I went back to Danebury on the Sunday night and, much to my relief, found all my kit had got back safely, although even then there had been some hitch with the truck going to Brockenhurst, much to my annoyance. I found that Gilling had left the same day to go on the Course I had just finished. I would have liked to have seen him to put me in the picture, if nothing else. The weather was perfect and I thoroughly enjoyed the tent life after the garish seaside hotel. Actually, I had the only tent as the men had gone into Nissen huts. I soon learnt that we are to strike camp on 27th September, going straight on to BUMPER* and then returning to Lymington. This left little time for training during the few remaining days, but in between maintenance and packing stores, etc., we managed to do some. Everyone enjoyed the scheme, the weather was perfect and, despite the tiring journeys (mostly night), we managed to get through without serious mischief.

Meanwhile, outside our own little affairs, the battle in Russia seems to be getting grimmer, with Leningrad and Odessa hanging on, and counter attacks in the centre of the line, which, except for the Ukraine, was fairly straight. But now Hitler has put in a massive offensive in the centre and he is not much more than 100 miles from Moscow. The whole situation is grave but the Russians fight on; such names as Brynish, Vynasma and Orel (lately evacuated) figure largely in communiqués.

14.10.41   Up till today the weather has been glorious this leave, an echo almost of our July weather. We had a splendid weekend and a memorable one, for it was the first time that Percy,* John* and I had been together since the war began, and also the first time we had been together as married men.

Dulcie and I had two expeditions up the Blackcap valley, one to pick spindleberries, another blackberries, which were still numerous. Despite a lot of ploughing, the downs are much the same as in pre-war days, except perhaps that fences are more numerous. Large areas of hawthorn and scrubland have been uprooted and ploughed, and yesterday, when we walked over the ridge to Falmer, we could see to what extent this had been done above the Blackcap valley.

---

*Scheme.
*Brothers.

Last night we had our first winter fire, not absolutely essential perhaps but nonetheless delightful, homely and friendly. Snug we sat down to a game of solo, our thoughts far from war and the grim Russian struggle. What food for thought there, for what of the people of Brynish, Vynasma and Orel? Where were they tonight? Had they food, shelter, warmth? It was a grim contrast but we can only suppose that the big-wigs are seeing that all that can be done is being done to help Russia. A major offensive in the west is highly unlikely yet, for we have not the equipment, nor the air superiority necessary for such a vast operation.

We turned on the news and, instead of paying attention to it, were soon sitting up all ears, for in the pauses between the different items came a mysterious voice with a good English accent making remarks as 'Oh rot', 'lies', according to what the announcer had said. Although we had heard so much of the Russian ghost voice on the German radio, I think this latest piece of German propaganda, copied though it is from the Russians, came as a complete surprise to the complacent British news-listening public. I think its first effect will be a stimulating one; for it brings the enemy into each home, it makes one more 'enemy' conscious, and that is a great thing in wartime, when too often the enemy is much too impersonal a being. Later, no doubt, if the Germans continue it, it will be laughed at just as Haw-Haw was. The voice was on the Forces programme and seemed to have jammed the Home programme so that people would switch over. What counter action the B.B.C. will take remains to be seen – or heard.

29.10.41   When I got back from a combined Operations course in Scot-land, I learnt that the battalion was going overseas and that embarkation leave was to start on Tuesday, 28th October. There was, of course, much speculation as to our destination, but all that we know definitely at the moment is that we are being issued with ARCTIC kit. Discussion in the mess as to probable places have so far produced Iceland, Norway, Russia and the Caucasus. Personally, after thinking it over, I rather favour Iceland, although, of course, I do not know for certain if other divisions are involved. The 4th Division is certainly going, and if this is the only one concerned then it seems quite possible that we are relieving troops in Iceland. Norway and Russia seem highly improbable to me; however, who can tell?

Dulcie, naturally enough, was terribly upset when I told her over the phone that I was coming home on embarkation leave. It had come absolutely unexpectedly to both of us, and I'm sure we had thought of my going overseas as a very distant improbability, and had consequently hardly ever mentioned it, and indeed why should we have done?

Nowadays it is no good living in the future, and we have always enjoyed our happy times while we could.

However, here I am at 'Benallan' on embarkation leave till next Tuesday. Dulcie is much calmer now that I am at home with her and now that we know it is not the Middle East. She is also coming back to Lymington with me to stay with Mrs. Harvey again, so this leave loses a lot of that sad and horrible finality. Rumour has it that we have to be ready to sail by about 20th November, so that will give us at least another fortnight. Nevertheless, it will be a worrying time for Dulcie until she hears where I'm going.*

1.11.41   I suppose of all leaves embarkation leave would go more quickly than any other, not only because of its special significance but also because there is so much to do. However, the greater part of our time has been spent together in our dear home. Shopping, naturally, has called for a good deal of attention. At a time like this one has to consider necessities first and luxuries last.

Gloves and underclothes have been first on the list; boots I hope to get from the Quartermaster on repayment and I shall be highly annoyed if this doesn't come off. Such other things like shaving soap, razor blades, notebooks, writing pads, aspirin and a whisky flask have been well to the fore. The only thing is that I hope I shall be able to pack it all. I have bought a new pipe – a Parker Veteran – which I hope will do me good service. So far I have managed to get eight ounces of tobacco and I hope I will be able to get it wherever we go. I still plump for Iceland and, in fact, have gone to the extent of studying Ernest Lewis' list of birds as observed in his Gyr-Falcon expedition to Iceland. However, his was a summer trip and what a winter list would look like I don't know. Curiously enough, the last volume of the *Handbook of British Birds* has just been completed and Dulcie gave me it today. This includes the terns and gulls, species I am likely to see a lot of, especially if I am far north next summer. Unfortunately, I have no reliable small pocket bird book which would be most useful for reference. However, as this is no ornithological picnic I may not get as much chance to study birds as I hope to, but who knows? The fortunes of war are indeed extraordinary though, and it may be that instead of looking for Germans through my glasses, I may be watching arctic terns.

3.11.41   And so inevitably the last complete day at 'Benallan' has arrived. Thank God Dulcie is coming down to Lymington with me, as it makes it easier to leave home with her. In the Army one gets used

---

*Later learnt to have been Murmansk.

to saying goodbye to the luxuries of home life, but when you are on embarkation leave and not knowing your foreign destination, or when you will get back to England again, then the break is not easy. But, if it is hard for us, it is even harder for the dear wives or mothers left behind in surroundings full of rich memories.

4.11.41   It was lovely defying the fates by bringing Dulcie back to Lymington with me. The journey went smoothly and to schedule, and at Lymington I managed to hire a respectable bicycle for a week. Mrs. Harvey welcomed us as warmly as ever, and we had scrambled eggs for tea. Afterwards I cycled to Pylewell to find out the latest news but really there was a scarcity of it.

28.11.41   Three weeks back at Pylewell have gone by and so much seems to have happened. Dulcie went back on Thursday after being here three weeks, three lovely weeks when I cycled to 'Bealah', Mrs. Harvey's home, every evening and stayed with her till the morning. It was so peaceful and homely sitting and talking in front of the fire, that sometimes it almost felt as if we were home, and I was in a peacetime job. We had a lot to talk about with various rumours flying round almost every day about the battalion move, but the most discussed, and the most exciting thing was the coming of Nicolas, for Dulcie was now pretty sure she was pregnant. A Lymington doctor, although he would not guarantee it, was very confident too. By the time she left I believe she was a hundred per cent certain, although so amazed were we that we kept asking ourselves if it could be true. If so, it certainly was like a miracle, coming as it did in this difficult time of separation, as Dulcie was so anxious to have a baby if I went abroad. My own reactions about Nicolas were at first those of amazement and incredulity, then when I became more certain, I felt a profound gratitude.

A few days ago the C.O. spoke to the Battalion and told us we were moving to Aldershot. Actually, this is our last night at Pylewell for we move early tomorrow. We are to come out in G.H.Q. Reserve. The C.O. said that the original expedition seemed to have been put into abeyance, but that it was still on the cards that, being fully mobilized, we may be the first to go abroad if needed. Imagine how thankful Dulcie was when she heard this. It seemed almost like a second miracle in three weeks, but who can tell one's luck? So soon after we get to Aldershot, 'C' Company go to Inverary as was the plan before all the embarkation business started. Let us hope that regular leave starts again soon.

Just recently I've had rather a big personal surprise for Bob said I was to be Second-in-Command of 'C' Company, with the rank of Acting

Captain. From a financial point of view it's an absolute godsend, especially with Nicolas coming, but I hate going over people senior to me.

Our offensive in Libya has been on about a week now, and the battle still seems confused. The Germans are slowly making ground towards Moscow.

13.12.41   A lot of things have happened to the world in the last few days.

Japan has declared war on the U.S.A. and has made several landings in various Island groups. She has also done much damage by aerial bombardment. We have lost the Prince of Wales and the Repulse, sunk by Japan, a heavy blow. Germany and Italy have followed in Japan's wake and also declared war on the U.S.A., so literally in a few hours the war has become a world war, a war of vast strategical complications needing perfect co-operation and masterly skill in its direction. Perhaps the most cheering time of late is the wonderful Russian offensive on the Moscow front. The Germans seem to be in retreat in several sections and their losses have been enormous.

16.1.42   Well, 1941 has come to its end with the world situation perhaps a little brighter than a year ago. The Russians are still advancing on practically the whole front, and we have driven Rommel to the borders of Tripolitania, where he is making a firm stand. The sting is in the Far East where the Japs are tightening the ring round the naval base of Singapore. It is taking some time for America to get on her feet but Churchill has been over there and had conversations with the President, and presumably plans have been worked out for some combined effort. We now await his return and a reassuring word or two from him.

20.1.42   What a peaceful restful leave this is, after a fortnight's Brigade training in Inverary. There has really been no incentive to go out since the weather has proved rather a stumbling block. There has been a fair amount of snow – a heavy fall last night, and that, coupled with the fact that Dulcie has a cold, is sufficient excuse to take full advantage of the comforts of home life. And, indeed, how better could one spend one's · leave. All the time at Inverary I was comparing the drab hutment life of our stay there with the friendly, book-filled, rug-floored rooms of home. And so it has been a quiet round-the-fire leave, reading, listening to the wireless, talking about Nicolas, talking about the future, sometimes just ruminating. Somehow I have been put in mind of the early winter of 1940 before I was in the Army. God, how happy a man can be in his own home if he so elects. Two years have passed since that hard winter of 1940 and much has happened since. Many Nations have fallen, many men and women have lost their lives in the grimmest of circumstances in the greatest of causes. Now, in 1942, the whole world is under arms, one half fighting for the light, the other half striving to plunge everything into abysmal darkness. The death lock has been joined. What shall I be recording in the early winter of 1944? It is too much to hope that victory will be ours, and that the fight for the peace will have begun?

Churchill is back, and Halfaya has surrendered, but the Japs are only seventy-five miles north of Singapore. The Russians are still slowly carrying out their avowed annihilation of the German Army. Singapore is vital. Either we had not sufficient men and equipment to defend it more strongly, in which case it was a question of priorities, or there was a maldistribution. A debate is coming off in the House which no doubt will clarify the position. The Far East has become a definite diversion.

29.1.42   And so once again on a moonlit Sunday night I said 'good-bye' to Dulcie and home. It was a grim and impassionate business. It has to be. We hate it bitterly; what lovers don't? We know each other's unspoken thoughts, they are best unsaid. If Hitler had caused no more misery than the separation of millions of people from their loved ones, he would deserve a ghastly death. What fate then is good enough for him and his clique now? It is impossible to say.

So once again back to the negative existence of Army life; negative because it is a dead life. We can be enthusiastic about the ends to be achieved, but can we be so enthusiastic about the soul-destroying means to these ends? One of Hitler's greatest crimes against humanity is that he has created a great wastage of living hours, days, months, years, and has thereby caused a great mass of energy to be maldirected. And all the time we are very conscious of this energy-wasting process. We do not live in the Army; we exist. To a great extent our individuality and our freewill is merged and lost because of the exigencies of the military necessity of some sort of unified control. We give ourselves up, so to speak, *in toto.* Freedom of action must remain in cold storage, and the ensuing frustration causes a profound mental conflict. The reaction of the individual must vary in degree according to the strength of will and intellect of that individual. But, nevertheless, the sum total of this great mental depression can have a very dangerous and damaging effect on morale. The outward signs of this inward affliction are now always manifest but of necessity there must be a tremendous loss of efficiency and power. In the Army we refer to this stage as being 'browned off'. It represents and reflects the daily drudgery of a soldier's life in Britain today. The soldier knows he has to prepare for war, to be able to use the weapons under his command, but is his training sufficiently enlightened, sufficiently vital enough to enforce in him the spirit, the mental energy, to overcome the sad 'browned-off' state of mind? I think it is not. I think that the present-day system of training is so antiquated, so unbattle-like that it has a direct bearing on the present-day mood of many soldiers. Familiarity breeds contempt, but worse, it breeds indifference.

7.2.42   Churchill, after the Tuesday debate in the House, warned us to expect more bad news, more set-backs. He maintained that he was perfectly justified in giving priority of supplies to Russia and the Middle East, adding that at that time they were the main theatres of war, whereas we were still at peace with Japan. There was no doubt that we had tried a big bluff on the Japs which unfortunately hadn't worked out. French collaboration in Indo-China was, of course, a grave set-back from the start; this enabled Japan to build up supply bases and to assemble large concentrations of troops for their attack on Malaya. Japanese fifth column activity, too, must have now reached a very high state of perfection, enabling them to get much valuable information. In war someone is always trying to find someone else to take the can, and Churchill said that if any blame was attachable, he himself was entirely responsible. His set-backs came sooner than most expected. We have been driven out of Malaya, and Singapore is now in the throes of a siege. The news of H.M.S. *Barham* being sunk on 25th November has only recently been released. The Navy is having a hard time. Perhaps, however, most surprising and most disappointing of all is Rommel's energetic counter-attack, which has so far brought him back to El Gonzola. With fresh reinforcements he sprung from the defensive to attack the Eighth Army when they themselves must have been in a highly disorganised state after the confused advance. The Russians, in the grimmest weather conditions, continue to advance, but they seem to be meeting stronger German resistance. It must be the Russians' aim to prevent the Hun from preparing for a vast Spring offensive.

Our move to N. Ireland turned out, after all, to be a clever ruse to cover the landings of American troops there. With the help of American planes and pilots we ought to be able to step up the bombing of Germany to a great extent, although weather conditions recently have put a stop to a great deal of this work. It would be interesting (though perhaps disheartening) to know our shipping position, for this is bound up very closely with any possible invasion we may make.

8.2.42   I have often wondered how difficult it is to put a certain impulse into practice. For instance, in these terrible tragic years of the history of civilisation, there is so much to tell, so much to record, so great a fund of the human story, that it seems a terrible crime to let it all slip by without putting some of it in book form, enabling the reader at a later date to see how things seemed to our minds at the time. Histories will be written and compiled, sure enough, but histories are normally such impersonal affairs. What I think is wanted is something written now that will reflect the day-to-day life and thoughts of the people at the time. I know it is being done, of course, but going back to the question of impulse, I see and feel so much of life today, that I feel very strongly at times an urge to put it into writing; yet in what form? And have I the ability? The most difficult question to me is the central theme of such a work.

17.2.42   The mad wind of war has hurled ugly laughter at us during these past few days. We have suffered the greatest military defeat since France, for Singapore has fallen, after only seven days siege. Think of it. Singapore, the stronghold and key naval position of the Far East, has fallen after SEVEN days. Why, we ask? Food, water, and petrol were short, they say. When the sad history of that short siege throws more light on the matter, will that be the only reason given? Obviously not. For then we shall hear of lack of weapons, lack of foresight, lack of air support, and, in fact, general unpreparedness. Look at our losses – 60,000 men, nearly four Divisions, and much war material. It will take many lives and much time to get back what we have lost, even if we are strong enough to do it. Meanwhile, the Japs push on. Burma, Sumatra, Java, all are threatened. Already the great oil centre of Palembong has fallen to the Japs. Will ever the great still pond of British complacency be stirred to wrath and action, or are the ripples of each new defeat going to settle down until real defeat comes, and then it will be too late. This is a war to the death, and there are never two winners in war. We either win or lose, and at the moment we are losing bit by bit, a very dangerous and paralysing process, for the position in the Middle East is none too strong, and there are certainly no prospects of any immediate victory there. To add to the list (realistic and not defeatist) comes the news that the *Scharnhorst*, *Gneisnau*, and *Prince Eugen* have sailed through the Straits of Dover, and got away with it. But negative criticism is so easy, especially in a time of trial and defeat. I know only too well that at heart we are not a warring nation. We hate the regimentation of our men and women for fighting, but we know it to be essential to beat Hitler. It is easy to list our misfortunes in a spirit of despondency, but I do not do so, I mean only to show the terrific task ahead of us, both mental and physical, in the hope that it may instil an urgency to meet any hazard.

1.3.42   If one was to write down the day-to-day life of present day
wartime existence, not only events but retrospective reflections
and reactions, what a volume it would be, and probably, if anything, on the
morbid side. Yet it might be of great interest in better days to come, as
come, I hope, they will. There is so much happening around me these days,
so much to think about, small personal things most of them, no doubt, not
generally significant, but rather genuine reflections and worries, if you
like. I don't think we talk enough about things, but brood inwardly. It is a
bad thing to do this. It makes for fear, for everything becomes an unknown
quantity and is enlarged unnecessarily. We should speak our minds more.
How better to get rid of a complex than by discussing it and reducing it to
simplicity. Discussion carried out in the right way is refreshing and invigorating to a degree. But no, we hunch ourselves up, talk commonplaces,
and lose thereby a great means of expression and fulfilment. Why do I
write this? Perhaps I am a victim, perhaps I see lost opportunities. It's easy
to talk like that, but what to discuss? 'Life,' I say. Here we are living
(rational) beings and we must assume, of course, here for a reason. Up to
date we have made poor use of our opportunities. We are at the moment
fighting that we may live again in the future. But what for? The subject is
endless and endlessly interesting. There is much to be done, and even in
wartime I contend we can lay the foundation of an intelligent attitude
towards the art of living. There are so many of us, so varied in type too.
Can we form a standard by which to live? I doubt it in the accepted sense
of the word. But we can at least, all of us, adopt certain principles: certain
rules of conduct most conductive to the attainment of our aims.

Back now to daily events. The Russian fighting is still fierce with a
claim that the 16th German Army is encircled. Progress is slow and the
Germans are counter-attacking in some sectors. It is a grim and deadly
business.

Our shipping position is graver than it has been for some time; how
grave is not known. British Paratroopers have been landed in France
where they destroyed a radio location station; most of them seem to have
got back.

The 9th Battalion of the Royal Northumberland Fusiliers was captured
at Singapore; poor devils. I wonder how Q.S.M. Johnson is feeling, and
his wife too. The Japs are hammering away and Burma is now a vital
theatre of war. We are withdrawing again there. Australia has had its first
air raid at Port Darwin.

There have been Government changes here, the most notable being the
inclusion of Sir Stafford Cripps; and so it goes on relentlessly.

I got home on Friday last when I had to go to a demonstration near Firle Beacon, most handy! I stayed till Saturday night. Dulcie is well, thank God, and Nicolas kicking more than ever. It was a Spring-like day with chaffinches and hedge sparrows singing in the village.

13.3.42   I suppose there are not many other Nations with such a capacity for bad news as Great Britain. Recently, for instance, the fall of Java, the fall of Rangoon, and the severing of the Burma Road by that route; now the threat to New Guinea. So that now both Australia and India are directly threatened. The Hongkong atrocities have acted, despite their horror and bestiality, rather as a stimulant than as bad news in the accepted wartime term.

At home, white bread is to disappear entirely, and the basic petrol ration, too, after June. These things will be readily accepted as necessities of economy. Sir Stafford Cripps has gone to India with proposals of self-government by that country. As yet, they have not been made known, and the outcome remains to be seen. Whatever the result, though, India cannot easily become a highly organised country for war, and with the Japs so near the position is very grave.

The loss of Java means the loss of much of our quinine supplies, a serious problem for our medical services. The Russians hammer on relentlessly, and the position of the 16th German Army is precarious, to say the least of it. The Russian effort is without question the backbone of the allied strategy.

17.5.42   The last month has been in the field of war a very eventful one. India has refused our offer of Dominion status after the war, a disheartening affair in the critical stage of the Far Eastern situation; however, the offer is still open. Burma is in Japanese hands and they are advancing up the Burma Road; our troops have withdrawn to Assam, after a bitter struggle against great odds. Laval has once again been installed in the French Cabinet, nominally under Petain, but virtually its head; we have landed a large force in Madagascar, a wise move in view of the Japanese threat. The R.A.F. have kept up a terrific hammering in the West, Lubech and Rostock being very severely damaged. St. Nazaire was raided by a combined force and the lock gates destroyed. Corregidir has fallen after a grim stand, but Malta still holds out, causing the Axis to pay a heavy price in aircraft, etc. The Germans are attacking in the Crimea but the Russians are doing likewise in the Donetz region. There has been a big naval battle in the Coral Sea off Australia which resulted, it seems, in a victory for the Allies; no full details have been published as yet.

Dulcie thinks now, after her x-ray, that the baby may be a girl, partly because of its apparent smallness. If so, we have decided to call her Christina – why, we don't know, but we think it to be a very pleasant and poetical name. The time is drawing near when we shall know.

14.6.42   I often wonder what our ancestors would have thought if they could have seen me examining the x-ray photograph of Nicolas – or Christina. It's simply incredible to see the outline of one's child like that before it is born. The shape of the head was extraordinarily clear, even the spine and ribs could be seen. For Dulcie it must have been amazing to see it thus. It should not be much more than a week or so now before the baby is born. How I hope everything will be all right.

The war is going its grisly way as usual. Rommel is testing us severely in Libya. The Free French have fought magnificently at Bir Hakenir on our left flank and caused a considerable diversion of Rommel's forces. They withdrew on orders from Ritchie. It seems now that Rommel is exerting everything in his new northward push with the aim of either cutting our communications to Gonzola, or of reaching and capturing Tobruk. The last two days have seen very heavy fighting around Acroma and El Aden, but so far we have held our positions. It looks to me as though reserves may decide the battle which is getting very tense now. If we have the reserves, Ritchie may get the opportunity of a great counter stroke, but in our reserves we need armour and armament. The Germans have renewed the offensive on Sebastopol and Kharkov but with the usual Russian grimness they are being held and killed in hundreds. This all definitely seems to link up with Rommel's efforts in Libya.

21.6.42   A year ago today Germany declared war on Russia. Who could have foreseen their position as it stands today? Least of all Hitler, I think, who had banked on a quick success. Granted he had had his successes in Russia, but he must be thinking today of the price he has paid for them, and that he is still fighting a Russia stronger than the one on that Sunday in June 1941. He is still on the offensive in some sectors in · Russia, chiefly Kharkov and the Crimea, where a bitter and tense battle is being fought for Sebastopol. He seems to have gained some ground there but the Russians are contesting every inch of ground. How critical the situation is, it is difficult to say, but from the communiqués it seems that Hitler is throwing masses of troops in without consideration of loss, and it must, I think, be nearing a critical stage for the Russians.

In Libya, the other pincer of the fight for the Middle East, things have been very grave, and we have suffered a heavy tactical and strategic defeat. Just recently one of our convoys taking supplies to Malta and

Tobruk suffered heavy losses, and although some of it got through, it was described officially as a 'limited' success.

That brings us to the most serious aspect of the war, our shipping position, which is undeniably grave. Our losses have been terrific, far beyond our power of replacement. Tanks in Britain are useless to Ritchie in Libya. To get them there is our greatest problem. This week it was announced that Churchill was in America for discussions with President Roosevelt. No official announcement has yet been made, but there is no doubt that shipping is one of the problems to be decided upon. The 'Second Front' question has been prominent just recently, especially after the Anglo-Russian treaty just concluded in London with Molotov and Eden. This treaty deals with supplies, conduct of the war, and the post-war period, and is to be effective for twenty years. One of the clauses was that agreement had been reached on the necessity for the opening of a second front in 1942. That, to my mind, is rather an ambiguous statement. It is maintained that 8,000,000 tons of shipping would be necessary to maintain a second front. Could we do it? I doubt if we have the shipping, or the necessary superiority of arms. It is easy to talk of opening a second front, it is another matter to put it into execution. So when Churchill says, 'We can see the ridge ahead', that ridge in the last few days has clouded up and there is no doubt that we are passing through some of the most critical days of the war. The Axis are all out for a decision this year; we must go all out to baulk them. We wait expectantly for Churchill's return and for his decisions. And into this maelstrom of devildom I expect a child of mine to be born next week. God, let us hope that never again will *they* see such madness amongst men.

10.7.42   At just about 1.30 p.m. today I heard that Nicolas had been born earlier in the morning, and that both Dulcie and the baby were doing fine. How glad I was to hear the news, how thankful too that all was well. According to the first reports he is a bonny baby and I am just longing to see him. It is strange and unsettling to be so far away on such an occasion. I felt out of it all, and somehow my mind could not grasp it all. How do other people react when they are suddenly told they have become a father? For myself I felt very excited and proud, and then later frustrated at the thought of not being able to do anything about it. I wanted to run about telling everyone I had a son, but I had to suppress myself of this expedient. Of course, I couldn't concentrate on anything to do with the Army and all I could think of was Dulcie, the baby, what he looked like, what Dulcie's experience had been, how she felt, and how soon I could get leave. What do you look like, Nicolas? I expect at this early hour a funny little thing. You must look funny, anyway, because they say you look like me, which is absurd, isn't it?

And so, Nicolas, I wonder what you will think of us bringing you into such a grim materialistic world as this. Times are very hard and bitter. But your coming has brought great joy to us, although I know you may say that is a selfish view. I think that, though the road is hard, you will enjoy life. Life is wonderful if man cares to make it so; it has, until quite recently, brought wonderful happiness to your father and mother, but now the clouds of war and separation hang over us. There are desperate years ahead of us, and it may be some time before our little family is united again and pursuing a happier existence. We are fighting for those days.

I am writing this in a hut at a place called Duncow in Dumfries. We have just moved here from more comfortable billets and although we do not object to being in tents, we do object to the flies which abound in this particular vicinity, breeding as they do in a large stagnant pond nearby. It is rather depressing outside, dull and raining slightly. My camp bed is broken, which means I sleep on the floor, and get tickled all night by various insects which wander over my anatomy. So I think, Nicolas, that when you are 'tucked in' for the first time in your life tonight, you will be much more comfortable than I am. And when I get to bed tonight I shall be thinking of you in your little cot and Mummy in bed, and I shall thank God for this happy day, the 10th July. As the flies hum over my tent I shall be thinking not so much of the present as of the future, and all that it holds for us. And I shall be hoping and praying that war will never come your way.

And you, my darling, what can I say to you? Whatever I tried it would not be enough. I long to see you, kiss you and hold your hand, see how happy your face is, and listen to you talk. So it was Nicolas after all, sweetheart; are you glad? It is getting cold and I must go to bed. Goodnight my darling; goodnight, my son.

14.7.42 I had my first letter from Dulcie today, written after Nicolas was born. He is apparently a small baby and weighed five and three-quarter pounds. He has a lot of darkish hair and deep blue eyes with, Dulcie says, a broad nose and remarkably long hands and feet. Tomorrow I go on leave for ten days. I look forward with longing to seeing Dulcie and my little son.

17.7.42 And so on the 15th I took the long wartime train journey from Dumfries to Lewes, starting at 11.50 a.m. Had I not been going on leave, and a very special one at that, the journey would have been a very wearying and depressing business, but, filled with the keen anticipation of seeing Dulcie and Nicolas, I hardly noticed the vicissitudes of

wartime travelling. The Dumfries-Carlisle train was filled to overcrowd-
ing with standing in every carriage and corridor. The people looked so sad
and ill, mainly women with their young children; the whole scene was
flavoured with war and its repercussions. I tried to think out why they
were travelling at all, and where they were going, but no doubt most of
them could not help the journey, following their husbands to different
factories, or moving from their homes for some reason, directly or indi-
rectly as a result of the war. Nevertheless, it was a pitiful and sorrowful
sight, and I couldn't help hoping that Dulcie and Nicolas would never
have to take such a journey. This was a slow train to London and at
Carlisle I nipped into a fast train, and managed to get a seat, a wonderful
comfort after standing all the way from Dumfries. Near Lancaster I had a
lovely view of the Langdale Pikes from the train, and that brought a great
flood of memories of those two glorious pre-war Lake District holidays of
ours. Travelling through the countryside like this, one realises what tremendous work our farmers have done in these last two years, God bless
'em. To me the crops looked magnificent.

How often have I walked up that lane in Kingston in darkness, in light,
in snow, in rain, in beautiful sunshine. How varied, too, have been my
moods, my 'leave' moods, mostly excited ones, each step up the hill and
down again bringing me nearer to 'Benallan'. And then as I reach the
bottom of the hill, through the thinning trees and lower hedges, I see the
little house on the hill, waiting patiently and stoically, it seems to me. But
my mood as I walked up the hill on that warm night of 15th July included
something else besides excitement, mingled with it was a sense of wonder
at what was in store for me. In a few minutes I would be seeing a wee mite
of flesh and blood, a little thing born of Dulcie and myself. I would be
seeing my son, Nicolas. And more than that I would once again see my
dear wife who had brought him into the world. It was all so incredible and
dreamlike. One's life is so enshrouded with mechanical devices, especially in wartime, that one is apt to get a mind that thinks and works and
explains things in some sort of mechanical and logical way. But the birth
of a son, though biological, is, at least to me, something quite outside this
sphere of thought. It seems to transcend the physical limitations of this
life. It goes beyond mere sanity, it is something exceptionally marvellous,
even miraculous. That is how a layman and just a father felt, anyway. A
doctor would laugh, a cynic would sneer, but to most humans, I think, my
reaction is the normal one.

Then I turned the corner, and walking along the path saw Nurse in
Dulcie's room standing by the window. She waved, and I waved back and

laughed with joy. No Dulcie to run down the path and meet me this time. I rushed straight upstairs to see her, to kiss her, and be amazed at how well she looked; brown as a nut, a lot of colour in her cheeks. It was good to see her looking so fit and well, and she was full of smiles and happiness. Soon I was enquiring Nicolas' whereabouts. He was asleep in his cot in Nurse's room next door. I crept in and peeped over the edge of the cot, and there for the first time saw his tiny little head, and was astonished at the mass of hair he had on it. He had side whiskers and on top it was formed like a comb-like ridge. Next I noticed his little nose, and his puffed eyes, which I believe is normal in such young babies. But the rest of him was well tucked away. I don't believe I've ever seen such a young baby before, and I was agreeably surprised not to find him ugly, but he was definitely funny, 'an extraordinary little chap'.

But my late arrival had upset the strict routine as laid down by Nurse, and soon after I said goodnight and went along to the Critchleys' house where I am sleeping on this leave. Dulcie had a lot to say to me and we looked forward eagerly to the next morning.

23.7.42   The next day Dulcie showed me all her telegrams and letters and the presents she had received for Nicolas. Then she told me all the circumstances of his arrival, and how at ten o'clock she had rung up her mother about the butcher, and when the meat arrived at two o'clock the baby had arrived! He has a funny little staccato cry, most unusual and quite unlike anything we have heard before in young babies. The shape of his head reminds me of Daddy. This week has naturally been a busy one for everybody, and I have been helping as much as possible in the house, and doing shopping, etc. There were many odd jobs to do, like registering the baby, getting out some sort of insurance, letters to write to various people, etc., and prospective godfather and godmothers to be approached. What a happy week it has been. To have seen one's child in wartime is alone a miracle, to hold him in your arms, as Lin Yutang says, 'Ah, is not this happiness?' It was fun, too, shopping for Nicolas, buying things that admittedly he won't enjoy till later but buying them because they may be unobtainable then. Such things as a woolly lamb, gollywog, books, jig-saw puzzles and the like gave me great enjoyment in their selection and purchase.

But the days pass by and it will not be long before I am in that old train going roaring up to the north. But such is the life of a soldier in this country today, and he has much to be thankful for, and knows it.

And what of the future? The Eighth Army are attacking in Egypt against strong and determined resistance. It is a good sign, however, that we are in a position to attack at all after being pushed back so far with such heavy losses in men and armour. The threat to the Caucasus grows daily, the Germans claim to have taken Rostov by storm. This has not yet been confirmed by the Russians but is evident that the situation in the Don valley is highly critical. What reserves the Russians have on the south bank of the Don is not known, but it is to be hoped that knowing the vital objective of the oilfields they have made full preparation. How can we ever repay the Russians for their grim sacrifices?

11.8.42   Since my leave I seem to have been tremendously busy. I got back to find that Bob was on leave (his son was born the day after mine) and for the next week I was mainly concerned with the preparation for exercise 'Dryshod', which was planned to practise the administration and maintenance of the First Army in a Second Front role. It was well planned with the peculiar feature of a Dryshod channel, a strip of Scotland representing the English Channel. It was full of interesting possibilities and tests of endurance, but, unfortunately, the 2 Royal Northumberland Fusiliers were given a very low priority in the landing table, hence we didn't see any of the fighting.

We got back on Sunday night. It was a hellish dark night, and it was a hellish run with a lot of other stuff on the roads. But we got back to Duncow safely at about 2.00 a.m. Monday. Somehow the wet old tents seemed like home and everyone was happy.

Letters have been difficult on the scheme, but I have had three today from Dulcie. She and Nicolas have gone to St. Michael's* for a few weeks. Nurse left on the 8th, so Dulcie has Nicolas *in toto*. How I miss them both.

6.9.42   Nicolas was christened today. It was a beautiful autumnal day. The sun rose in a clear blue sky and I woke early to hear the cockerels crowing. There was not a stir of wind, and the day before there had been almost a gale. The garden looked beautifully fresh, the grass dew-spangled and glittering with the early morning light.

The Rev. Rhodes officiated at this simple service. Nicolas behaved wonderfully, not a cry at all. He is a dear little boy now, with a sweet smile, and hardly any bother to Dulcie. In the mornings we put the carrycot on the bed and he smiles and gurgles to himself so happily. It is a joy to see him thus. Dad and Kathleen gave him a lovely silver serviette ring for his christening. I took a photo of him in his christening robe. I hope it comes out all right. After tea there were many planes about, and we saw two German ones and puffs of the A/A fire.

---

*Wife's parents' home.

27.9.42   Traise* quite recently called me the gypsy. It was very apt for
          indeed I had not been back from leave more than a week when
I was sent to Selkirk to partake in a 3" Mortar Course at Battalion H.Q.
The fate of the good old Vickers seems to have been decided, at least for
most M.G. Battalions. There are apparently exceptions where Battalions
are on special defence duties. Instead they are giving us 4.2 mortars and
a 20 mm A/A and A/T gun and changing the establishment completely.
But it is a curious time to be changing over, for indeed the Division to
which we are attached presumably, is under orders for the Middle East.
All ranks have been told that they can tell their next of kin that such is the
case, but as far as we are concerned, no official dictum has come out from
Orderly Room, and presumably everything is hanging fire until we do
change onto something or other. But where or when 4 Division is going
seems very debatable, and, who knows, the whole thing may be a big
bluff. Another thing that has put an extraordinary complex on our position
is that we are sending a draft of 100 to the Middle East, so at the moment
2 R.N.F. are in a bit of a shambles. No wonder then that I have not
informed Dulcie about this Middle East business; the whole thing, especially as far as we are concerned, seems most remote, although, of course,
it may not be.

The whole war, except for a big convoy to Russia, has been focused on
Stalingrad. As one paper put it, 'Has any people ever defended the ruins
of their city so heroically as the Russians are defending Stalingrad?' It is
magnificent, and they have held for five weeks. Timonshenko has put in a
strong attack from the northwest of the city to cut communications and
generally relieve the burden on the city. So far the attack is making
progress.

The topic of the day at home, apart from the above, ironically enough,
is the shortage of coal, the only thing we don't have to ship to this island.
Many restrictions have been imposed and the whole business is a pretty
lamentable effort on the part of the Government.

2.10.42   And so it seems that fate has decided that I finish this Selkirk
          diary on my 28th birthday. It is extraordinary that for about
one quarter of those years the world has been at war. I have just read
in today's paper that in the first three years of this war, 47,305 people
were killed in this country by enemy air raids, and that nearly half of
those casualties were suffered by London. The misery this foul war has
caused will be immeasurable and its tragic effects on civilisation will be

---

*Batman.

so far-reaching as to make the 'good old days' almost unrecognisable. I think it was Sir Samuel Hoare who said quite recently that if the war is much further protracted, the whole framework of civilisation will be irreparably damaged, or words to that effect. And when one reads of the pitiful conditions existing in Nazi-controlled Europe, one cannot help but agree with him. Mass killings, mass deportation, sterilisation, the mass removal of children from their parents, the slavery and hunger, the brutality and torture, all these things and many others will help to break up the very foundation of any society, i.e. the family. And yet the human spirit is almost unbreakable, and in various ways these poor oppressed peoples are fighting back for all they love. We are in the fourth year now and there is much to do before the end. And this time, for God's sake, let us make it the END. Let not the next generation see this wantonness, but let US learn from OUR bitter and costly experience.

Stalingrad still holds.

28.11.42   It is nearly two months since I finished my last little diary and nearly a year since I started it in Lymington on the day Dulcie came back with me from embarkation leave for Russia. I did not think then that I would still be in this country a year hence. I certainly did not think it possible that I should be on leave again at 'Benallan' the following November. But it was to be, for the tortuous chain of events has kindly led me back again to this happy home of mine.

Nicolas then was just a possibility; Nicolas now is much more than that – he is a personality, a cute little fellow with a dear little face and a strong, well-made body. Looking back, one is amazed at the incredible events of the last year, seemingly too many to be crammed into such a short space. And what of next November? What will I be writing then, and where will I be writing it, if I am there to write? It is difficult to say, and stupid to speculate, but somehow I have a very strong feeling that wherever it is, it will not be Great Britain. By that time I fancy the great battle of Europe will have started. A battle, perhaps the grimmest and most desperate of all time, but come it must, and not later than 1943. Yes, there lies ahead of the soldiers, sailors, and airmen of the United Nations a terrible fight to the death in the greatest combined operation of military history.

The war aspect has changed considerably over the last month or so. Alexander and Montgomery have chased Rommel back to El Agheila in record time, and he hasn't much left now after his tremendous losses in men and material. Timed with this attack was the landing of the Americans and the British First Army in Morocco and French West Africa. The

First Army are now only a few miles outside Tunis and Bizerta, and their fall is not expected to be very prolonged. The Eighth Army is preparing to attack Rommel's El Agheila's position and this time it looks as though Monty is making sure of it. Churchill said in a speech last night that he expected North Africa to be cleared of the Axis in the very near future. Genoa and Tunis have suffered terrific bombardment by the R.A.F. In short notes like these one cannot go into all the details and repercussions, but, naturally enough, the North African campaign forced Hitler to occupy all France, at first with the exception of Toulon, Darlan came over on the side of the Allies without a shot being fired. Then Hitler got nervous about the French Fleet in Toulon and he decided to occupy it, whereupon the French Navy scuttled all their ships. The position of Darlan in Algiers is worrying a lot of people, especially the Fighting French under De Gaulle. The appointment, however, was agreed to by General Eisenhower commanding the forces in West Africa. So, mainly it is an American decision. Italy is definitely beginning to feel the effects of the war now, and a lot of peace propaganda has been thrown at her over the air. It was the chief theme in Churchill's speech last night.

6.3.43   Time just gallops along these days, and it hardly seems three months since I last wrote. This is an excellent thing in some ways but not in others, especially leave which I have just been enjoying during the last nine days. Much has happened in these last months, and there is no doubt that the dominant feature as regards the war has been the gigantic and successful Russian offensive which started in November and is still continuing. Hanging grimly on to Stalingrad, they mounted the offensive using that city as a sort of pivot. They attacked in force north and south, surrounded and almost annihilated the German garrison and swept on to the Don and the Donetz, smashing counter-attacks on the way. In good time other offensive actions took place on the Moscow and Leningrad fronts. The results of this splendid achievement can be summed up by the many towns retaken. In the Donetz heavy fighting is still going on, the Germans counter-attacking very determindly to prevent encirclement of the entire German forces here and in the Crimea. Will the Russians reach the Dnieper, I wonder?

Regarding ourselves, the Tunisian fighting has been more prolonged than we at first thought. Hitler will no doubt put up a good fight here to save time in Europe. Monty has captured Tripoli and is now in part of the Mareth line, and we await his offensive. The Americans got a nasty knock in Tunisia, but the Hun is almost back to his starting point. The British First Army has been attacked but they have held their ground well, and caused heavy casualties. John* went out to Tunisia with his Division on 6th January and from all reports seems pretty happy and well, and confident in the future.

Then came the Casablanca Conference between Churchill and Roosevelt and Service and other Chiefs. Roosevelt called it the 'Unconditional Surrender' Conference, and Churchill has said that offensive action against the enemy would be undertaken within the next nine months. All plans were made and decisions taken for these operations. Churchill came back and went to bed with a touch of pneumonia, poor fellow.

It has been a happy, glorious leave, with weather almost incredibly beautiful. Dulcie and I twice managed to get out into our favourite woods – Chailey and Warningore. Primroses were prolific; the wild daffodils were almost out and we found kingcups and ladysmock. At Warningore we found a long-tailed tit building, and there is a thrush's next in Kingston lane. The cowslips in the garden are well advanced. I have enjoyed a spell of digging on this leave and Dulcie's father can now put in whatever she wants.

It's good exercise, digging, and yet steadily ruminative. We have had flowers in the garden all the winter, one of the mildest I can remember. Some things like marigolds have not stopped flowering.

Nicolas now weighs 19 lbs. and is beginning to talk a lot now. He seems to react quickly, especially to animals, the cats in particular fascinate him, probably from a mischievous point of view.

2.4.43   After my leaves, I returned to my new abode at Stob Camp.

This is situated on a windswept hillside about four miles south of Hawick, and the roar of the wind is so terrific and continual that to go down the valley was just like walking away from the roar of a waterfall. Although it wasn't the best of camps, somehow the company liked it a great deal; perhaps because it was the fact that we were together again after being split up in Hawick and Selkirk. It was a wonderfully healthy spot, and in the evenings we had splendid walks over the hills and in the valleys. It was good to be able to step out of the mess and start your walk right in the hills, with magnificent sunsets over the Cheviot hills. Altogether the view was lovely, especially to the Eildons. The curlews were beginning to come back to their nesting grounds and their haunting cries were already to be heard.

4 Division were leaving for embarkation ports and gradually Stob Camp began to empty. It was pity we were not going with the Division to which

---

*Brother.

we had belonged for so long but it was almost inevitable. Bob was away on a mortar course and we settled down to our normal training.

Then came one of those surprises; I was summoned to the Barony, i.e. battalion H.Q., on 13th March and there was informed that the battalion was moving to St. Germain in Cornwall, with advance parties to move off on the Monday and the main body on the 18th. I had never been in Cornwall before and from the ornithological point of view it seems pretty good to me. We are right out in the country, only three miles from the sea, and there are some lovely wooded gorges in the vicinity.

9.5.43   A weekend that will be remembered for a long time as the Tunisian campaign has to all intents and purposes been brought to a close by the swift capture of Bizerta and Tunis. This was the work of the Americans and the First Army. The Eighth Army has been mysteriously inactive but now that the remnants of the Germany Army are in the Cape Bon peninsula it is possible they may be deployed for the final kill.

It has been a long and hard fight but once the Mareth line had been broken, the pressure became increasingly too much for the Axis. But the defence was particularly strong and determined at Mejez El Barb, Long Stop Hill, and they took a lot of shifting. Then the Americans made a sudden thrust and captured Matru, then the rot set in. The R.A.F. support throughout has been magnificent.

The Russians in a similar situation are attacking in the Kubair, and our bombers have been making extremely heavy raids on Germany. What next on the bill?

16.5.43   A beautiful day and one that I am not likely to forget as we have been warned for overseas. The battle of Tunisia is over, with 170,000 prisoners in our hands, including Von Arnim. It was a spectacular victory – 'a classic example of the military art', as it has been called in the press. The air support was magnificent and must have gone a long way towards the end, especially as the Luftwaffe had retired.

And now Churchill is in Washington with Roosevelt, and all the military bigwigs, planning the next step, or the battle of Europe as it has been called. We were to have moved to Littlehampton at the end of the month, but it has now been cancelled and our leave has to be over by 9th June. Naturally, we are all hoping we will rejoin 4 Division in Tunisia but that remains to be seen. I hope it isn't India or Burma, anyway. It came as quite a surprise in a way, as we are in the middle of our reorganisation. We may get the men before we go or get them out there; much will happen in the next few weeks. I expect it will be a shock for Dulcie but she must be more ready for these nasty surprises now.

The C.O. comes back from the War House tomorrow and we will then know what establishment we are going out on. I hope we go to North Africa, as I may see John. What a pity we are so far from Kingston here as Dulcie could otherwise have come and seen me after my embarkation leave. Littlehampton would have been ideal for weekends. But no, all this wishful thinking will have to be forgotten, and, anyway, I expect there will be much to do and I won't have time to think. This is where Dulcie is at such a disadvantage, as, being at home all the time, she has time to think, and the environment to remind her of things.

25.5.43   And so I am home again for the second embarkation leave of
           the war, but this time I do not think it will be a phoney one.

We cannot really get used to the idea that this is, in fact, embarkation leave, and perhaps it is for the best. We are both much more prepared for it than we were in 1941, and now, too, there is Nicolas (thank God), and he, with his happy little ways, is enough to take our minds off the future.

It has been a beautiful leave. We have even spent one day in the country on our cycles, and visited a lot of our favourite haunts of pre-war days. To be prepared for the future these days is wise, but to muse on the future is

Embarkation leave, May 1943.

foolish. However, we cannot help at times hearing the 31st May knocking at the door. Already nearly a week has passed. All arrangements have been made and now there remains a little more shopping and one or two more relatives to see; then we can spend the last day or so by ourselves. And soon it will be a happy, very happy memory, and the reality of the long separation will be upon us. Yes, the words 'embarkation leave' must have haunted the hearts of many a wife and mother in the history of these islands.

29.5.43   And so the time of my departure from 'Benallan' after my second embarkation leave of the war draws nearer, and my heart is heavy at the thought of leaving my dear Dulcie and little Nicolas, my home and my native land. How I shall miss the soft beauty and green freshness of the downland; how I shall miss the highways and byways of Sussex, the county that has succoured me for nearly all my life. But I could not have better memories to sustain me on my new journey, perilous and long as it may be. It will give me solace to think of my family in these sweet surroundings, though memory is not always sweet for those left behind. However, I go with good companions and that indeed makes one's lot much easier to bear.

Today we have had a strange mixture of happiness and sadness. Dad was to have come over but he was taken ill in the night with his bladder trouble, so I went over to lunch at Newhaven to say goodbye to him. He looked very poorly but as calm as ever, as he always is. He must have been terribly lonely since mother died, and now the war is splitting his family up even more. He never vents his feelings but I know how he feels and thinks about these matters. He gave me a letter to open when I got home, and it will be a letter I shall cherish all my life, so noble is it in its unselfishness, so calmly dignified in its tenderness and purport. That letter has given me greater strength to face the future than anything I have so far encountered in the written word. It is written from the heart and has affected me deeply.

15.6.43   I knew we should be entraining tomorrow and consequently confined to barracks, so, with a heavy heart, I went down to my old 'phone box to make a last call to Dulcie. I shall never forget those brief 'six minutes' and the inevitability of their passing. It is difficult to know what to say at these sad times of one's life, and perhaps even if one did know, the words would be better left unsaid. Goodbyes are difficult and painful and I hope this is our last one. Tonight we started to load our stores on the railway vans, and it will be my last night in a bed in this country for some time to come.

17.6.43   I arrived at Avonmouth near Bristol, at about 0630 hours this morning, and immediately detrained, formed up, and after slight difficulties with the embarkation staff, began to embark. The ship was H.M.S. *Tamaroa*, of about 9,500 tons. It was a pretty tight squeeze to accommodate all of us together with small batches from other units who were travelling on the same boat. Practically the whole day was spent in getting the men settled into their mess decks, stowing their rifles, packs and topees, and, in fact, generally settling down. In the evening we had a practice 'Boat Station', during which the ship was inspected, and it was pretty late before we eventually retired to our bunks for a well-deserved rest. After the accommodation in Bake House, our cabins seemed small to a degree, and it was quite an art not to get in each other's way. However, so tired were we that having once got into our bunks, sleep came straight away.

19.6.43   At about 4.00 a.m. this morning I was awakened by weird banging noises and men shouting, and I realised at once that we were at sea. Yesterday we had moved out into the Bristol Channel and lay off the south Wales coast, which we could see quite clearly. This morning we had hit a rough sea and in my half-awakened body I could feel the rolling and lurching, a not too comfortable feeling to the person not accustomed to the sea. Putting on a brave face, I went down to breakfast, but there were so many white faces, and that, coupled with the first taste of a piece of bacon and two enormous rolls of the ship, sent me scuttling back to the lavatory. I felt a lot better afterwards and went up on deck to get some air, which helped enormously. By lunchtime I was very much better and managed to finish my lunch which was, as usual, a very good one. Today I saw, for the first time, a gannet, a single bird. How powerful and fierce they look.

20.6.43   The day started gloriously, sunny and warm. We seemed to be lying off the coast of Scotland somewhere; so it seemed anyway from the shape of the mountains. We had joined up with some more ships and farther out to sea was our escort of destroyers and cruisers, a wonderful sight indeed. It was a fascinating game studying all the ships and watching the manoeuvres of our escort ships. I had seen many pictures of convoys and I found it difficult to believe that I was really in one.

The convoy did not delay long and once it had formed up we proceeded on our way out into the Atlantic, catching a glimpse of Northern Ireland as we did so. Unfortunately, the weather began to deteriorate and I missed my lunch, tea and dinner. I had had a good breakfast, though, which

included a real grapefruit and eggs and bacon, how luscious. Two Spitfires flew over for quite a while today. They looked so tiny.

25.6.43   The weather has been getting progressively hotter every day,
            and each day has brought its various stages of undress. For the
last two days the daily routine has barely been upset at all; we have simply
been ploughing through the vast seas, repeatedly changing course, and so
hour by hour eating up the miles that separate us from land. The weather
has been calm, the sea deep cobalt, magnificent to look upon. I have
written to Dulcie and hope it will be despatched within a day or so. I have
nearly finished Vol. 1 of *War and Peace*. What absorbing conversations
he gives his characters. I had rather hoped to play some chess on board,
but no-one has a set handy, and the heat is a bit detrimental to clear
thinking.

Today the convoy broke up, one part turning to the south, while our part
continued in an easterly direction. The first part was presumably on its
way to West and South African ports, and I was glad we were going to
North Africa. It was rather sad to see the familiar ships leave us though.

26.6.43   The fact that the convoy has split up meant, of course, that we
            were not so far from Gibraltar. We were told that we should
pass the Rock at about 3.00 a.m. this morning, an extremely annoying
time to those who have not seen it before. I hoped to get up in the night
about that time and go on deck. Actually, Thomson wakened me at 2.30
a.m. and I got out and could see the Rock quite clearly, with a lighthouse
at the southern end flashing its beam. I was glad I had seen it. Looking
south we could see the lights on the coast of Spanish Morocco, an extraordinary sight after the blackout in England. What a magnificent sight too
the stars presented, especially the Milky Way where nebulae looked so
clear they might have been misty clouds. There was a crescent moon too,
very yellow and very low, casting its phantasmal light across the sea. And
so we were entering the most disputed sea of the war, the *Mare Nostrum*
of Mussolini's Empire. I had looked at it so often on a map – it seemed
incredible that I was actually sailing on it.

This morning it is very hot and we all paraded on the decks in our khaki
shorts, etc. There was no land in sight, last night might have been a dream.

27.6.43   Today everyone was up early and there was a general feeling
            of excitement as the end of the journey was evidently near.
Traise brought me a beautiful cup of coffee early in the morning and I
relished it. Then I got up and went to see the new view.

There was actually very little to see of the coast because of a heavy
mist, but where the coastline was high it was easily discernible, a differ-

ent, burnt-up-looking line of hills. So it went on till about 1100 hours, when the outskirts of Algiers came in sight, and after that for a long time we could see what appeared to be a continual line of villas, white with red roofs, looking very hot on the slopes of the hill. As the ship lessened speed, it got hotter and hotter, and we began to realise how the movement of the ship had helped to keep us cool. Soon we could see Algiers proper, and the docks, and we berthed at about 2.00 p.m., putting our clocks on one hour as we did so.

It was strange to look over the side of the ship and watch the natives unloading the boats, the British M.P.S., and the U.S. troops, some of whom were playing baseball. The town too looks so different from any British port, the white and red houses seemingly piled on top of each other, and the brown bare earth all around them.

North Africa

27.6.43 (Cont'd.) There was great activity in the port, many ships were there, mostly American of a type to be used in an opposed landing. It was a great sight and on it all the sun beat down with unaccustomed fierceness.

It took some time to disembark the battalion down the gangway, with all the kit a soldier carries with him. However, eventually it was done and all the kit sacked.

We had all hoped for a short march to our reception area, but soon after arrival we were informed that a seventeen-mile march was ahead of us – pretty much after eleven days on a boat, spent most of the time in P.T. shoes. C company started to land about 1655 hours, when I actually walked on African soil for the first time. (I met John* on the road; he had been looking out for me all day, and how brown and well he looked. It was strange meeting him thus.)

By about 1730 hours the Group moved off, looking rather odd and new in their topees. It was a long and strenuous march, unused to heat as the company was, and not being feet fit. My impressions were not many. The heat I shall always remember, the dustiness too, the bare dried-up ditches, the Americans and the girls who always seemed to be in their vehicles; walking on the right side of the road, the Casbah and its horrible smell, and filth, as we marched through, and the incredibly dirty and destitute little Arab boys who followed us. I remember, too, the joy of seeing martins and swallows, swifts and goldfinches; the strangeness of the countryside, with the vineyards, the orange and fig trees; the funny little horses and traps; the surprise that my shoes weren't giving me blisters, the

---

*Brother.

35

sweat and discomfort caused by my topee, the different-looking earth, and always the different and stuffy smell that seemed to pervade everything.

And so wearily for five hours we marched away, and marched well in my opinion under the circumstances; three men only falling out towards the end. We were told to go to W. Camp in O area, and this proved to be the furthest away of the lot, but it turned out to be good. The last mile or so was the worst and seemed very long, but at last we reached W. Camp, turning off the dusty road down a lovely avenue of trees to a big farm. It was dark, but there was much noise going on. Troops getting into barns, getting a blanket issued, drawing a mug of tea, shouting of orders, and all the usual turmoil of troops getting into a billet. We were 500 strong and there were many men to each barn. The barns were rather lovely, very low buildings, red-tiled, whitewashed walls, but we were too tired to take note of our surroundings.

After the troops were in, I got a table top, put two mosquito nets and a blanket on it, erected a mosquito net over the lot, then to the chirping of many cicadas, thankfully laid my head down on my haversack. My legs felt like lead weights and I was too overtired to sleep, so I thought of Dulcie and home. I was amazed at the ever-changing scene of life and its curious ways. The general reaction after the march caused a lot of talking, as is often the case, so sleep would have been difficult in any case; the dust and dirt on the floor, too, seemed to set most of us coughing.

2.7.43   Yesterday C company supplied duties for the Camp and little training was done, not that we can do a lot until our stores are unpacked. Our vehicles haven't yet arrived in N. Africa. It seems that we are moving from this Camp to another about thirty miles north of here, the other side of Algiers and near the sea, and I'm afraid we'll have to march it – phew! We are attached to 46 Division, John's Division, who seem quite pleased to have us.

Today we all have to be vaccinated as an Arab boy at battalion H.Q. has been taken away with smallpox! *C'est la guerre!* Battalion H.Q. have had to move, of course.

5.7.43   Nothing of note has happened during the last few days. On Saturday morning we got up at 3.30 a.m. and did a twelve-mile route march on a cup of tea. We went through Sidi Moussa and Arbir and there was none of that early morning freshness of an English dawn. The air was muggy and the villages and huts smelt badly. I had only one halt and the men did well, though there was a bit of shuffling and grumbling towards the end. I saw several birds new to me, one particularly rather like a small thrush, light in colour, with a beautiful fan tail.

Every day I look forward to mail but as yet none has arrived for me, though some have had air mail. It has been somewhat cooler of late, quite cloudy, in fact, but when the wind dies down it becomes very close and most unpleasant. Oh, for the fresh greenness of England; oh, for a shower of gentle rain; oh, for the clean smell of 'Benallan' and the garden. I hate the intolerable lassitude of after midday with its heat and sweat and heavy limbs.

Tomorrow we are moving to the Foret de Ferdinand and C company is going as advance party. It is a pretty new site and a lot of work will be involved, including the laying of pipes and latrines, etc. However, I don't think the men will be sorry to leave here, chiefly because they do not like being with 1 Group. We are all longing to get our vehicles and do some decent training, but so far there is no sign of them.

7.7.43   Yesterday we all got up early, packed our kit, and after a bit of delay, tumbled on to some R.A.S.C. trucks and set off for the Foret de Ferdinand. How I hate these hot dusty roads with their continental straightness and on either side the dry brown ditches, and the brown fields. The forest is between Maelma and Zeralda and is in view of the sea and altogether a most pleasant and airy place with the sweet smell of pines pervading everything. We soon got into our temporary camp, and the rest of the day was spent settling in and recceing the area for our new camp. Best of all we went down for a bathe, and it was incredibly warm, and so delicious to get all the dust and dirt off our bodies. This will definitely be a daily institution for the battalion.

14.7.43   I have now received two letters from Dulcie. How wonderful it is to have contact again with home; mail certainly has a tremendous effect on morale.

The chief news of the past few days has been the invasion of Sicily by American, British and Canadian troops. Monty is in command of all British troops which must include several Divisions from the Eighth Army. The invasion began on 0300 hours on 8th July, and so far we have a bridgehead of about 100 miles in length and twenty miles in depth. Several ports have been taken, including Syracuse, Augusta and Gela. Over 2,000 ships were involved, a mighty procession it must have been. 46th Division is in Army Reserve for this attack and its exploitation, but as we are still not complete with our kit, and thus not ready for active operation, we can hardly say that it affects us directly. Monty issued one of his typical dramatic messages to all troops and I had to read it to the company. It finished with the words, 'Good luck, good hunting in the Hun's country of Italy.' Sicily is now being referred to as the doorstep to Europe. The British are now fighting their way north to Catania.

21.7.43   My fourth letter from Dulcie; how wonderfully happy it makes me to see her dear homely writing on the envelope, and know that for a few moments I can forget my present life and environment and go back to the things and people I love.

Nicolas had a beautiful little birthday with a cake with one candle, and lots of presents. Dulcie has now heard from me direct, and I am now receiving B.N.A.F. mail and by now she will know that I have received her letters. No surface mail has yet arrived, and as Dulcie has written several ordinary letters this is highly aggravating, for we never know when we may move away, though at the moment we are so short of transport and kit that it seems unlikely. I shall never be able to express how profoundly I miss Dulcie, Nicolas and my home life, and how proud I am of the way in which Dulcie is carrying on, for she indeed has much responsibility on her shoulders.

28.7.43   Ever since Mussolini's resignation, everyone has, I believe, been secretly waiting for significant events to follow. So far, however, there has been no official indication that Italy is about to sue for peace. In fact, Badoglio the soldier says the fight goes on, and he asks the people to rally round the King. Badoglio is not particularly pro-German but will, I think, make Italy fight for her soil. How much longer she can resist I do not know, but without German backing she must be pretty helpless. She has her choice, making herself a battlefield for Germany as Churchill put it, or making peace and thus escaping further privation of war. In the meantime, 'she can stew in her own juice' and we will wage war against her with all our increasing might. Already in Sicily we have encountered German Divisions in all sectors, a pretty good advertisement for Italy's warring strength. Those Germans are fighting stubbornly, a reminder of the long way we have to go before we beat our worst enemy – the Hun. Day by day, though we may not be consciously aware of it, that battle draws nearer for us; we are, in fact, training for it now.

This new Group, scraping together vehicle by vehicle, hopes to go with its parent Brigade, the 139th, and there is not much time left, a month, perhaps more, perhaps less. And suddenly the day will come, as all things seem to come in war, when the ships are loaded up, and we sail to make a landing on some foreign beach, and there we fight and die for the ideal of freedom. Somehow war seems to numb the brain, and the very business of doing things seems to delimit one's mental comprehension and imagination, which is just as well!

I wonder where it will be when we go? It is quite obviously going to be mountainous country and that, of course, entails much sweat and swearing, and transport difficulties. It may be Greece, Italy, anywhere like that, and I think on balance we would prefer Italy. We have been told jokingly to prepare for a land of typhus, dysentery, etc., so it sounds more like the Balkans than Italy, but, of course, we don't know really, and it may now depend on the political situation in Italy.

2.8.43   As usual, there has been another sudden change in our arrangements, and this one looks ominous. We are changing with 1 Group and going to 128 Brigade in a show that is to come off shortly. 2 Group are handing up all their new vehicles and on Thursday we are moving to Djidjelli, which is about 200 miles east of here along the coast somewhere. The 128 Brigade is the Hampshire Brigade. In a way it's a nuisance as we were just beginning to get to know the 139 Brigade, but I believe we revert to them in a later stage of the proceedings. I don't think any of us will be sorry to leave the Foret de Ferdinand with its flies, dust and horrible diarrhoea. At the moment we are lucky and have only six in hospital, the lowest we've had for some time.

5.8.43   There has been another sudden change of plan, and we are not now apparently going to Djidjelli. It is not certain exactly what is happening but Graham has gone off today with an advance party for Tunis, and it is said that we may be the only Group to go at all with the Division. All our vehicles have arrived, and they are being painted and waterproofed. Bob Gray has just come in, having been sent back no doubt from Djidjelli. I wonder what news he has?

The Divisional Commander is coming tomorrow and, as usual and quite against the general policy, we are doing some window dressing for him. How I hate this 'quack' training, and how appalled I am that it hasn't at this stage of the war been stamped out by the Divisional Commanders themselves. Why they ever warn a Battalion Commander of an impending visit utterly defeats me, and surely must defeat the object of the visit.

8.8.43   (Cheers, a two-letter day.) It looks after all we will be moving on the 10th. I hope so anyway as this waiting is most annoying, especially as our vehicles are loaded ready to move, which means we can do little training. I think we are going to the Ferryville area in Tunisia, and it seems we are definitely being attached to 128 Brigade, the assault Brigade for the next operation. What this is, no-one can definitely say, but my guess is that after the fall of Sicily we will land in South Italy. If Italy capitulates in the meantime then I also think we shall land there but probably in the north. With any luck we may have a fortnight for intensive

training with the Brigade before embarking, which means that the operation should take place early in September, but who knows? I often wonder
from the blankness of my letters whether Dulcie feels something is brewing.

10.8.43   Last night we moved down to Arbir and so saved an early move
            today to join up with the Gunners. We stayed in a field very
close to our previous exercise camping ground, but much better as it was
off the road. After we had our evening meal and made all arrangements
for the morning, I went to bed, thankful that this time it was to a camp bed
and not the hard, heavy, smelly soil of North Africa. It was moonlight and
I remember how lovely the shadows of the leaves were as they lay straddled across my mosquito net. Beyond the leaves I could see the splendid
African night sky, and I could not help wondering at the strangeness of
life's uncertain ways. A cicada called in the tree above. If Hitler had not
made war on mankind, that cicada would have still been there in just those
same surroundings, but I and my truck and the cookers and the men
wouldn't have been there.

17.8.43   For the last two days we have been frantically preparing for
            exercise 'Jennifer', an obvious prelude to the real show, and a
big one at that. Waterproofing has gone on apace and we have been
working out assault plans and serials for crafts. That is one big snag, that
men and vehicles get split up, which means a considerable delay at the
other end while they are being assembled again. It's a pity they cannot
come off the boat as a fighting unit.

I managed to write to Dulcie but I feel it was a poor letter. It is difficult
to express oneself somehow with so many restrictions and a great lack of
peace and quiet.

This morning we moved off to our assembly area, where I am writing
this and we now await for instructions to move to the docks which
probably won't be till the 19th. I heard that Messina has fallen today, so it
is over in Sicily. It looks as though we may be destined for Italy. There is
certainly much happening here, a terrific concentration of troops and
shipping, and the Hun knows it, as air raids are fairly regular now at night
and the barrage is a pretty show but highly dangerous in the open. I
wonder if Dulcie thinks I am in this area; it must be most aggravating for
her not to know where I am, and I hope she doesn't worry too much.

24.8.43   The exercise was not a very happy one in many ways. First we
            were all put off LST 357 and had to stay in the assembly area
for a night, and then we were all put on LST 386 the next day. My
stomach and general condition were very low and had been for some time.

I felt depressed and very weak. Food I hated the sight of, I could not face it and then I was sick again, not from the sea, but because of my stomach trouble. We were on board until the morning of the 22nd. There was nearly a four-hour delay but eventually we got off and got to our assembly area. The platoons were eventually assembled and got into action. Denny had very bad luck; one of his chaps, Dixey, when getting the stuff off the truck, tripped on an Italian landmine, injuring three, and catching the truck alight. Everything in it went up in the ensuing explosion and the fire spread to another truck and destroyed that also. Luckily no-one was killed, though Dixey was pretty badly hurt and Denny got a bit in his nose. Replacement is the difficulty. Saw the doctor yesterday and I have slight jaundice.

30.8.43   (BLACK) For an unmilitary person, today I have had what so far is my biggest military disappointment. They won't let me go back to my unit – 'not justified' were the words – and so having got the company so far, I shall miss their first big venture, and what is more, I shall miss the assault of Italy proper, which I know will not be long delayed. My spirit rebels at my misfortune, especially as I feel pretty fit and am the mildest case of those of us sent to hospital for jaundice. If only this had happened when we were in the Foret de Ferdinand, when I should almost have welcomed a spell in hospital. Perhaps I should have gone anyway when I had a bad time; not doing so probably led to this. So today I feel depressed and frustrated, and all the time my thoughts are with the company, and the excitement and bustle that must prevail there. How miserable to have to desert now of all times; my jaundiced liver will forever be remembered with many cursings.

To cap it all, we are all being evacuated again, and we know not where, except that we go by train. It may be Constantine, Souk Ahras, anywhere. Also, the whole affair produces problems of kit, and when I shall see all mine again, I don't know. Some I have sent on with the company but I shall have to retain my bed, etc. It is one of those annoying domestic problems that without Traise will cause me much worry and annoyance. I am a bad patient, restless and lacking the ability to enjoy a scrounge when it is offered to me. My only consolation is this little diary, where I can let off steam.

What a wonderful trade war has in diseases; last night the ambulance delivered a lot more new customers. Some here were wounded in Sicily. Tony must write to the C.O. when we get to our new hospital to make sure we get back to the Division. The food is good here and is planned to cope with the 'yellow peril', as we now call it. The Sisters – V.A.D. – are excellent, and it is pleasant to hear their voices and to see them make the beds in an English way.

Tony and Coutts look very yellow today. My legs ache with boredom. We have an Italian prisoner of war who acts as orderly and brings food round. I get very hungry now, quite a change.

2.9.43   We were taken by ambulance to entrain at Tunis. By a miracle the ever-loyal Traise turned up just before we left, and with all my kit too, so I was able to sort out what I wanted, and that was one weight off my mind. German medical prisoners of war helped us on the train with our kit. We were supposed to be evacuated lying down, and I'm glad we were as it was certainly the most comfortable way for such a tedious journey, as it proved to be. It was two hours before we started and then we kept stopping for various reasons – once because the brakes wouldn't go off! The stretchers were in tiers, placed in a sort of hooped iron frame that reminded me of a Russian sledge. I was on the top of one tier and had a good view of the country. Being up so high it gave me the impression of being in an aeroplane. Eventually we discovered we were going to Souk Ahras, the 72 General Hospital. It could have been much worse and much further away. We all got very hungry on the train and managed to get lashings of bread and jam, but little else except jelly and salmon. This fat-free business ties us down somewhat. We didn't arrive at Souk Ahras till after 2200 hours, and the last part of the journey was rather trying as we had to go through many tunnels, and the smoke was terrific.

However, we were soon in the hospital and, after the usual reception procedure, were taken to a magnificent ward. The building is an old school, I believe, with big rooms, big windows, all very cool, clean and dust-free.

Well, the doctor saw me and prescribed no treatment for me as my jaundice has, to all intents and purposes, departed. I am now up and NON-FAT-FREE. I shall be here for a few days to recover my strength which is reasonable enough – and then to get back to the company, but that will be another story.

5.9.43   On the 4th, after a mad rush of 190 miles in unexpected transport from hospital at Souk Ahras, within twelve hours I was on the last landing craft to leave the shore at Bizerta.

At such times as these, when the future is grim and uncertain, when, in fact, you are going to war for the first time, you cannot help but think of your family, your sweet wife, and your baby boy. All the beautiful things of life that were once yours, now seem so remote. Yes – all these things flood into one's memory and then the great tragedy of it all is borne upon you. Oh God, may the day soon come when men can govern themselves in a way worthy of your teaching. And then you pray that those loved ones across the seas may find strength, faith and patience, to face all these tribulations.

7.9.43   Monday morning the convoy sailed out of Bizerta harbour and formed up at sea, just off the coast. These flat-bottomed, heavily laden LSTs roll like the devil, and it was decidedly unpleasant waiting thus in the swell. We anchored all day and most of the night. I had just got into bed last night when 'General Quarters' sounded on the alarm bells. Soon an air raid developed, more on Bizerta than us, and never have I seen such flack. Smoke screens were put up by the ships, but it was a very light night with half a moon, and above the smoke you could see all the tracer and the heavy stuff and searchlights. It was a tremendous sight from the sea and I don't expect the Jerry pilots relished it much. It lasted for about a couple of hours, after which I could see two fires on the shore, one a fairly big affair that looked like ammunition.

We moved off early today eastwards along the coast and what an impressive sight we made. Hundreds of ships and their escorts in line ahead plunging through a blue sunlit sea; a convoy stretching far beyond the eye could see, will remain for me one of the most memorable scenes of my life.

Except for the escorts we were the leading LST and so we had a grand view from the boat deck looking back on the convoy. We passed the Cape Bon peninsula, and I must confess I hoped it was the last time I should see N. Africa.

I decided to brief the men tonight after tea, and symbolically enough as I did so, we were passing Maretimo, a stately island indeed, like a massive crag. As I spoke to the men, their eyes were alight with interest, and I could feel the excitement that was passing through them as I described to them the various phases of the attack. It was, for me, a memorable occasion.

8.9.43   Today we have been sailing peacefully northwards through the Tyrrhenian Sea. The sea had been like a millpond and so far we have had no enemy interference, which to my mind is absolutely amazing. This morning we passed the island of Ustica. It is now nearly 1700 hours and it is between now and dark that it is so important we do not get spotted, and there is a tense atmosphere about the ship. But what impunity to be sailing like this in a vast convoy in an Italian sea?

Tomorrow is 'D' day and zero hour is 0330. We land at Z+240, so in about fifteen hours' time, with any luck, we should be on Italian soil. It is incredible. Anyway, I shall go into battle nice and clean as I washed my hair and had a wonderful hot shower this afternoon. Then again I got one of my Fusiliers to wash a lot of dirty clothing I had, so I am well set up.

I spoke too soon for there goes the alarm bell. It turned out to be some aerial activity, and we could see a great pall of black smoke on the horizon. The alarm bells went again afterwards during our evening meal – more planes – and several chaps saw a bomb dropped, but it was a feeble effort altogether. However, the enemy must suspect that something is up!

This time last year I was on leave, the first I had had with Dulcie up after her confinement. I can still remember the excitement of catching the train from Hawick. Oh God, those leaves were fantastically beautiful and exciting, and sometimes I cannot help picturing my homecoming after this great wartime venture – and, being human, I cannot help hoping I shall be there to go home when it is all over.

This will be my last entry before we invade Italy for I have much to do in the way of preparing for battle, and generally getting myself and my kit into some sort of order. May I wish myself good luck!

Italy

10.9.43   If I had time I could probably write pages about the last forty-
             eight hours. Needless to say, they have been pretty hectic,
especially yesterday. The convoy arrived at its destination in the Gulf of
Salerno about one hour earlier than anticipated. We were very near the
coast; in fact, not long after sunset we passed in view of the Isle of Capri,
which we then thought to be a risky procedure. In the early hours of the
morning the outline of the hills behind the coast was plainly visible. There
surely never was a more beautiful night with the moon shining over an
exquisitely smooth sea.

But once in the Gulf all that was shattered by the sound of gunfire and
A/A fire, which was pretty terrific. A duel seemed to be going on between
naval and coastal guns and this intensified as zero hour approached. At
0315 the Navy put down five minutes gunfire and then came the rocket
guns which were a tremendous spectacle, and the blast was very great.
Several fires were started, one in Salerno itself, but after zero it was
impossible to tell what was going on, but there seemed plenty.

We were due to land at 0730 and about two hours before this they let
down the pontoons. Just before we were due to land we heard the astound- ·
ing news of Italy's capitulation, but with very little detail. We were now
in the process then of clearing the Germans off Italian soil, and they were
fighting desperately well. They were apparently Grenadier troops. As we
drew into the shore we could see that they were shelling the beach and the
ships and it was a most unpleasant experience. Several shells missed us by
only a very minor margin. Things were definitely tense, but the worst part
was when the ship hit the shore and sat there – a perfect target. I decided
to bring the men off by themselves and leave only the drivers and vehicles. We mustered on the tank deck and moved quickly along an R.E. road

45

and got safely off the beach, which was being mortared. It was a curious way of visiting a country for the first time! – and I can see now the ditched vehicles and the bulldozers. I soon had 4 platoon mustered in the assembly area, and I remember being impressed by all the fruit, especially the apples and pears, several of which I devoured on the spot. Yes, I can see myself sitting in a ditch with Hollo and Bob eating them.

I then went back to the beach to see if the vehicles were getting off O.K. (very warily as it was being pretty heavily shelled and mortared) and soon I saw Graham and gave him directions as to where he was to go. Eventually, except for our three-tonner, we had the whole company more or less assembled, but it was a hell of a game as the roads were very bad and there were many ditched vehicles and trucks; the congestion at times was appalling. The Germans were still fighting on Green beach and apparently the battle was grim there. As we were moving up to the assembly area, I saw John Deighton looking for his platoon. He had heard and seen nothing of them but somehow or other he had managed to get a gun. He saw the C.O. 2nd Hamps. badly needed support and he and Denny went off to see what they could do for him. It was later that Quinn came up and told me that John had stepped on a mine and both he and Denny had been badly wounded. It was a cruel stroke of bad luck. They were both evacuated to the hospital ship. Steve took over 3 platoon and very soon they were sent to the Ponticagnano area to support the Hamps. Company H.Q. remained in the assembly area near Brigade H.Q. I shall never forget walking up from company H.Q. to visit the platoons at night – there were snipers in the vineyard, and the narrow dusty lanes from the beaches were full of infantry and trucks of every description. It was very eerie and I was glad to get back to company H.Q. But we had no peace from the Luftwaffe that night.

19.9.43   And still the battle for the bridgehead goes on, and it certainly isn't the piece of cake we had hoped it would be. In our particular sector we have managed to secure the first main line of hills inland from the beach, and there our infantry has stayed to attack and be counter-attacked. These hills are vital to our position as they give us observation posts, and also give us cover from fire view for our mortars and artillery. The country is a mass of vineyards and cover is plentiful. In fact, it is said that planes in the way of close support are useless in this wooded, hilly country. Soon after we arrived, the group reverted to 139 Brigade, and ever since then the company has been in action continuously. I have not had time to write a letter or any diary for ten days, and I find it practically impossible to reconstruct the ten days we have been here, so intermingled have all the days been.

We have moved our H.Q.s several times, chiefly to be near the platoons, but partly to escape shelling, as soon after we left our H.Q. at Pastena, a shell made a direct near hit, so we were lucky then.

It has not only been tiring physically but mentally, and I just cannot connect up accurately all the main events of these last ten days – the great support given by 4 platoon in Salerno, for instance, is now a dim memory of long ago, and I cannot remember the day; the shifting of our H.Q. from Ponticagnano to Mersatello, and then to Pastena, and finally to this farm east of Salerno by about a mile and close to the platoons; the amazing bomb consumption by the platoons and the great work they have done – forty-eight hours firing in one platoon; the wonderful way in which they have organised themselves, for we are in a proper defensive position with line to our observation posts, and now a line to Brigade, and between mortar position officers; the shelling and mortaring of our positions; the little hopes and fears one has in tense moments; the legendary status of Monty and the effect on the morale of the troops when they knew he was nearly with us; the arrival of Light and Fuel scales; Tommy going to hospital; Bob getting sniped; seeing John* in the opposite bed to Tommy at the C.C.S. (he had tonsilitis!) ; the furious attack on the 16th when things didn't go too well for us, but the mortar platoons did excellent and gratifying work; the splitting of our company H.Q. to A and B Echelons; – all these things are jumbled in my brain, and really I have not had time to realise my first impressions of Italy, except that it is a thousand times better than N. Africa, and I feel very fit.

27.9.43   The attack for the northern exits of the Vietri defile duty went in on the 23rd, and a heavy barrage preceded it, helped strongly by the mortar companies of both groups. The 138 Brigade had a difficult task as they more or less had to fight for their forming-up place. The Durham Light Infantry on the left, however, got on well, and Paddy was brought out in the morning and moved his platoon to Dragone where he had some fine shoots. I moved my H.Q. up to Vietri.

Slowly, bloodily, we were pushing the Hun out of the hills; soon we were ordered to concentrate in Vietri, ready to move forward to support another attack further up. At 1800 hours that night we supported an attack of the Hamps. on San Martino, an attack which I do not think was very successful despite the creeping barrage. The ground was bad for mortars, and positions were few because of enemy observations from the surrounding heights. Company H.Q. and the two platoons were very closely

---

*Brother.

situated and we came in for a lot of mortaring. Company H.Q. was under a semi-courtyard – a pleasant enough place – but slightly overlooked. I remember thinking how beautiful the surrounding scenery was – Nevana and the clouds and the trees – and for the first time I had the feeling that one could live here. The next day Steve moved up to Epitaffio de Cava and got a position for us there in the grounds of a big factory-looking building which had been a German Divisional H.Q. It was lucky he did, for in the afternoon the whole area of our company position was very heavily shelled and Paddy lost six men, three killed and three wounded, a heavy blow in a mortar platoon. Two of them were buried on the mortar position and Wright died on the stretcher going to the Advance Dressing Station. And so the war goes on – inexorably – and each day more steel helmets are placed on mounds of earth – a grave in a corner of a vineyard by a wall under some trees – an English grave, a soldier's grave.

Company H.Q. decided to move back to the extent of 400 yards, and Graham found a house, the back of which was still pretty substantial, while the front was badly shelled and bombed. I shall remember this place because we had to get in the window, and it was extremely dusty with the floor a mass of plaster. There was a gigantic double bed in the room – the Italians certainly set out to enjoy married life all right! Mortar bombs were falling all around us soon after we got there; they were after the gunners who had been supporting an attack on to San Martino again. I went out to see 3 platoon with some information about defensive fire tasks, and it was pretty dark – the clocks went back on the 16th. On the way back we got caught in the Square with more mortar bombs and made a dash for cover; in fact, we found a shelter with old Newman in it holding a quiz with his platoon! We stayed there for a while, and then walked back to H.Q.; it was too dark for my bad driving to risk it. I had just started my apple stew when down came another lot all around us and one incendiary bomb was burning in the garden, a bloody near thing for our vehicles. However, all quietened down and I slept long and well. This morning all seemed quiet and I had a good wash – feet and all! I shall always remember the little garden of this house, the beautiful dahlias, the marigolds, the roses, and the fuchsia. It was almost English.

This morning things moved forward a bit; Paddy moved his platoon under Martino, or thought he did, but map reading went a little astray – very difficult in some of these well-tracked areas. Company H.Q moved, too, a little, to a delightful house with a lovely calendar garden with steps up to it. It was occupied and how many families I don't know – maybe they were flats. The house was in fair condition, windows, etc., gone, of course. We were well received and had a room given us. Steve had to move forward to a new position and he found a good one, but it was being mortared and sniped, and he had to lie doggo for some time.

28.9.43   Last night company H.Q. had a fantastic soirée with our Italian hosts. It was, to me, very unreal and rather beautiful; it could almost have been taken out of something of Chekhov's or Tolstoy's. I had heard a piano being played during the day, and in the evening when I had finished my meal I asked if we could have some music. Soon we were all asked into the sitting room, where an enormous gathering seemed to have collected – grandmother, grandfather, brothers, sisters, and young children.

The curtains were drawn and the candles lit by the piano. The chairs were drawn round and we all sat down full of laughter and happiness. One old lady held a candle for the pianist, a clever woman who spoke French well and conversed with Graham, and was, in fact, a method of interpretation. On the top of the piano I remember was a doll, shining smooth in the light of another candle. We sang, or tried to sing, 'Thy tiny hand is frozen' and 'Ave Maria', and then lighter themes. The whole affair was most alfresco and it seemed incredible to me that these homely people had been made our enemies by political duplicity. The son was an artist and we were shown some of his works, very vigorous painting.

4.10.43   I had a most pleasing gift today, a drawing of Nicolas reproduced from a photo of him. The artist, F. M. Vartino, has done a magnificent reproduction, an enlargement of about four times of his head and shoulders. It is a wonderful piece of work. Vartino wrote underneath his drawing in Italian – 'To little Nicolas, with admiration'. My only wish is to get it home to Dulcie in good condition and I feel very nervous about sending it through the post, and that I cannot do until the Censor lets me.

7.10.43   We left Cava early yesterday morning, and after the usual convoy hold-ups, especially at the start point, made good progress. We took the coast road and I was very disappointed with Pompeii, except for one Cathedral building but, of course, I did not see the old Pompeii. It was extremely dirty and smelly and most incompatible with the beauty of Vesuvius in the background. Vesuvius' white plume of smoke was in evidence, and it was a lovely sight, visible for many miles away. I was very impressed with the fertile plains around the volcano, fruit being especially prolific. Tonight we are up at the front, and the now familiar sound of guns is with us again. Graham managed to find a farm here in the village of Villa Literno, and at the moment, round two lamps, a game of solo is being played by four of company H.Q. It was a terribly slow convoy and it rained like hell nearly all day. But, dear me, I am sleepy.

9.10.43   Yes, Vesuvius was a magnificent sight. I was very glad to see the farmers still working, about the only section of the community who still seem organised. The roads were crowded with people all the way, walking, riding in carts, sitting about in doorways, dirty, ill-fed, and now without leadership. Here we are witnessing the stunning effect of capitulation. A social order has been smashed, and now masses are suffering from the political duplicity of the last thirty years. As Churchill had said, 'They would stew in their own juice.' The towns were dirty (I believe they are in peace time, but I am not sure), they smelt strongly, and there seemed to be no drainage system. The people, too, were of the same tone, dirty, slovenly, listless. I saw literally thousands of men who weren't stirring a muscle to help get things in order. As we approached Naples, the masses grew, thousands of people along each side of the road; in fact, American troops were lining the road to get the people away. Here one could see what happens when the government of a people is *non est*. Cohesion and civilian discipline become a thing of the past, and I can see how easy it must have been for Hitler to come into power. The greater percentage of the people in Naples looked wretched, and after our terrific bombing, after the fighting, and after the Germans had smashed all water, sewerage, and lighting installations, who wouldn't be wretched? They looked ill, hungry, and without hope, and yet a lot of them had laughter in their eyes and somehow tried to wave a hand. The food and water queues were a sad sight, but I think these things are now gradually being organised. The destruction in the factory area was terrific, and was a good tribute to the accuracy of the R.A.F. bombing. Altogether it was a messy sight. A dead horse, a dog left dead, did not make the picture any more attractive. And yet in all the chaos one could see how smartly a lot of the girls were turned out, lipstick, etc., all laid on.

As we got north of Naples, the people were more attentive than ever, and they threw apples and cheered, and very often it was quite uncomfortable in the truck with about ten apples flying in the windows, but they were lovely! When we got to Calvizzanio we were handed slips with 'Friends, Liberators – Welcome' written on them. It was an extraordinary experience altogether, but rather depressing.

11.10.43   I started my last diary on leave at dear 'Benallan', and finished it in a queer two-roomed, two-storied cottage in Villa Literno, which lies just south of the river Volturno. At the present rate of writing, coupled with this slow progress of our advance, I ought to finish this little book in Italy too (God willing). I've had to resort to it as I cannot obtain anything else at the moment, and for the last few minutes I have been rubbing out notes on conferences referring to Exercise DRYSHOD, a queer twist in the chain of events.

We had a good Church Service yesterday in the farmyard just by, and I was very struck by the sincerity and profundity of our padre - Capt. Parks. The men seem to enjoy these services very much and sing the hymns well, and I admire more and more the work of the Army Chaplains under all kinds of conditions.

John* had been in quite a bit lately and since his job takes him to Brigade a lot we get red hot news, and we are always eager for that.

I had a letter from Dulcie today in which she says she thinks I am in Italy as she hasn't had a letter for a fortnight. Dear girl, how right you are, and how I long to be out of the place and the war too, and get home to your kindly companionship and love.

12.10.43   And now things are beginning to happen again! After sitting here doing nothing in particular, I was called to a Conference yesterday and told of the big show that was coming off tonight. What infuriated me, however, was that the Brigadier wanted to put my mortars at so and so. I wish he would give us the tasks and let us do our own selection of position. Anyway, from the map they looked highly untenable and very bad base-plate ground. Bob had pointed this out to the Brigadier, but, no, he was adamant. Anyway, to make sure he wanted me to go out with an infantry patrol to see the ground for myself. David Brook was to come as well, to pinpoint his position. And so from the peace and quiet of the last few days I was suddenly shot into a patrol – never a dull moment.

We accordingly reported to the C.O. Foresters, and got as much dope as possible, studying a large scale map of the area, which showed a fosse not marked on the smaller maps, and a possible position(s) for a mortar · platoon. I was still unhappy about putting my platoons there, however. From there we went on to D. company H.Q. who were providing the patrol. This was a recce patrol, its job being to cross the river, find possible crossing places, etc., and bring back as much information as possible. Two men were detailed as our guardian angels and were to return with us. At a certain point the patrol would break away from us to the river, while we were to continue our recce along the river bank. We set

---

*Brother.

off at about 1930 hours and it was then bright moonlight, although there was some cloud about. We left our map cases at the H.Q., a typical infantry H.Q., candle burning, rather murky, forms lying around, tea on the brew, the Company Sergeant Major swearing down a Don. 5, and kit all over the place, but, on top of all, a cheery atmosphere.

Well, it was an experience being out for the first time in my life with a real action service patrol, floundering about in muddy ditches, creeping over roads, freezing, hugging into a bank; the mosquitoes were a plague and I was very glad I had my cream with me. We went through the forward company where dim shadows were cast by rifles and Brens in this no-man's land. Well, we were lucky and met no Boche. The fosse certainly gave cover but the sandy road was bad for us, and so were the approaches, and, as we learnt on the way back, it was very near a nasty German mortar task and a Gunner task. We got two lots of mortaring on the way back, and were pretty quick into the ditch. We were out nearly two hours and I remember seeing the amazing red glow of Vesuvius in the distance. But I felt sorry for the Foresters who had still to cross the river in a rubber boat. They certainly have a bloody time, these chaps, and they are wonderfully cheerful and high-spirited about it all. To our right there seemed to be several fires but I could not say for certain whether they were the effects of our shelling or the enemy's. The Volturno meanders in the true sense of the word. It was queer to look back and see the flash of our own guns and hear the shells whining overhead. Yes, the infantry man is still the hub of an army.

And so we were glad to return to H.Q., get our map cases, have a nip, and after a pleasant chat, return 'home'. I managed to get a lift back in a jeep, and there was old Gorman waiting to cook my dinner, lovely fish cakes and chips, nice fruit and a cup of char. I sat by the light of the lamp and read some 'boomf' and felt pleasantly happy as I went to bed.

14.10.43   Zero hour for the attack on the Volturno was 2100 hours on the night of the 12th, with the Foresters doing a diversionary attack on the right, the Durham Light Infantry doing the assault, and the Leics. following through them. The mortar platoons were to move up at night and be ready to do observed shooting by day. So, as 2300 hours I left my H.Q. at Villa Literno (I had got quite attached to this place, despite the depressing surroundings) and took the platoons to the mortar positions I had previously recced the night before the patrol. It was a cold, brilliantly moonlit night, and standing up in front of Paddy's carrier, I was glad I had my battle dress and scarf on. The attack was going in on the whole front, so as we approached the river, we could see, looking back, a multitude of gun flashes. My thoughts were very much with the infantry on that bright night; it must have been a nasty feeling going across in small boats, in a swift current, not knowing what was waiting for them.

We got up to the position behind the fosse, as arranged, and soon got cracking in slit trenches. Mortaring and shelling seemed to be going on the other side, and we heard occasional small arms fire. The Padre had come up with us and went on to the M.G.s, who were on our right. When I saw all was going according to plan, I picked up the Padre and we returned, I to my new H.Q., a small building about two miles back, which we were going to use for that night, and he to 1 Group to go round there. A good chap, our Padre, very conscientious and very human. He had supper with us before the attack and had actually brought a pushbike with him to go up to the forward troops. When we left the position the carriers were ferrying bombs up from the road, the nearest point to which we had brought soft-skinned vehicles.

The following morning I was about early, enquiring over the air whether observations posts had been established. I sent up the O.P.O.s who had to cross the river to see the C.O., and went back to send up their O.P. carriers, and a 22 set from our rear H.Q. When I got back, we had established ourselves in a big farm house, the Foresters' old battalion H.Q., and in a very quick time all these things were going into motion, including the sending up to 4 platoon four O.P.A., another sergeant and a despatch rider.

I hadn't been there long when Steve came back rather shaken after a lot of shelling, mortaring, etc., and said that the C.O. wanted a mortar O.P. officer with him the whole time, and Steve was to relieve him. One platoon was therefore to come out of action, and go up the following night to relieve the other and so on. They had spun a coin as to who should stay, and Paddy lost.

In the afternoon the situation deteriorated very rapidly when tanks broke through, followed by infantry. We had nothing to stop them, the line broke, and we withdrew over the river. Many were left on the other bank, dead and wounded, and those who got away had to swim for it. Jack Kysh was hit fighting his M.G.s and believed killed. His poor wife had only just had her first baby on the 30th September. Paddy's O.P. party were tanked over and they got away leaving the 21 set behind them. Again we were lucky and had no casualties. It has been a most unpleasant action and the Foresters must have suffered heavily; in fact, I think nearly all the officers were killed or wounded. Paddy got his platoon out of action and pulled back to Villa Literno, but 100 bombs had been left on the position.

Luckily, however, the Boche stayed on his side and the Rifle brigade came up to fill the gap.

16.10.43   The battle of the Volturno can now be considered to be over.

The German's counter-attack was no more than a local affair, a common trick of his infantry when he is on the withdrawal.

On the night of the 14th, Bob, David and I went up to see the Brigadier at his H.Q. at about 2100 hours. It transpired that he wanted an A/A platoon, a 4.2 platoon, and a M.G. platoon brought up near his H.Q. to be at his immediate disposal. We were also to bring up our advance H.Q. We had to come up that night, hide ourselves away behind the tiny farmhouses that the Fascist Regime had provided. I got Steve up from Villa Literno, and at 0035 hours we left my H.Q. In the morning (spent a cold uncomfortable night in my truck) we learnt that the positions had greatly improved and trucks were moving along the road the Germans had called Macheusen Street.

On the evening of the 15th I rejoined my old H.Q., now shared by Division Tac. H.Q. After the miserable night I had spent behind that smelly farmhouse, which was crawling with mosquitoes and flies, and where the occupants lived on the top storey and the farm animals on the bottom, it was pleasant to go to our reasonably clean room and go to bed in a camp bed.

20.10.43   A really beautiful day, with a lovely Italian 'blue sky'. It was just like a September day in England, and it made me feel I wanted to go up on the downs to Black Cap valley and pick some spindleberries. But here, alas, there is not incentive to walk anywhere, the surroundings are depressing, flat, murky, and military. The Padre came to tea, and later Bob and Mac came in for a chat. The front is quiet and no-one knows what is happening. What a queer mixture this military life is? You have long periods of boredom, rest periods so called, in which it is impossible to rest mentally, for you have more time to think of home and all its delights, of your loved ones and their blessed companionship. On top of that, you feel that you may be called at any time to fulfil some task, which is full of danger, suspense, and a strain on the nerves, certainly to an unwarlike person like myself. So you get the double pull! The precious hours do not seem so wasted when you are actively engaged.

23.10.43   Yesterday morning we had a Service followed by Holy Communion in Paddy's farmyard, and again I was full of admiration for the Padre's talk. He gave us some tricky hymns to sing though.

In the afternoon I had enjoyable time buying presents for Dulcie – my Christmas shopping, in fact. I was able to get her some stockings, powder, lipstick, and I also bought a beautiful breakfast set of Florence porcelain. I only hope I can get it home safely. It seemed fantastic to be shopping like this only fifteen miles from the front line, and it all seems so unreal, as so many things do nowadays. It's a queer war for us at the moment. We are still on the canal north of the Volturno, and it seems we are making no determined effort to push on, and we rather deduce from this that there must be some less obvious plan afoot, a flanking movement, but then all army movements seem to be either frontal or flanking. Maybe we hope to encircle the enemy?!

4.11.43   On the 29th I had letter No. 52 from Dulcie, a small thing to write down, but a wonderful thing in the daily life of a soldier.

Recently I had started a habit of getting up early and going round the platoons before breakfast – rather pleasant, giving one a good appetite. I visited 4 platoon that morning and was disappointed at the few bombs they had fired. In the afternoon I went with Steve to Nocelletto to see the C.O. again, and it was rather unhealthy there, shelling and mortaring. One horrible sight I shall never forget – an Italian mother and father, helped by a soldier, carrying in their little boy to the Field Dressing Station. He had been badly wounded. The mother was demented, poor creature, and it is these sights that make one so sick of the war and all it means.

6.11.43   We have a lot of dead cattle in our new billeting area (east of Sessa), most unpleasant, horribly obnoxious and smelly, and today we have set light to one or two, but it takes a lot of petrol. The Germans are doing this a lot as they retreat, a sort of vindictive scorched earth policy aimed at the Italians as much as us. Cases of Italian civilians being shot are now frequent, and one can well imagine how the German mentality will work out even more as we advance. But they are doing themselves great harm in this short-sighted policy; they will not be loved by many after the war.

7.11.43   At the conference yesterday we learnt that we should probably be back in the line on the 16th, and the rumours about the division coming out to rest seem now to have been definitely squashed. Still, they are allowing us to run recreations into Naples, and that gives the men a chance to buy things to send home.

The war goes on steadily; our patrols are over the Garigliano, and the Americans are pushing up the centre, threatening the Arunci position. Demolitions are the bugbear and someone had said that we have had to face more demolitions than any other army ever.

There has been a relief on the German side and one of the divisions, the 276, is apparently one that has reformed since Stalingrad, so they are probably pretty good. Sam Enderby has flown back and is now C.O. of the Leics., and he says that battalion H.Q. 2 Group are on their way to Bizerta, so they should be here shortly. How glad they must be to have left that horrible Foret de Ferdinand. It is raining very heavily now and our sunken lanes will be a bit tricky in the morning for vehicles.

I wonder what Dulcie is doing now; it seems so long ago since I saw her last. She may even be sitting at our old desk writing to me, or is she slipping quietly into the nursery to see if Nicolas is asleep? Yes, this separation is a hard thing to endure, perhaps the hardest of all of wartime. And now to bed and Tolstoy, God bless him; and we have a roof over our heads.

10.11.43   The Russians drive on past Kiev, that wonderful victory which may yet be the turning point of the whole war. In fact, the day may not be far off when Hitler will have to withdraw (if he can) his whole army in South Russia, but I feel that the Russians will have a lot to say in the matter. Churchill, in his Mansion House speech, says that, 'if no error is made in our strategy, then 1944 should see the climax of the European war'. He says that the hardest fighting for the British and American soldier is yet to come, presumably he means the second front; but we must not be complacent, he says, for the Germans still have 400 Divisions. Eden confers with Turkish Ministers; what brews in the mind there, I wonder? There is no smoke without fire.

20.11.43   For the last eight days I have been in hospital. It all started, I believe, with the stupid TEWT, when I'm pretty sure I got a chill. On the night of the 12th I went to bed early and didn't feel well enough to eat our lamb, which was a great pity! I got very hot in bed, and when Graham took my temperature it was 103.5. So, very kindly, he went to see a doctor, and came back with an ambulance, and orders that if my temperature was still as high I was to go to the M.D.S. that night. I argued that I didn't want to go; I was beautifully warm in bed and it seemed stupid to move me. However, they prevailed over me and I was duly installed in an ambulance and soon we were bumping along the lane, and I remember trying to judge exactly where we were by the turns and the Bailey bridges we had to go over. It was not long before I was at 184 Field Hospital, and in the reception room I was soon telling the doctor that it wasn't much and I was sure it was a chill plus infected tonsils, and I would soon be all right. They then moved me to a marquee tent and I got into a cold bed and was unable to get warm for some considerable time, but I did get a hot water bottle.

On the 13th they had still not diagnosed me, but I was gargling and felt that at least they were on the right track. I had several blood tests for malaria, all of which proved negative. The Padre and Traise came to see me and I got some little things settled up. That night it poured with rain and the old tent just couldn't hold it, and there we were, shifting our beds from place to place, trying to find a dry spot, not much fun for people with chills and temperatures, and it's most annoying to have water dripping on your pillow! By the 14th they had decided I had got 'Clinical Malaria'; how they arrived at that decision I cannot imagine but I don't think medical skill had anything to do with it. 'That's what it usually is,' seemed to be the keynote. On that day the rain just belted down, and in the afternoon one half of the tent capsized and before long we had a miniature lake inside. They gave us plenty of hot drinks but the food, generally speaking, was poor and often is in these forward clearing stations, but I don't know why it should be.

On the 15th I was transferred to 21 C.S.S. and then put in a smaller (Italian?) tent, which was very warm and comparatively dry despite the fact that it had been raining for about three days and nights. The doctor gave me a thorough overhaul and apparently came to no other conclusion, and I was put on quinine.

Once you are in hospital you soon get used to the routine, and before long you are enjoying yourself – if you are not ill, as I wasn't by this time; even the horrible 5.00 a.m. wash is taken in its stride.

And so I waited there till the 18th, when I was transferred to the 92 hospital in Naples. We came through Capua and Aversa, and it seemed a slow business. We missed our lunch and had to wait in the reception tent quite a time while we were sorted into our various categories. However, once we got to our ward, all was comfort, a tremendous change from the mud and wet. It's a colossal place this, meant to be one of the most modern in Italy.

25.11.43 Yesterday we left the 92 General Hospital. After a somewhat irritating delay we at last got an ambulance to take ourselves and our kit down to the docks, where we got an American craft that was to take us across the Bay of Naples. It was a cloudy day mostly, but with some sun, and the air was wonderful, and I rather enjoyed the trip. The views, of course, of Vesuvius, Saunamarte, Capri and Ischia were magnificent but visability wasn't too good with the clouds swimming all round the heights. As we ploughed across the Bay, the towns of Tore Annunciatre, Castille Lamare and the Sorrento came into view, clinging as most of these places do to the cliffs and seashore. The little ship tossed and heaved and waves poured over her bows, and altogether it was most exhilarating. There is such a poetry of motion about the waves, and the gulls float so gracefully just above them. The sea was too much for the doctor and it made him sick and very off-colour finally. It was his first case of seasickness and it made him remark, 'that he wasn't so fit as he thought he was.'

After an hour we approached the tiny harbour of Sorrento, and how it reminded me of Ardrossan in Scotland. We approached it but couldn't get into it, and the arrangement for doing so seemed to be very haphazard. In fact, the American officers were asking if we knew anything about the place, and there was a signal station there! We milled around waiting for something to happen and tempers began to get frayed at the thought of having to return to Naples. The Captain said he couldn't get in with such a wind and rough sea. However, all was well in the end. The Captain took the ship into the harbour and bumped his bows on several occasions against the breakwater. We were getting highly annoyed by now, for soldiers are very intolerant about what they think may be bad seamanship. Soon they began to shout their advice; most of them were sick men who wanted very much to get on *terra firma*, and consequently their nerves were much on edge. The Italian fishing boats left very little room for us, and finally one of them moved to make more room, and came to our aid. The little boat, a small trawler, came alongside and we all got into it after a bit of leg stretching. It manoeuvred alongside the quay very easily and soon we were handing our kit over to the little Italian boys and getting ourselves on land again. There were four officers and we got into an ambulance with our kit and were taken up the winding hill to the hotel 'Tramontano', which had only recently been opened for convalescing officers.

This morning I saw the M.O. and heard that I should be here for a week or so, and for the next three days I have to take some special pills, 'pamacine', I think they are called, and then my treatment is complete. It was a very leisurely and cheerful consultation. Afterwards George showed the doc. and myself round the town, and we visited many shops; it is a place that caters for visitors. The local trade apparently is woodwork, and we saw some wonderful engraving work. I bought Nicolas a money box and a pencil box, and Dulcie a velvet chiffon scarf and shawl that rather attracted me. I had great fun bargaining for Nicolas' pencil box; they wanted to charge 450 lira but by various signs and writing down the sum I considered a suitable price, I eventually got it down to 267½ lira, which I thought was a pretty good effort. It's amazing what one can do by this bargaining, a thing I have never been able to do before, and I believe the Italians love it too!

27.11.43   Life goes on steadily, quietly and comfortably. It is so pleasant
to wake up in the mornings and hear in the garden the familiar
pink of the chaffinch, the sad cadence of the robin, and the cheerful staccato trill of what I believe to be a blackcap. In the mornings we usually write letters until about 10.30 a.m., then we stroll up to the town to see what we can buy, and already I am broke! In the last two days I have purchased three metres of silk, two tobacco boxes, a knitting bag and two playing card boxes, beautifully inlaid. My only hope is that all my little parcels duly arrive home, but good quality paper is just not obtainable here, and so it difficult to make a good secure parcel.

This afternoon we walked along the road towards Castellilarie and the orange groves on either side of the road make one of nature's loveliest scenes. The contrast of the golden fruit against the dark green leaves is so beautiful, and I suppose, to an Englishman, seem very fascinating. We seem to get a tremendous appetite here and we eat all day, filling in between meals with nuts, sweets and chocolate, and then wanting more than our share at meals. How good it is to enjoy food like that.

1.12.43   A new month and my last day at the Tramontano. Tomorrow
we return to our units. George Pearce found a book in the library about this hotel, which unfortunately he's mislaid. I had intended to copy out some passage relative to our little stay and it vexes me that I cannot find it. It mentions the fascinating underground passage that leads down under the hotel to the sea. We explored it ourselves the other day, and it is truly an exciting walk. One begins to forget here that there is a war on, and I must confess I am loathe to leave, but the longer the stay, the more difficult the return. But I shall be glad to see my fellows again, and to get some mail.

4.12.43   Last Thursday George, the doc. and I left Sorrento soon after
11.00 a.m. and along the coast road it took us about two hours to reach Naples.

We came back via Aversa, Capua, and I had hoped to go by Francolisi, but we turned off before then, and finally reached Sessa where the doc.'s M.D.S. was. Then more delay. First, no-one seemed to know much about the whereabouts of Brigade, let alone our Group H.Q., and then there was some trouble about a relief driver to take us on. At last we got one and, being moonlight, we decided to set off in the direction of what was supposed to be the location of Brigade H.Q.

We got out of Sessa and took a left fork, but soon after I stopped at some wayside unit, who thought that there was a 53 H.Q. somewhere back up the road over which we had come. Brigade anyway, they said, had moved two days ago about eight miles up the right fork road. So we turned the car and by continual stopping and questioning eventually found our B Echelon, and got all the dope from Swill and Tony. Fortunately for us, C company B Echelon was in Sessa; in fact, billeted in the police station. So it wasn't long before we were with Steve, who was acting Second-in-Command. Of course, the first thing we asked for was mail, and I had seven letters from Dulcie. The company was doing great work and only the night before had fired 1700 bombs. The R.A.S.C. had made a dump of something like 8,000 bombs up there and altogether things seemed to be pretty hectic. The battle, which started a day or so ago, seems to be pretty bloody. Travel on the road past Ponte by day was not permitted, so I decided to stay the night at Sessa and go up on Friday night. As usual, when you return to your unit in the middle of a battle, you are plastered with all the terrible stories – bad roads, trucks and tanks going over precipices at night, shelling, of chaps you know killed and wounded, and you are not put in a very good frame of mind, but personally I have found it better to ignore these stories and wait and see for myself. It's just no good worrying in wartime, it doesn't help a scrap. So Traise made up my bed (on a policeman's iron bed, well-sprung), Gorman made us some tea and for that night anyway we would be comfortable. Steve had to go up to take some drivers as ammo carriers, and when he came back he said things were very much the same with plenty of 'stonking' going on. What annoyed me most of all on my return was that two pairs of boots of mine had been lost!

Yesterday morning Swill managed to get through to Bob, who said he didn't want either George or myself to go up. He didn't give any reason and I felt bloody annoyed. As Company Commander I felt quite out of place back at B Echelon. In the afternoon I went up to Ponte and tried to phone through from there, but was unsuccessful. Swill went up on a bike and I told him to give Bob a message that I was most desirous of getting to company H.Q. When Swill came back, he had orders from Bob that on no account was I to go as Ginger had given him orders to keep a reserve of officers in Sessa. So that was that, but I shall try again today to see if Bob will let me swop over with Graham. I hate being out of things like this, it's all so dull and detached. The weather has been simply appalling since yesterday, and it has been raining for twenty-four hours. Conditions up at the front must be horrible. The fight for Rome in this country and weather is going to be no easy walkover, and I hope they don't expect a cheap victory at home. But slowly and inexorably we are pushing the Hun back, and that, I think, is bloody good in a country so ideally suited for defence.

8.12.43 When you are landed plum in the middle of a battle and, to say the least of it, a rather confused and bloody one, it takes time before your mind really gets adjusted to what is happening. All the more difficult if you arrive at night, as I did. But I have gradually picked up the threads and now have a reasonable picture of what has been happening in the past few days.

When I arrived on the night of the 5th, the platoons had just finished moving out of the gully position to new ones south and north of Vandria. In fact, they were in the middle of a three-hour shoot. We had jeep trains allotted to us to get to these positions, also to get ammo up; in fact, throughout the operation we got practically everything we asked for.

After stumbling up the wet gully and climbing through terraced vineyards, I eventually got to Graham's 'Hovel Farm' H.Q. Thank goodness, there was some moonlight; in fact, a beautiful night, white fleecy clouds against a velvet sky. I remember how the incongruity of the roar of the guns struck me. It was a queer-shaped farm, built into a bank, and the bottom room, the cattle room, gave good protection against shells. There was Graham in his blue pullover, with a snivelling cold, sitting in an improvised table made out of logs and a bit of board, kit and Don.5s all around him, and beds on the straw. I could not stand upright in this place. We sat and talked and he told me what was happening; of 1 Group mortar H.Q. joining them for a while; of the shambles it involved; of Martin and Sgt. Smith going forward with a section of mortars and doing good work in knocking out a Jerry mortar. Base plates were continually giving way, and on many occasions we only had one mortar in action. Every night Steve would be taking one or two base plates to R.E.M.E. The Padre had called previously to see Graham and had described his company H.Q. as the 'Gnomery', and it certainly was an apt description, with Graham as the gnome. They had had a pretty hectic time, getting hardly any sleep, and he was in good form on the Don.5, telling people just what he thought of them. But tonight we were lucky; there was little shelling, no call for defensive firing tasks, and we all managed to get a reasonable sleep.

On Monday morning I went up to visit platoons (thank God for the jeep, for S. Clemento and Croce were in a hell of a mess, and so were the roads), and I saw for myself the very difficult conditions under which they were working. However, they were cheerful enough and I was glad to see them all. They all looked dirty, unshaven, and very tired indeed; they had had a bloody time. Both platoons went into action whilst I was on the position, and it made me realise how long it was since I had heard the familiar sound of 4.2 fire. After the gully position, the new ones were a paradise, for they could at least get some shelter from nearby cottages. Then I went back to Sippicciano to see Group, and saw Bob and Hollo, who were in good form. This village was a hell of a place, for the small cobbled streets wouldn't even take jeeps. But it was in good condition, and I decided to move my H.Q. there at once.

This took some time as we only had the jeep and all the kit had to be manhandled from the 'Gnomery' to the gully, and from the road to the new H.Q. In the early afternoon I received orders from Bob as to new targets on which we had to fire for 120 minutes, and on and off all night. This was to support the attack which finally gave us the Calabritto basin, including the wood that had held the Leics. so long.

The next day I went with Hutch and Bert to Calabritto to see if it would be possible to get a platoon forward. On the way, we called at Sam's H.Q. and it was a pretty sorry sight. It was an old church on a bit of high ground, behind which had been dug many a 'bivi'. All around were shell and mortar holes, the church itself had had five direct hits; several soldiers' graves were to be seen; German steel helmets too, and masses of kit of killed and wounded lay strewn all over the place. In general, it was pretty depressing but typical of war. The Corps Commander was with Sam and the Brigadier when we arrived, so we waited. I spoke to the Brigadier, who seemed delighted with our mortar fire. We had a chat with Sam, who looked very tired – he had had a lot of casualties, and I think he did damn well. He said it was all right to go to Calabritto, but that a lot of wounded were still being brought down. We had already seen many in the hills, jeep ambulances and several prisoners of war. We thanked him and took the jeep slowly up to Calabritto. It was a sad journey that, wounded men coming down, dead men laid out on the roadside, just collected from the battlefield, mud and kit and burnt-out vehicles, and the tired faces of men who had suffered great strain.

'They died for their country' will be written on the memorials. If only the people could see some of these places, these corners of a foreign land where the men of Britain are laying down their lives for future freedom. 'Lest we forget.' How easily we forgot those who fell in the last war; we must never forget again.

Up there we saw the Divisional Commander, who said it was no go for mortars, about which I was extremely pleased as it would have meant a tremendous labour for the men, and they were already dog tired. Here was a good chance for some rest. We returned over the horrible 'bog track' and I gave the news to Bob, and he said he would try and get us out of action if possible.

We slept well that night and the men got their first real rest for several days. The 139 Brigade, less the Durham Light Infantry, were being relieved and the next day Bob informed me that he had got the O.K. from Brigadier Harding, 138 Brigade, under whose command we had come, to get out of action and return to Sessa for maintenance. All that day we were preparing for the move back, which took place at about 1800 hours. It was a very light night, thank goodness, and we all got back safely to comfortable billets.

13.12.43   Our rest and maintenance periods do not seem to last long, and as the Camino battle had been pretty bloody we were hoping to be out for some days. But it was not to be, for on Saturday we were informed that we had come under the command of 128 Brigade with effect from 12th December.

This was bloody annoying, especially with 2 Group in the country. We hate being switched from one Brigade to another, and until all Groups are in action this is always likely to occur.

15.12.43   We are now in S. Carlo. When I say 'in' that means company H.Q. and 4 platoon. Steve is down on the Mortala feature, which is about three miles from here as the crow flies, but a hell of a sight further by the twisting rather diversional road. We came up last night and up to Ponte it was reasonably light but beyond that up through S. Martino it was pitch black and no joy ride on the mountain road. Still, we arrived without mishap and soon got about unloading and setting up our new H.Q. which was a tiny one-roomed cottage up a cobbled lane.

17.12.43   Things have been reasonably quiet since we've been in S. Carlo. There has been a lot of shelling, and the infantry are doing pretty extensive patrols. In fact, we are not quite sure what Jerry is doing over the river, and I sometimes wonder if we know what we are doing!

Mail is particularly scarce these days, which makes life much less bearable. However, I am very comfortable in my little one-roomed cottage shaped like a loaf. It is clean, reasonably warm and, of course, we have made it well lit. So, compared with some, we are well off.

This phase of the battle allows us good nights, and I go to bed in pyjamas (Graham's rule is that if within shelling range – no pyjamas) and sleep like a log. Traise usually wakes me with a plate of porridge, which I devour before I get up for the next course. Then the sun gets up over the hill and, shining straight into our door, takes the nip off the early morning air. For the last two mornings I have walked up to the farm to see Brigade with Bob. This is a pleasant walk along and up terraces treed with oaks

and olives. Woodlarks abound, their mellow song is to be heard everywhere. The weather for the past few days has been delightful, like September in England, and this no doubt accounts for the woodlarks singing.
Chaffinches and robins are common round here and I have seen a few tits.
I heard a stonechat near Steve's platoon yesterday in an area with margue-
rite daisies – and propaganda pamphlets our artillery had sent over.

I hear from Dulcie that Nicolas is beginning to walk now, how incredibly quickly he is growing up; it is such a horrible business missing all
these different stages of his childhood. I can see he will be a real little boy
before I get home again. Home again!! How remote that does seem, how
terribly remote. We all ask for how long this madness that is called war
can go on, but it goes on day after day; no wonder we are sometimes
browned-off.

20.12.43   The chief news of late is that it is planned that 2 Group come
up on Thursday night to relieve us. At the moment things
aren't settled as to exactly what is to happen; the Brigadier has one policy,
or is it the General's? The C.O. wants so and so to happen, and I'm afraid
I get very annoyed at times with all these various people and all the
complicated channels by which we deal with them.

I have just heard that 139 are taking over and we stay out. In many ways
I'm glad. It will be good to be back again with the old Brigade; the
'Bishop', as the Brigadier is called, is a delightful fellow, very helpful
and very easy to get on with. News of coming events is nil, but surely
something must happen soon; I plump for a big push towards Cassino,
as the Yanks are doing quite well in that sector. Mark Clark and Alex
were up here the other day and that usually means something is in the
wind.

I visited Steve again yesterday afternoon; it was a warm and beautiful
afternoon. There was a sad scene outside the Advanced Dressing Station,
two signallers lying there, killed by mines, and later I learnt two more had
been killed. How I hate these things, to see those blood-spotted, blan-
keted-dead, to see in fact what war really means, the sacrifice of youth.
They lay there, their duty done, at the edge of the olive grove, the serene
blue sky above, the mountains beautiful in their austerity, looking down
impassively, and indifferent to man's insanity. We passed them by and I
was glad to get out of the jeep and pursue my walk on the now well-worn
track to the five positions. I like this walk the more I do it. It is becoming
like a favourite walk in England. Yesterday, near the wood and stream,
there was the smell of England, the smell of dead, rotting oak leaves. That
smell brought back vivid memories.

21.12.43 'Coming events cast their shadows before them.' Things have been happening today, a day of preparation. In military parlance, an attack is being mounted, and a pretty big one I should think, the probable intention being to break through the Mignano Gap and get to Cassino and the easier country beyond.

24.12.43 It is Christmas Eve and I am alone in my 'loaf' cottage. Outside it is raining but otherwise all is quiet. I suppose this is the unhappiest Christmas of my life, for I certainly don't feel very joyful. We are still in S. Carlo under the shadow of the mountains, and lately warlike activity has decreased somewhat, and there is no doubt that the Hun is withdrawing to the Rapido line. However, one of my platoons has to fire for three hours tonight, and tomorrow, and the other one has to do a shoot. So things go on much the same, largely due to the wet weather, the extremely wet weather in fact, and that has probably saved us from heavier fighting over Christmas.

But it is not the loneliness of the war or the weather that has made me unhappy; it is the fact that I have received information today that I may have to go to 1 Group within a week or so as Second-in-Command. That has depressed me beyond words; it has rocked me out of my happy groove. I don't know why I am such an immobile fellow. I feel so inflexible, but I have no military ambitions and I should like to keep the job I have for the rest of the war. I hardly know anyone in 1 Group and I shall feel almost as though I am leaving the Northumberland Fusiliers. I only hope and pray that something will happen to avert this personal catastrophe. I shall certainly let the C.O. know my feelings about it. I have got so fond of my company and its work that I feel it would be worth risking my majority by refusing the job. I've had enough of Second-in-Commanding anyway; it's a horrible job and am I capable of filling the post? Such is my nature, such is my immediate reaction, it remains to be seen what follows.

Christmas Day, 1943. The most unusual Christmas I have spent, perhaps will ever spend. Last night there was a bit of a drinking party in my cottage. We had a merry evening but to me it was a very artificial one and all on the surface. I experienced no real natural joyfulness myself; in fact, deep down in me was a great sadness. It was hollow festivity, but I think the others were happy enough, certainly inebriated enough! I was not sorry when they left, and I could open a window to let out the smell of humans and stale tobacco smoke. I slept well, helped no doubt by the 'Vermut Bianco', but I did not wake in an exalted mood; my first thoughts were very depressing, they preyed on my future transfer to 1 Group.

Christmas greetings from Italy.

Yes, what a strange Christmas morning; it was dry and looked promising, and as I lay in my bed waiting for the sun to rise over the hill, I studied the alien Christmas scene through my open door. The little tree on top of the wall just outside, the olive groves climbing in terraces up the hill, the trees on top of the hill silhouetted against the rising sun, the Italians walking by, some women carrying great urns of water on their heads as they do every morning, collecting it from the well further up the hillside and then walking back in this graceful fashion down the most rocky of lanes. How easily, and with what poise, they do this. Yes, I lay there and thought of other Christmasses, and the next, and wondered where I would then be.

Later I wandered down the village to see 4 platoon, who had got a shoot at 10.30. How terrible to shoot on Christmas day? Yes, it was a strange feeling. Some of the Italians had given the men roasted chestnuts and other fruit as a Christmas gift, but they were dismayed when they saw we were going to fire our mortars.

After the shoot – and Jerry had been using a house and we and the M.G.s were ordered to have a go at him, just to spoil his Christmas dinner I expect, but anyway we have the wrong weapon for the job; still that's often overlooked by military geniuses – I went to 3 platoon. We got to the jeephead, after which I had to do my old walk, this time in a hurry, with a sack of cauliflowers over my shoulder. I had to get back by 1.30 to get my own dinner. I arrived O.K. but old George Pearce had filled me with gin, and I was definitely on the happy, but seemingly unsteady, side when I bade them farewell and a happy Christmas. It was an effort getting back in that slippery mud in gum boots, and with too much gin on an empty stomach. But I made it, and very relieved I was to sit down in the jeep. How glad I was that it was a dry day for 3 platoon, for they certainly have had a tough time, and doing a lot of night firing as well. But they were happy and the cook had prepared an excellent dinner for them. I hope to relieve some of the men on 27th December.

26.12.43   I spent all the morning looking for another position for Paddy.

He and I walked over miles of muddy country, which was just about jeepable, but only just. We got down to the forward companies in difficult map-reading country, even with a 1.25000. The maps here are, unfortunately, not very accurate and the conventional signs are poor too. Even the Durham Light Infantry were a bit hazy themselves. There was only one possible place, a track, which looked as though it may have been a supply route. However, I managed to discourage Dudley on the phone and Paddy stays put. This afternoon I had a very narrow escape in some shelling from Jerry's long-range guns. A bit of stone landed on the back of my head!

29.12.43   Still at S. Carlo waiting for the impending push. I don't know what the delay is but I have heard that we are waiting for the Yanks to capture more high ground in the S. Vittore area. I went down to 3 platoon on Monday with the Padre, and he stayed for an hour or so. He was very lucky on his way back when at 'daylight jeephead' he had some nasty shelling, added to which he was unable to find Cox and so had to walk all the way to S. Clemento. I had walked back with him to the old jeephead when I met the C.O., Dudley and David, and so I walked back to 3 platoon with them.

During the afternoon the C.O. whispered rather apologetically into my ear about the possibility of my having to go to 1 Group, and I, of course, told him I didn't want to go a bit, not mentioning, however, that I was willing to lose my majority. I wasn't brave enough for that and, anyway, I want to stay in 3 Group and be a Major! So I had to go steady. Still, he knows my feelings but, if necessary, I suppose I shall have to go, a military subjugation of the will. I still hope it may be avoided. It will be my greatest regret to have to leave all my friends at this stage of the war although, of course, it will usually be possible to see them fairly often. Apart from that, he saw the platoon under the best conditions, dry sunny weather and not much doing. There was something rather hollow and artificial about his visit; the organisation of a support battalion makes the C.O. a very distant figure and one who has no bearing whatsoever on the battle.

I was most pleased today when I saw a letter from Ginger to Corps agreeing to all my recommendations about the mortar company; that was most gratifying indeed. Better still though was his strong recommendation that battalion H.Q. be abolished *in toto*!

Our supply problem to 3 platoon is a damn nuisance, as we can only reach them by night. Bombs and batteries head the list of bugbears, as rations and water are taken for us by the infantry. This means that poor old C.S.M. Cook is up nearly all night with a bomb party and it's not fun in the dark. It's certainly bloody hard work. He has worked like a slave without a decent rest ever since Salerno and his cheerfulness and efficiency have been a godsend to the company.

31.12.43   A foul night, not in the least festive as New Year's Eve should be. One is apt to forget that it is possible after such beautiful weather as we have been having. Yesterday I walked down to Steve and the scenery was perfect; a warm sun, a clear blue sky, which together gave the hills that purple glow, and in the distance beyond Mt. Cassino, the Appennines laced with snow. For the first time in Italy I heard and saw long-tailed tits. 3 platoon were happy in such friendly weather. Today they must be cursing it, cursing the rain as it leaks in their flimsy bivouac, cursing their wet squelching clothes, cursing the mud, cursing the war.

And so ends the not uneventful year of 1943. Eisenhower says that this will be the last combat Christmas in the European war, and I hope he is right. Certainly things look promising, despite this slogging up-hill campaign in Italy. The Germans are at least beginning to feel the weight of our air offensive (another 2,000 tons on Berlin last night), and on the Eastern front the Russians are advancing in all sectors. The Second Front Commanders have been nominated, and the Hun cannot be waiting too eagerly for that massive assault. I only hope to God that next New Year's Eve I'm not sitting in a small cottage on a hillside, with the rain pouring down, my feet as cold as hell – no fire – the prospect of going to 1 Group, people coming in and out, mud, darkness, guns, and wondering what comes next. No, pray God 1944 sees the end of the chaos and misery of war. Funny I had hardly finished writing these words when a despatch rider came in with the fatal message headed – 'Inter-Group transfer – Officers', and then at the top was 'T/Major E. H. Parkhurst transferred from 3 Group to 1 Group, and appointed Second-in-Command' – as though that was an honour! I stared at it blankly for several minutes and then said, 'All right,' to the D/R. So it has come, earlier than I expected, and even now my mind is trying to absorb what the wrench will mean.

I shall go, of course, without demur, as I knew I would at the beginning, but I am not going to try to seek out advantages of such a move. How I shall miss them all – all of them in those two platoons of mine who have been so grand ever since we landed. Surely it would be difficult to find better men in the whole Army. But I take old Traise with me, a good reminder that I am in this fine 'Geordie' regiment. Yes, it will be difficult to leave all these men, all the memories of the past years that they bring back to me. The break is a human one, the great link of comradeship that means so much in war. To start again now, to build up this spirit in 1944, is the task that so immobilises me, but it will have to be done, and done quickly. And so on this New Year's night, as the rain spatters on the door, I am in a sad mood; queer how one becomes so attached to things and people, and emotional experiences, all of which I had never even contemplated four years ago. Somehow it makes the future seem so much more uncertain for me, and great loneliness haunts my soul. God give me the

strength to do this new job well, and God bless C company for all that
they have done for me.

2.1.44   A series of fleeting impressions as usual in a change like this,
            which it's difficult for the old brain to absorb entirely: arriving
at the old house at S. Clemento, a biting wind blowing, dark steps, and
then bursting into Tony's office. Tony's military aura and his exactness of
speech and thought; old Ellis surrounded by maps and air photos, beautifully kept, situation reports too, all of which I was to take on; going round
the company with Coutts, strange people again, and then coming back as
Tony was ready to give me the low-down then. I shall never forget Tony
telling me why I had come as Second-in-Command, and all the history of
his officers, etc. etc. And as I listened to all this, nodding or shaking my
head as the words required, I remember so well the roaring wind through
the draughty window and wondering what would be the warmest part of
the room to sleep. Sometimes I asked questions, could Knight take over
the MG company, or Mac the mortars? Other memories – Tony's brisk
'Fall out Wright' when he was interrupted, his 'B – lake' when calling his
servant, and the bloody good dinner. Later trying to sort out Ellis's air
photos and situation reports, and thankfully going to bed. Today has gone
quickly too, despite the fact that we rose at 6.15 a.m. (that, apparently, is
normal in 1 Group, great Gods!) I went with Tony to Mignano and saw
country the far side of Camino. Mignano was shattered and last night B
company came in for some shelling and had one sergeant wounded. The
Yanks have turned the old railway line into a road – now called railway
road – and along this we struggled against a strong side wind and we had
to de-jeep at Mignano station. We visited Brigade first in a good shell-
proof gully, and then proceeded another mile or so to a battalion H.Q. of
the 6 AIR, a company of which a M.G. platoon of ours is following up in
the attack on Porchia. The battalion Commander was not in his H.Q., so
we hunted for him on the Raconia feature, and there we found him
eventually with the Regt./Cmndr., a Col. Paul Steele. The battalion Commander was a Lt. Col. Ringsaid* and I took an immediate liking to the
man. His whole personality exuded vitality, intelligence and friendliness,
and he struck me as being right on top of his job. Before going back to his
H.Q. we studied the battle ground to be and had a fine view of the Porchia
and Cedra features, and behind, Trocchia. The country otherwise was flat,
well wooded, good going for tanks, by the look of it.

The Americans were highly optimistic and thought this a chance to have

---

*Ringsaid, poor fellow, was killed in the Porchia attack.

a real crack at the Hun. On the way back Ringsaid and I talked about homes. He liked England and wanted to live there. He didn't like N. Ireland where he had first landed from America. He came from S. Dakota. At his H.Q. we discussed the plan for the attack, and again I couldn't help admiring their intelligent approach to the tactical situation. I offered him some of my baccy and in return he gave me a packet of Edgeworth – the Q.M.S. issue! Paul Steele, a regular, I remember had a fighting face and deep voice, typically American. Their whole approach and readiness to tie up all 'Q' problems, the help they were willing to offer, was a most refreshing experience. The Red Tape Worm seemed to be almost non-existent compared with the British Army. Everything was finally fixed and I was sorry to leave.

5.1.44   So, on Monday we left S. Clemento to take up our active stations northwest of Mignano for the Cedra battle. I came up in the morning and got our railway road farm prepared as an H.Q. We were lucky to get the place, as there was nowhere else. It was a bit shell exposed, however, but we were willing to take the risk for a little warmth and comfort. The grey hills loom up on both sides of this Mignano gap, and make the guns scream and roar like express trains. The weather, thank goodness, has been dry up to now, but damn cold.

All night the guns roared, both ways. It was a restless night, with the telephone and the booming echoes from the hills. Literally, it was guns to the right of us, guns to the left of us, guns to the front and guns behind us. The din was terrific. The British attack was successful but the Yanks were held, so 138 Brigade did not do the final phase on to Cedra and Casamannio area.

Roy Gibson's company received casualties, about ten in one platoon, and three in another, none fatal however. Only two guns out of six got into action on Maggino and 11 platoon were, of course, pinned to the ground behind the Americans, and were still there this afternoon. The 6 Lincs. received a direct hit on the RAP and the doc and padre were killed. Padre Parks visited us this morning on his way up to the lines. Poor Padre, he looked tired and depressed and a little frightened; how I should hate his job. We went up together for moral support to A company and I was very glad we did for there was shelling on the railway cutting and a jeep had already been hit when we got there. It's bloody frightening to walk along a road, knowing it to be under observation and shell fire. After the jeep exploded (it was armoured) we started on our way again, rather gingerly with ears flapping for that hateful whizzing sound. We were glad to get off the road on to the jeep track, although the Germans had shelled this also, and did again when I was with Coutts. All was well with Coutts, he had had no casualties and had not fired from that terribly exposed position. I had my pow-wow with Coutts and decided to leave in what I thought was a lull from what Tony calls 'Teutonic Aggression'. I had that horrible frightened lonely feeling as I walked back along the jeep track to the railway road. I walked quickly, not stopping a minute. The Hun had apparently only a few minutes before shelled this cutting and several casualties were suffered. I saw three dead lying there as I hurried by, poor devils, they were hit horribly. All up the cutting were new shell holes and I expected to have to dive for cover any minute. But I got through O.K., telling Dusty to get back too. Dusty had been going up to pay a social call to A company but the shelling and my warnings finally deterred him, and very sensibly he came back with me. Tony went to the companies in the afternoon, and forward to 3 platoon. He's a bloody brave fellow is Tony Dewhurst, full of energy, fussy but not obstinately so, a tartar for discipline, an excellent sense of humour, and an amazing walker.

Tony came back from Brigade with the orders to withdraw 11 platoon from the Americans. Later we got orders to bring 9 platoon and 3 platoon in, and we hope that 139 Brigade will be taking over from us tomorrow night, thank God!

10.1.44   It was finally confirmed that 2 Group come under command of 138 Brigade when they relieve 128, so, with any luck, we should have about ten days' rest, which, of course, is just marvellous. Although we are out of the line, we are not completely idle, for we run cadres and refresher courses on operating M.G. work, etc., so as to help out on badly needed specialists, who are never forthcoming in reinforcements. Still, when the mind and body are occupied, the old time goes quickly and we'll do anything out here to make home seem a bit nearer, to make our dreams a little more solid.

I had another letter from Dulcie today, an ordinary one with a sweet photo of Nicolas with Ellen. He looks as happy as a coot and it's the first time I've seen him in his winter leggings. I now look forward to seeing a photo of him with his hair cut. Dear God, I miss that little lad of mine, and the lass who brought him into the world. He seems to have such a natural joyousness about him; may he continue thus throughout his days. It must be terribly hard for Dulcie at times, not to be able to share with me all his antics, all the signs of his growing up, for the joy of children is the sharing of that joy. Yes indeed, we face this cruel separation most bitterly and may it soon end.

18.1.44   As I expected, a lot came to light today as to what we may be doing in the future. There was a good old cannonade all last night and it appears that 56 Division and 5 Division were making an attack over the Garigliano in the Minturno area, and further up, too.

Tonight the Boche still holds Castelforte, and after a pretty bloody crossing it looks as though we may find ourselves down that way before long. Air activity has been on an increased scale of late, and this morning I had the best view of a plane crashing that I've ever had in my life. It was a Jerry FW 190, I'm pleased to say. There had been a lot of aerial machine gun fire and we looked out of the window of Group H.Q. and there was the plane falling down, slowly like a leaf, very unreal, very toy-like as a child's glider, and impersonally, impassively, we watched it crash on to the hillside not far away. It did not catch fire. As it was in our area, I went over to see what the results were and, of course, by the time I had reached the spot there were already a lot of soldiers there. The pilot was dead, had been killed in the air I believe, his body terribly lacerated, almost unrecognisable. Already his boots had been taken off as booty, his parachute too for a table cloth, his maps to the Y. & L.H.Q. It was an unpleasant sight, a mass of twisted machinery, a mangled body; the scene typified war and civilisation today, a messy bloody twisted sort of existence. Already the soldiers, quite unconcernedly, were digging the pilot's grave.

20.1.44   So, as often happens in war, the plan went awry; the 128 Brigade attack was a failure, a failure not so much due to the enemy as to nature. The river, at the points selected for the crossing, was too fast running, and the boats were swept away and ropes broken.

On the left only a few men managed to get across; on the right about three-quarters of a company succeeded. Then the Boche got wind of it, poured small arms fire and threw grenades onto the boats as they struggled to get across. It was a heroic effort, which had to be called off. I heard later that the 'little company' was still fighting on the other side and had even counter-attacked when surrounded. Let us hope that some of them manage to get back under cover of darkness tonight. I cannot help feeling that the attack in this particular area was based on faulty appreciation, especially as all patrol reports had stressed the difficulties of crossing the river here. However, such is the confusion of war. As a result, Tony was called to a hurried conference at S. Carlo and there met the Corps Commander and the General, who were (or had been) making a new plan. The Support Group was to come under command of 46 Recce! All as clear as mud, I thought, especially the 'clear' orders as to our task!! Still, I suppose like most things in the Army It will all come out in the wash.

Tony put Group H.Q. in a bit of a whirl by sending a note back warning us to be ready to move by 1200 hours. But I'm used to these things and I told Traise to leave my stuff here until he came back, and lo and behold we are still here. When Tony did get back, he ordered Order Groups and straightaway went off to recce for positions. Why he does not leave the company and platoon commanders to do their jobs, God only knows, but that made a total of seven officers all doing the same job. They were off at 1100 and got back at 1600 hours, pretty hungry and exhausted. When we had eaten something he then pushed off to H.Q. Recce, and after dinner tonight has gone off again to see the platoons. The energy of the man amazes me. I certainly hope I'm not doing his job at his age.

26.1.44   Well, things haven't changed much as yet. The 138 are putting in an attack on Mt. Fuga, which we are supporting with M.G.s and mortars. It is a slow gutty business and terrible country for infantry. I heard today that Cassino had fallen. It was very clear as I walked down to Coutts H.Q. this morning and I could see Cassino very clearly with the St. Benedictine Monastery above it. The big massif that towers above was mantled in a greyish snow. War seems ludicrous in such beautiful country. Sometimes when it is warm I hear the delightful song of the woodlarks and I stop and listen, and my heart bleeds for England. Oh God, how easily I conjure up those blessed haunts I know so well. The birds are very numerous now and are a great joy to me whenever I go to visit companies and platoons.

28.1.44   And so the battle for the Gustav line goes on fiercely and relentlessly. We have not got a firm hold over the Garigliano and at the moment are in the process of getting the enemy out of the hills beyond, no easy job. So far it has been going well and today Rotunda, the first objective in phase 4, was taken. The enemy are suffering pretty heavily in casualties and prisoners of war. I saw several of the prisoners today and they looked bedraggled and tired, very young a lot of them.

4.2.44   And so I spend my fifth wedding anniversary at San Clementi. That wedding day seems a long time ago now, but how vividly I can remember it; much has happened since and I feel quite a bit older, not physically as much as mentally, but I suppose that is not surprising after four years in the Army. How I long to be back with Dulcie, out of all this misery, chaos and destruction. All the time there is a certain amount of strain, sometimes conscious, often sub-conscious. Sometimes there seems no end to it all.

We are out of the line just now, but a letter from the Brigadier mentions the important part we are taking in the next vital operation, so we shall be back soon. Tony is at Ravello, having a well-earned rest. Now to my lovely bed.

6.2.44   Our respite was not to last long, for yesterday I had orders from Division that our M.G. platoon was to move up to Masse Valle di Fuga tonight to concentrate there with the 2/4 K.O.Y.L.I., and that I was to go to Brigade myself at 1000 hours today. The mortars would not be required for this next battle, but that did not mean they would rest for we had to provide our own porters out of the mortar and A/A companies. So, with Roy and Martin this early bright morning, I set off in the jeep to the foot of 'Fleet St.', the name given to the rough track leading to Masse Valle di Fuga. The ground was hard from last night's frost and there was a nip in the air which made walking quite pleasant, and once we were up the steep part it was easier going.

What a lot is hidden away in these hills. Farms and terraced cultivated plots of land and rocky tracks all come to life as you proceed. At a distance all seemed barren, and it is, in fact, not nearly so fertile as this side of the Garigliano, but I couldn't be certain about that. I saw Michael Holford, who put me in the picture as far as possible, but no definite plan had crystallised for the forthcoming attack and, in fact, it all largely depended on the 5 Hamps., who at that moment were being counter-attacked in Dimitri. We witnessed some of this as we climbed up the line.

8.2.44   A pretty horrible day for a non-warlike fellow like me. I left S. Clementi with Traise at 0700 hours and got up to Mass di Valle di Fuga to establish my battle H.Q. with Roy, leaving Tommy Prior to bring up the two despatch riders and two signallers with all the kit needed by some of Coutts' chaps. When I reached our rather smelly and dilapidated farmhouse, I found Roy and George Strutt had just left for a recce in the Cerasola area. This farmhouse, just recently vacated by the Hun, is a pretty evil place, with dead cattle all around and the remains of dead Germans, which we had to bury today. However, we have cleaned it up considerably and it is now quite habitable. Massi di Valle itself is rather a beautiful spot, a fertile wooded hollow in the bare rocky hills. Indeed, I thought I saw a blackstart tonight, and heard a thrush singing. Now the valley is a hive of activity, mule trains being organised, troops moving up to the battle in the hills, and Sikhs, Italians and Basutos are to be seen everywhere.

I went to Brigade and Michael told me that last night's attack had only been partially successful, the 5 Hamps. getting into Cerasola; the 6 Lincs., however, had a bloody time near point 803, just east of M. Faito. Most of our company got badly cut up and things were definitely sticky. I left

Brigade to plod steadily up 'High St.' As one climbs the rocky path, everything comes into view in a magnificent panorama; Rotunda is completely overlooked and to the south the Garigliano plain, the Gulf of Gaeta and the Massiro Ridge, to the east the M. Croce massif, with Carlo, Marini, Sipperiano and San Clementi are clearly visible, and, of course, all the low ground running down to the Garigliano, the old Mortola area being very unmistakable. The Camino massif stood out well, as did Cedra and Trocchia. But as I climbed near to heaven, I came in close contact with the work of the devil. The rocky graves, the stretcher bearers bringing down the wounded men, the sound of our guns, and the bursting of the Boche shells, and walking wounded making their way slowly down the long, long track.

All this effort to destroy life, all this effort to save it, seemed so mad, so incongruous that I could not understand it. If only the people at home could see these men, their surroundings, their conditions, what a deep impression it would have. As I looked down at the terrifying physical features which our men had won from the enemy, I was amazed we had progressed as far as we had. I proceeded up round Turlito into 'Cheshire' dump and there found 11 platoon, who had come up last night; Roy, with Strutt and Martin, had not long left them. They had got up without incident last night, thank God, and now were waiting to go into battle, and somehow I could see what the men were thinking as they sat there in the warm sunshine. The stretcher bearers (Sikhs, Pioneers, Medicals) continually passed them, not too happy a thing to watch while they were waiting. The evacuation of stretcher cases was a terrific task, taking hours to get a man down to an ambulance. It was a task nobly and untiringly carried out, and all concerned deserve the highest praise. I went on further round the muddy slippery track of Mt. Fuga to the Fuga-Orinto re-entrant, and there hell was at its best. Shells and mortar bombs were bursting near and on the track, throwing up showers of rock splinters, and in general making things most unpleasant. I watched for a time, terribly frightened, wanting to contact Roy, and yet knowing I might never find him in all that maze of rocks. I returned to 'Cheshire' and there found Johnnie Gubbin, who said he thought Roy was at Tac. H.Q. 5 Hamps. There was a telephone at hand and luckily I got on to Roy who said he was just off to recce for a position in the 5 Hamps. area with Martin. Strutt was on his way back. Roy told me not to come up as things were bloody hot. Roy is bloody brave and I take my hat off to him.

Tonight I had a little treat; my parcel of 4 Square Yellow tobacco from Nicolas arrived with a little note from Dulcie. Dear God, re-unite us soon.

12.2.44   The last three days have been pretty tumultuous, grim and
          depressing; but soldiers have a great aptitude for quick recov-
ery, and once they return to the fundamentals of life their spirits rise
rapidly. And in these Arunnci mountains I think things have been harder
than ever before, certainly the weather turned against us.

On the 9th, after a very wet night in which my room got soaked out, I
woke feeling definitely queer in the tummy, a touch of sciatica in the left
thigh, and mentally I was depressed; my immediate surroundings didn't
help a lot. The next day – the 10th – was one of the bloodiest any Group
has ever spent.

Tony and I went to Brigade and were informed that a completely new
plan had been made. One M.G. platoon could be withdrawn but we
couldn't get the O.K. for the other in Cerasola. This was sickening and
Tony went up to 'Cheshire' to see the Guards Brigadier, but even he
wouldn't give the O.K., saying it was a matter for the relieving C.O.
Luckily Tony knew the C.O. and arranged that the platoon come out. The
whole of this area was being heavily shelled by the Hun, and, unfortunately, by our own artillery; it was pitch black and it was snowing and
sleeting. In fact, things were pretty miserable and rather tense, and all this
was going on in the height of a Boche counter-attack on the 5 Hamps.
Meanwhile, Roy and George had gone up to 11 platoon and arrived there
as they were engaging the enemy at point blank range. The men, despite
heavy casualties, were in the highest spirits and seemed to be enjoying it
all. The Hamps. also were in great form, despite their small numbers. It's
so bare to put this in writing, but it was all going on at the top of a rocky
mountain in a sleet storm in the pitch dark. It was about 1740 when Tony
arrived to say they were to be relieved. The platoon had suffered three
killed and thirteen wounded. Roy went to 'Cheshire', or shall I say stum-
bled over the rocky track, and organised 11 platoon and some of B
company to return to Cerasola to lift 9 platoon out. They arrived back at
about 2115 hours. There was heavy shelling all the time and why there
weren't casualties, God only knows; they'd had pretty well enough. The
one horrible track was strewn with stretcher cases left on the side with no
bearers to attend them. Roy said all the rocks were spattered with blood.
And on the way back men of other units had become so exhausted they
just lay down on the side, put a blanket over themselves and stayed there
in the pouring rain and sleet; not for a long time has there been such a
miserable night. Our men carried all their kit and got back to this farm at
0445 hours on the 11th. Every man was drenched to the skin, absolutely
tired out, and filthy. All their blankets were soaked through and all they

could do was to borrow a blanket from some of the men already at the farm, and cuddle down together in the dirty old rooms we had managed to find them. About half 11 platoon had come back and several were badly shell-shocked. For me it was war at its worst and yet the men stuck to it magnificently and were actually singing on the way back. Roy Gibson's courage, energy and leadership is, to me, beyond the highest praise.

Our room was completely flooded that night. Tony and I slept with Roy's chaps, where, thank God, there was a fire. Roy and George were absolutely perished, hungry, but wonderfully cheerful. Ginger Martin had been wounded in the face and had to be evacuated.

11 platoon had shot up and killed several Boche, knocked out a M.G. post, and killed a sniper who was himself about to kill a company commander of 5 Hamps. It was a damned fine effort. Whilst all this had been going on, and how poorly and weakly I have described it, Coutts and I had been to another part of the front held by the 2/5 Leics. to recce for further mortar positions, should we be required (and, of course, we would be) in that area. There was a battle going on there (a part of the one on Cerasola) and we had a lot of small arms fire come over our heads. Luckily we met Dudley who gave us a lot of useful information about positions at present occupied by 2 and 3 Groups. I hobbled along behind big old Coutts, for my sciatica wouldn't allow a good speed, and when the fire came down, or we came under observation, I had a hell of a job to keep up with him. On the way down our gully Coutts pointed out some snowdrops – so beautiful they looked, so gentle, so remote from all that had been going on around us. I could not resist standing and admiring them for a little while.

Yesterday, the 11th, it was still wet and miserable and the men had considerable difficulty in drying their soaked clothing, but fires were lit in the farmhouses and a great improvement made. I visited 11 platoon in the next farmhouse to mine, and I think it's one of the dirtiest places I've seen for some time, the result of very recent Boche occupation. What a place to return to after a night like the 10/11, and yet it was far preferable to what they had been experiencing. How can I describe this horrible place? It was the usual small dirty Italian farmhouse built on the eastern saucer slopes of Masse di Valle. Just outside three donkeys (presumably killed by the Boche) lay bloated and cuddled in death. Strung up outside the farm on wire lines were sides of meat, weeks old, left stinking and rotting. An old Boche latrine was near, still uncovered. On top of these things there was masses of equipment in the form of rifles, Boche helmets, papers, letters, bombs, grenades; inside was filth – bits of bedding, dirty straw mattresses lay strewn on the musty floors, and it was in these rooms that our chaps had rested for the night, or what was left of it. There was an Italian farmer there with his wife and baby – God, how ill and macabre their child looked. My heart shuddered, for there was something pitifully revolting about the whole scene. How sickening, how soul-destroying war was, how easily it blotted out all the decencies of civilized life. I thank God it has never come to England. The men lay there cuddling together for warmth, dirty, worn out, wet through, but happy and relieved to be out of the line. I told them that a hot breakfast and dinner was on its way, and that helped a bit, I think. Yes, I take my hat off to those fellows; they were bloody marvellous after all they had been through. And so they spent the day, trying to get warm and dry, and resting. Tony, meanwhile, had gone over the river to see Brigade and came back to say we should probably be in again on the night of 13/14th. So, despite the wet, the cold, the filthy mud, we were glad to be all out for a day or so and we decided to stay in Masse di Valle to save the labour of getting all the stuff to Lamasti and back again. I have known better spots but I suppose I shall see worse!

Today, the 12th, was fine and dry, and whilst Tony was away I went off to recce for M.G. positions in the 2/5 Leics. area. I was in a sad and reflective mood, and took my time as I walked down the now familiar gully to 'Palm Beach'. I was glad I did so, for as I sauntered I was able to observe the signs of spring. I found a beautiful flower rather like a gentian, with the colour of a crocus, a very short flower that seemed to spread its petals out from the ground. It put me in mind of the Pasque flower. Then I heard a Dartford warbler and later saw one. What a friendly sound; I remember I was standing near the grave of a Hampshire laddie and somehow it all seemed so horrible and senseless, this war we are fighting. There are many birds in these gullies and they took my mind off the war. In a few weeks the hillsides will be a mass of flowering plants. Talking to Tony the other day about the futility of war, he summed it up by saying – 'When we reflect, all this effort could well be put down the lavatory and the plug pulled for all there is to show for it.'

15.2.44   Today I witnessed some grim history – the destruction by aerial bombardment of the St. Benedictine Monastery on Mt. Cassino.

17.2.44   A really beautiful day. I left San Clementi at 0715 to go over the Pateley Bridge to see Tony. The sun was rising behind me, lighting the hills with that lovely warm colour. To the right the snow-clad Apennines and M. Cairo looked magnificent. The battle H.Q. was on a tent basis and with the sun so warm, on a lovely hillside situation, it didn't seem an awful lot worse than billets. It was a colourful scene altogether, with the mule trains going up the mountain paths led by Italians and Indians. The scene reminded me of some of the films I have seen in colour, with the mules and men against the background of the green hillside and blue sky. It all seemed a bit unreal and unwarlike. I went along and saw Coutts, and from his H.Q. one gets a magnificent view of M. Cairo and Monte Cassino and the Monastery, or what is left of it now. Through glasses this ancient building looks completely wrecked. I saw a number of refugees, always a depressing sight with their under-nourished children, the ill and infirm being carried on some sort of home-made stretcher, and the inevitable cattle and goats. Yes, not a very happy sight.

19.2.44   Yesterday I spent all day in the hills with Roy to visit his MG platoons. It was a fine day and in peace-time would have been a beautiful walk. The views from Purgatorio and the slopes beyond were magnificent. Ambrogio, Cedra, Porchia, Trocchia, Cassino, M. Cairo, the Camino massif, all these were spread out like a canvas. Luckily there was little 'Teutonic Aggression' at the time, and I had a peaceful walk and enjoyed my sandwiches with 9 platoon. the Guards had had a bit of a fight in the morning and properly trounced the Germans, who had put in a counter-attack. These rough mountain paths and deep wild ravines make hard going, but I enjoyed it, and, of course, looked out for birds and flowers. There were many lovely gentians or crocuses out, their petals wide open to the sun. Yellow hammers and woodlarks were singing away in Masse di Valle. I used two tracks today that are new to me – 'Low St.' and 'Fleet St.'. Fleet St. runs down the steep side of Purgatorio and for a lot of the time you feel as though you might topple over into the ravine below.

Today has been a day of fairly heavy counter-attacks in our sector and on the Guards, but again the Hun has suffered and only just now, outside this tent, I saw about fifty prisoners of war being marched down. They certainly didn't look like members of an unbeatable army! I often wonder what queer reactions prisoners must have as they come back to our lines and see all our jeeps and mules and H.Q. signs, and hear our guns. I expect they are all bloody glad to be out of it. I may go to a rest hotel on the 21st, so that'll make a change. Roy had three more casualties.

21.2.44   And so for a few days I am again in a world of peace, this time at the Belvedere Hotel, Ravello. Ravello is on the Sorrento peninsula but on the side opposite to Sorrento, so to speak. It was a beautiful day for the journey down and we started at about 0720 hours. I called in at Division to see John because it seems that things are definitely happening, and I thought that he may have gone by the time I get back. I

went to the Information Room and, poking my head round the large
'situation' map, saw John seated at a table talking to an orderly. He was
luckily on early duty and as yet was unshaved and unbreakfasted. It was
fortunate I had called because he had received some tobacco of mine from
Nigel*, sent to him in error. He thought the dope was that the whole
Division would be away within twenty days, back in N. Africa to re-fit
and come back again for a later phase. This last seemed a bit thin, but he
didnt't know whether it affected us or not. The thought of two more
months in N. Africa does not please me greatly. It means that 4 division
are taking over our front, so they won't exactly be strangers to 2 Royal
Northumberland Fusiliers.

I have been rendered pretty useless by catching a chill in my right
shoulder (caused, I think, by riding in the jeep). As a consequence, my
right arm is useless, or was yesterday, when I had to get Traise to dress
me. I went into the M.D.S. and got some embrocation and last night was
administered by Cpl. Adams, who was a bit fierce and pugilistic, and then
before I got into bed I rubbed myself again. It was easier this morning and
I could dress myself. Traise said Dulcie ought to have been there to do it,
and the thought tantalised me. It was so cold in that fireless room. But I
had some gin, put on a pullover, and went to bed early and slept well, but
I was glad to be going to rest hotel; I felt I could do with it.

It was amazing to see how tidy the salvage campaign and the dry
weather had made the old battle fields. The farmers were all back at their
work and there was a wonderful atmosphere of peace, an atmosphere of
getting on with something positive, after the strange negative force that
had stormed the land. Yes, the newly turned earth and the leafless trees
looked fresh and clean in the warm sunlight. For some people the war is
already remote and forgotten. It is indeed strange to come out of the battle
areas into these quiet parts. I cannot describe this unreality, or reality,
whichever it is.

Our journey took us through Capua, Aversa, Naples, Turi Annuciati,
Pompeii, Nocera, Cava, Vietri, then along the wonderful coast road
through Minori. It was interesting to see Cava and Vietri again, after all
the fighting we had experienced there. One almost expected shells and
bullets in the old hot spots, especially 'Gauntlet' bridge at Vietri. To be
able to go across that at ease was wonderful. To see everything in its real
light as beautiful scenery, was a great pleasure. The coastal road to Amalfi
and Ravello is, I think, the most beautiful I have ever seen. Each bend

*Brother-in-law.

brings some lovely scene. We stopped once to admire the view of Salerno, and Salerno Bay is equal, I think to Naples Bay. 9th September 1943 seemed a long way away today, seemed an impossibility, in fact. The sea was blue and the sun was warm. Several interesting flowers caught my eye on the steep mountain slopes. Every possible piece of ground had been terraced and cultivated, oranges and lemons were everywhere to be seen.

The road from Minori to Ravello is even more twisting than from Vietri to Minori, and all the time one is climbing; I believe we are about 2000 feet up here. We are informed on arrival that the ex-King and Queen of Italy were also in Ravello, and what's good enough for them is good enough for us, we thought! We were unable to get the Utility right up to the hotel because the road narrows so.

The view from our bedroom is perfect and we have a terrace from which to enjoy it. We look right down at Amalfi and the sea, but it was too misty to see Salerno. The hotel itself is delightful, and has some magnificent paintings and ceilings, again beyond my description. Our bedroom is blue and very comfortable. But how I shall enjoy all these vistas much more if only my beloved was with me! Denis, who is with me, is enjoying this rest. He said it felt like going on leave, but I could not help feeling there was something very much lacking!

23.2.44   We did wisely to bring the Utility for in this part of the world
            distances are deceptive. A hillside across a valley looks very close but come to walk there and it takes hours of hard work. But not only because of that were we wise – the chief reason is that we are resting and one can still rest in a car but at the same time enjoy the many changing viewpoints. Yesterday morning Denis and I walked around Ravello and found there, quaintly out of place somehow, a village shop for all the world like any village shop in England; it had everything, but this one had a surprise for us. The wife of the owner came from Wandsworth, and could speak cockney in the good old-fashioned way. She was a benevolent looking woman and talked quite a bit. She had left England when she was 19 and got married out here, and speaks fluent Italian, of course. I think she felt a bit embarrassed at Italy declaring war on us. Against the Italian women of her age she looked incredibly robust. She said that they had had a bad time these last twenty years – with Missolini. However, this peninsula had been lucky and from the stock of stuff she had in the shop, things weren't too bad from what I could see.

In the afternoon we went down to Amalfi but weren't awfully impressed, rather dirty and seasidish after Ravello, and so we went up one of the craziest loveliest mountain roads I've ever been on. We kept getting out to admire the view, and once we climbed onto a small promontory where we looked down into a vast amphitheatre of terraces that came down in tiers from the high hills right to the sea. Up here a lot of wild crocuses were blooming, a lovely sight.

We were determined to go to the top, and very glad we were too, for, instead of barrenness as we'd expected, we came suddenly upon a fertile plateau on which lies the village of Agerola. it was astoundingly English. There was snow on the ground, a lot of lovely green grass and it was well wooded. There was some sort of religious festival going on in the village, and a lot of small boys had got masks on and dressed themselves up in all manner of ways. The whole village had turned out. We stopped and talked to some old men about the 'Deutsche'.

26.2.44   Back again to the slush of war. It was so cold at S. Clementi when I got back last night that I went to bed almost as soon as I had had supper. Thank God, there were two letters from Dulcie to break the cheerlessness of my return. But oh dear, what a difference the old camp bed is after the luxury of those superbly somniferous mattresses. There was not much news. The Hun has been shelling Pateley Bridge pretty heavily, and the bottom of Fleet Street too. Coutts' H.Q. had direct hits and he has since come back nearer 'Skipton' and I don't blame him. 4 Division has begun to take over and it seemed like old times to see the familiar sign again.

I saw John this morning, and it seems that we are not going with 46 Division, but no-one seems to know what is happening to us. I wonder if we will remain as part of 4 Division. This lack of information is very unsettling.

2.3.44   Things are still very much the same and as yet nothing definite has materialised about our fate. At the moment we are being worked as hard as ever, if not harder. George Strutt has been wounded yet a third time; he seems fated. The main activity on both sides seems to be shelling and mortaring. Pateley Bridge is now closed to all intents and purposes, and it's a terrible business going 'Skipton' way as 'Sun Track' is shelled pretty regularly. The favourite area is the nasty right bend as one comes up Sun Track on to the canal bank. Beswick and I had one about 100 yards away today, which made us spurt a bit! But officers and men are really getting a little tired of it all; we have been in too long and nerves and tempers are, to say the least of it, somewhat strained.

10.3.44   Ah well, I suppose it is very befitting to end this notebook of mine today, for this morning the command of 46 Division passed to 4 Division. Even now, when most of our old Division has left us, it does not seem absolutely certain that we are staying with 4 Division permanently. As yet we have received no orders to repaint our vehicle signs, or to remove the Division signs from our battle dress.

We are getting nearly committed in very diverse ways. Yesterday I went with Coutts and Hugh to recce for the new mortar position and found a good place, very well protected and defiladed, although the area is apt to get shelled occasionally. It was beautiful there, and a pity we could not linger because the recent rain and sun had brought our many lovely new flowers and I would have liked more time to spend on these botanical interludes. There are many strange-looking flowers coming up in the fields by the Garigliano, but of course it does not pay either to tarry on Sun Track because of the shelling, nor to wander in the fields because of mines.

John came to dinner last night and we had a small brotherly farewell party. It seems strange that I may not see him till the end of the war. He thinks that Cairo is their destination, but after that, God only knows. He is staying at a transit camp near Naples for about a week before they sail.

17.3.44   It was a lovely day yesterday despite the heavy rain of the night before. On the higher hills it meant snow, especially on M. Croce. I went up to C company H.Q. where I had my sandwiches with George Newman who has taken over from Roy, who is away at the rest camp. Then I walked up 'Low St.' and visited 3 platoon. The bowl looked lovely in the sunlight and the spring flowers were coming up everywhere. The clusters of violets are especially beautiful and so are the anemones. I had a hell of a climb up to the peak of point 433 where our infantry company was, but what a lovely view, the best I've had for a long time. Waves of bombers were going over continuously and the whole Cassino area was a mass of drifting smoke, as the battle of Cassino raged.

I got back to Group H.Q. tired and dirty and was thankful for a good wash. The C.O. called in the morning and had some news for us. 1 Group were to pull out on the night 20/21 March (unless the enemy withdrew from the Ambroglio area before then) and would move with 10 Infantry Brigade to an unknown destination. The snag of the whole business is that we get out by the night 20/21 and have to move as a complete Group on the 21st!

Tony and I, of course, both thought 'it's the beachhead' but after a little pumping from the C.O. we gather that we are going over to the Eighth Army front, or somewhere in that direction, and presumably we'll be moving by road, except possibly for the Carriers. I think it's definitely the lesser of two evils, but I do hope we get some time the other end to get things into order before going into action again.

20.3.44   With any luck, this is my last day in this damned Garigliano
battle, which has now been going on for too long for my liking.
The last two days have been very busy making arrangements to get the
Group out. The trouble is that we are not being allowed to lift any of our
platoons out until the relief of 2 Group is complete. However, we hear
now that we may not have to move off until 0600 hours 22nd March,
which gives us a bit of time to pack up. Tomorrow I take an advance party
to Qualiano just north of Naples, which is the Brigade concentration area.
From there we go by road via Benevento to our unknown destination,
which may be either Central Italy or the Adriatic coast.

Yesterday and last night were really noisy and we had quite a bit of
shelling, much shrapnel whizzing past our tent. The bloody French were
going up last night, preparatory to taking over tonight, and they made a
hell of a din. Sleep was impossible; no wonder the Boche shelled us, he
must have thought that a mighty attack was being mounted. A mule died
on Bond St. too last night and rolled down the terrace just near the
latrines.

The song of goldfinches and yellow hammers, the happy love flight of
the stonechats, the 'see-sawing' of a great tit, all bring back happy recol-
lections of dear old England, which even now must be beginning to taste
the beauty of spring.

22.3.44   What a sudden and amazing change of scene. I am writing this
at Qualiano, not far from Naples. It is a flat and well-cultivated
area, consisting chiefly of large orchards. Qualiano itself is dirty and
typically Italian. It's one of those places with masses of horses and carts
with large wheels which insist on travelling in the middle of the road. I
left yesterday with the advance party and we came down via Cascani,
Nocelleto, Camello, Villa Literno, and it was interesting to see some of
the old battle spots again; especially lovely were the narcissi growing in
the fields between Camello and Villa Literno. Soon after I arrived I went
to 10 Inf. Brigade H.Q. and got route timings for the main Brigade Group
and information about trains for the Carriers.

I had just got everything organised, had written a lengthy screed to
Tony, had arranged to move off at 0500 hours today, when a Brigade
despatch rider arrived with a message – 'No move until further orders'. I
confirmed with Brigade that this meant the advance party and not the main
party of 1 Group (actually, they didn't know), and this morning it appears
that we are not going to Lucera after all. Advance parties already there are
being re-called. We eagerly await fresh orders. The Group arrived well on
time at about 0900 hours and we got them safely into a harbour which I

had recced in the early hours of this morning. It feels just like a scheme in England, especially with no shells or guns at the moment. There was a heavy raid on Naples last night. Vesuvius is erupting madly too, lighting the sky at night.

Fresh orders have arrived and I have to go to Cariazzo with my advance party tomorrow. The Group comes up on the 24th or 25th March. It is difficult to deduce what this sudden change of plan means. We shall see soon enough!

1.4.44   We were moved on first to the Vairano area, then to the Belvedere section north of Cassino. Today, there is a terrific amount of movement going on, and I imagine that a big re-grouping plan is being carried out in preparation for another attack. The last Cassino attack can be called a failure, and the vast aerial bombardment doesn't seem to have had much effect, simply because there is a vast tunnel system in the Cassino area, and the Germans just stayed down until it was all over. We took very few prisoners and they reported very few casualties as a result of the air attack. The Boche has Jaeger troops in this sector, and they are bloody good, having been specially trained in street fighting, etc. But, my God, what a bastard place to attack. Kesselring certainly chose his winter line well, and he's certainly held it. But it is not a discredit on our troops who have fought splendidly and bravely and suffered great losses. To fight against all the natural advantages of defence as well as the Germans is a bit much. From what I can gather, the Rapido valley area is in a hell of a mess of knocked-out vehicles and tanks, and the smell of decaying bodies, and dead cattle.

So the Group didn't get the great change we so sorely needed, for ever since November we have been able to see M. Cairo and Monastery Hill. And now we are in the line just north of it. I suppose it is not too much to hope that 2 Group may relieve us, if we are here for any length of time.

Double summer time starts tomorrow, which will be a great help, except, of course, it means that to visit forward positions you have to go much later, but I suppose you can stay in bed longer! We are still waiting for units to move out of our area at Venafro, and I'm hoping to move in tomorrow, certainly not later than the 3rd. I hope the roads are quieter by then; the dust is something appalling, and very reminiscent of Africa. Everyone is asking now when the Second Front will open. We all hope soon!

3.4.44   I suppose one of the most amazing aspects of war is the contrasts it is continually providing. Yesterday in a farm, today in an olive grove camp under the Venafro hills. This side of the hills all is quiet, a piano is being played near a truck, and there is a happy, almost fête-like atmosphere about the place. It is a glorious evening, all is still and warm, larks are singing, bats are whizzing round the trees. The other side of the hills is hell; death stinks in the Rapido Plain, on the track from Acquafondata to Inferno, and over the other side to the shell-pitted slopes of M. Cairo. Here men can move freely; over there they daren't move a finger by day for fear of hundreds of shells being hurled at them. All around the German eyes are watching, and they miss nothing. We are in a horribly unhealthy salient up the shelled track and, thank God, up till now, by some miracle, our casualties have been light. Queer that fate has decided that I should 'stay back' this time, but who knows what may happen? Yes, by God, war takes some working out.

We left Alvignano yesterday and travelled in company blocks at hourly intervals. Rear Group started off first and we came up via Alefi, Pratella, Capua, etc., and the bridge of the Twenty Six Arches. It was a fine blue crystal day and the snow on the highest mountains looked beautiful. I was sorry to leave our peaceful green countryside and the night before I went and said goodbye to the Italians at the big farm. I showed 'Mama' a photo of Nicolas, which delighted her. It was dusty ride up, as we came up against a steady stream of a Brigade of 4 Indian Division who were pulling out. They looked a fine lot.

Tony and I have exchanged several notes. They are living in sangars built against the wall of a terrace and they get shelled frequently. Mercifully they have had only two slight casualties so far. Old Coutts has been firing away, but the Brigadier has cut him down to fifty bombs a day, a smaller return. The Brigade signal officer was killed up there. I met him a few days ago. I saw the C.O. yesterday and he told me confidentially that our organisation may be changed quite a lot. One suggestion was a mortar company of either four or six platoons, with a Major commanding. He said he was going to give me the command if it came off, and I was delighted at the thought. It would be a bloody good command and much more interesting than a Group second-in-command. However, it may never come off, but it was gratifying to know I had been considered for the job. And so the old time slips by and we wait hopefully, longingly.

4.4.44   The croaking frogs jeer in unison at the end of my fleeting happiness. That happiness ended at 2200 hours when the C.O. called in to say that B company was required to go in tomorrow night as infantry in the Belvedere sector. He had received a message from Tony to this effect which also stated that I was required, and he thought it was possibly to be 'Force Commander', but that hasn't been confirmed yet.

And so the bloodiness, the horror, the dull mental misery starts again. It always seems to be us. How well I know the strain, the fear of these things, that shell-shattered wilderness. We move up to Acquafondata by day tomorrow, and after dark move on to a debussing area on the Terelli road, there presumably to be guided into our positions. As yet I know nothing about whose command we come under, nor do I know our exact role.

Thank God I have written two letters to Dulcie tonight, and have received several from her, including one enclosing some beautiful photos of Nicolas. How my boy has changed; I could hardly believe it. Pray God that I seem him again some day, and may it be soon.

6.4.44   Well, it all took place as I supposed it would. It was one of the most eerie experiences I've had for a long time. First the dusty twisting mountain ride to Acquafondata, where we staged till after dark and had a meal. The basin in which Acquafondata is situated is very similar to Masse di Valle in its stoniness and general appearance. The town itself, very medieval in its architecture, is built up on a small knoll, and in peace-time might have been rather a striking place. But after the scourge of war had passed over it things were pretty chaotic. What must, this time last year, have been a lovely green bowl, was now a barren area of dried mud, tracked and pitted all over, and gun emplacements and litter in many places. Bomb holes, shell holes, masses of line, ruined houses, pathetic civilians, a lot of them children, gave the whole place a grim aspect. It was high up though and the air was much fresher.

We waited till the Division maintenance convoy came up and then we tailed in behind it and proceeded on our way. Once we were over the hill above Acquafondata we would, in daytime, have been under observation. Never in all my life have I done such a mountain road and I thanked God there was a moon. It twisted and turned in the most hair-raising way, and over the side one could just discern the deep valleys. It seemed to take a hell of a time, that ride, but eventually we got down into what has been called the 'Inferno', which in reality is a dried-up river bed at the bottom of a steep gorge. The surface had been made up into a good road, and of course the whole area was ideal for its purpose, as a forward dump. The roads in Italy are for the most part very white and this helps enormously at night. But the dust is terrible, and if one happens to get behind a tank, you just cannot see the road at all. Eyes, throat, both become clogged with it. At Inferno we had a bit of a delay while I found the signal officer 10 Brigade to get the O.K. to proceed to our lying-up area. And that ride across the Rapido valley was really rather grim. The whole valley, a large open, very fertile and well-populated place in pre-war days, was absolutely deserted, and in the moonlight it was most phastasmal. Once I saw a cat dash along the road. The gaunt shell-holed, bomb-cratered buildings stood silent and ghostlike. This plain is one big no-man's land, overlooked on all sides by the opposing forces. One of the worst features was the smell. It was the smell of death, of dead humans, of dead animals. The sides of the white road were littered with knocked-out ambulances, trucks, tanks, and all the paraphernalia of war. And in this tense atmosphere, all ears strained for the sound of shells, we drove on towards Cassino. We approached it to within about a mile, and as we did so, the noise of battle got louder, that nasty crack of shells bursting in the hills and on the road. Over Cassino (Monastery Hill) we could see a lot of tracer stuff. And then we crossed a small bridge over the Rapido and turned up towards Cairo and the Terelli road. This turning was a mass of littered tanks, etc., not a soul anywhere, and our fifteen hundred weights seemed very big and noisy. The shelling intensified but we couldn't make out exactly where it was. It may have been the village of Cairo. But it was quiet when we got through. But, my God, never have I smelt anything so revolting as that village. It was bloody horrible.

Then we started to climb up the winding road to Terelli. Not far up we were met by Bill Muir who had recced a place for us. For that night we were to live in a cave and the men in dug-outs in the gullies nearby. And so for the first time in my life I slept in a cave, and it was pretty good; a bit smelly from previous occupation, but as long as you got your bed in such a position that the water didn't drip on you, you were all right. You at least felt secure, and we were able to brew up. We got to bed at about 0200 hours. Tony was there to meet us. He said I have to take over the Group, whilst he took over command of the L of C Force, as it was to be called. It was rather an extraordinary experience waking up in a cave, for I had slept well, and for a while I couldn't fathom where the hell I was. Then I saw the entrance of the cave silhouetted against the light, the whole thing being broken up by the trees we had put over it for camouflage. Just outside a blackcap was singing away lustily, a heavenly sound.

Tony came down later in the morning and said that B company had to go into the line tonight, and that he would be moving into his Force H.Q. soon after midday. So, at midday I went up on the back of a motor cycle to Group H.Q., a strong terraced re-entrant, one of the few places not under direct observation from the Boche. The many shell holes in the area provided ample evidence that it wasn't exactly a health resort. Tony's sangar was built up against the wall of a terrace but it wasn't completely effective as its roof was, in fact, a 160 lb. tent, not as solid as one would wish. I went up to see Roy and Coutts, about twenty minutes walk up the line to jeep head, where they both have their H.Q.s, safely protected by well-made sangars.

9.4.44   My sojourn in this unhappy sector was fortunately only a short one for 2 Group relieved us with 28 Brigade. At about 0500 hours on the morning of the 7th we were heavily shelled, and it was a most uncomfortable feeling in bed hearing the bloody crashes above and below us, with shrapnel and stones flying in all directions. My ears were very much on the flap for that spiteful stinging sound of the 88 mm gun. Hugh poked his head into the sangar, having come up during the night, preparatory to taking over. He and I went to Brigade to arrange a few details and then went on to 'Bedpan' H.Q., the code name for Tony's Force. It was a warm day and quite sticky walking, especially as we went up to Roy and Coutts as well.

Breakfast this morning was the last meal we had in the open. As ever after that the Hun was too damned active, and we accordingly ate in our dug-outs. That evening at about six o'clock he gave us a good clouting, but we had only one casualty, in A company. It was most unpleasant whilst it lasted, and I retired to bed soon after dark. It wasn't really dark as it was almost a full moon, and when the Hun quietened down it was beautifully peaceful on those terraces.

I was woken up early again in the morning by shelling, and in fact the whole of the 8th was, except for a few short intervals, to put it crudely, a bastard. He shelled and mortared us all day long, and we were all wondering what the relief was going to be like. The whole thing had been planned to the last detail. Clem was bringing a convoy from B Echelon of six vehicles, which with the ten of 2 Group, bringing their heavy kit, gave seven to each company, and two to Group H.Q. for carrying us out. The men of 2 Group were marching (climbing!) up from a lying-up area near Hill 70 below us, having got there the night before. Guides for all these parties were duly arranged and so after sunset it was just a question of waiting. And the bloody Boche would not stop shelling. The men arrived between 9.00 and 10.00 p.m., and whilst they were moving up to the companies the Hun was still at it. Then suddenly, strangely, it stopped. It seemed like a miracle. All was quiet and there was a full moon. Coutts got his chaps off very quickly with Clem who arrived from Acquafondata in very good time. After an hour or so John Worthington arrived with 2 Group's vehicles, and with him the first big contretemps. He had only brought ONE vehicle for Group H.Q. I swore and cursed like hell, as I hate careful planning to go astray like that. By dint of much pushing, I managed to squeeze all except three in this vehicle, and the rest I had to leave to be picked up by C company, which they duly were. One's nerves are very strained on a relief, for you are itching to get out of the line, your ears are strained for the expected shells, and something going wrong on top of that doesn't help much. However, our miracle held out. Quietly our trucks slid down the Terelli road, through Cairo (touch wood!) and back the same way we had come, to the north road over the hills to Venafro. The plain stank to high heaven. We nicknamed it 'The Valley of the Shadow of Death'. I was never so relieved as when we were on that north road, despite the fact the Hun started some counter-battery shooting. It was so light we had no difficulty in seeing the road, and I took off my steel helmet, sank back, and thanked God. Incidentally, never in any sector before have I worn my steel helmet all the time. I shall not forget that area for a long time, with its shells, its smells, its chiff-chaffs, and blue flowers on the terrace wall above my sangar; nor the skeletons made by the camouflage net on my canvas cover over the sangar. Traise passed out that night.

17.4.44   It seems that with any luck we might have a reasonable stay out of the line, at least the prophecy is up to the end of April. We are all touching wood like mad, and we are much too wise to take anything for granted. The 'gen' is still not forthcoming but it is quite obvious for anyone to see that something is afoot. Jack Ormston told me today that 12 Brigade take over at Cassino in a few days, but whether 3 Group will be required is not certain. There is still a lot of talk and correspondence going on about the new plan for a Support Battalion, consisting of possibly three M.G. companies and one heavy mortar company, presumably designed to save manpower by cutting out the A/A. General Alexander was furious, I understand, when he heard of a movement to cut down the twenty-four mortars in a support battalion to sixteen, and it will be interesting to see what the hell is decided in the end. Such a reorganisation for us would be a tremendous business, weeding out the chaps we wanted, etc., and, as far as I can see, it would mean us being out of the line for at least a month, about which no-one wants to grumble as I feel we deserve a rest. It would be very hard on the fellows who would have to go, especially after all this fighting, and when such a good regimental spirit has been instilled into everyone.

Last night I went to our open-air cinema, the first I've seen in my life, and I enjoyed it, and Ann Sheridan's legs! Incredible to be sitting out in the open like that seeing a film, when over the hills you could see the flashes of our guns. It was a lovely change to see the female form again, though! By God, it makes you realise how the men miss their womenfolk and, not unnaturally, very much from a physical point of view. War means an unnatural life, barren and suppressed, and the things of the flesh become somewhat over-emphasised in men's minds. However, I suppose it's all part of the bloody game.

24.4.44   We had a magnificent St. George's Day yesterday, and, con-
                sidering that most of the Group are not Geordies, and for them
therefore it was their first, things went with the traditional revelry. We had
a Church Service in the morning with a ceremonial Parade, which included a march past the C.O. After the long period the Group has been in
the line, the turn-out and smartness was an absolute credit to all concerned. The men were in the highest of spirits and thoroughly enjoyed
every minute of it. In the afternoon we had the proverbial football match –
officers v sergeants, which the former won. It was played, shall we say, in
the convivial spirit, as, of course, it should be. The meals throughout the
day were quite up to the usual standard and the cooks did well. It was a
great joy to everyone that present operations had allowed us all to be out
of the line on this day.

27.4.44   The last few days have been spent in combatting the very
                changeable elements. On the 25th we had a high wind and
minor dust storm. The roads, and the track in the camp especially, were
horrible, great clouds of dust being thrown up by vehicles and the high
wind. Tony and I went to Brigade that day, and Tony received 'TOP
SECRET' instructions about the forthcoming operations, so secret in fact
that they were addressed to him personally, and he wasn't allowed to tell
his second-in-command! So, day by day we get nearer to something pretty
big.

29.4.44   I am writing this in our improvised mess built onto the side of
                the motor transport officer's caravan. I put this down because I
suddenly thought that when I read these things in later years I won't
possibly remember where it was written. I won't be able to see the same
dull sky, the view of the mountains, or hear the wind in the canvas, nor
will I see the dust being flicked off the road by the wind.

We are still resting. We are still ignorant of the operations to come. The
daily build-up goes on increasingly. We know that the Rapido has to be
crossed in strength and we have got to get the Boche on the run. It will be
a hell of a battle. Probably many things will happen elsewhere at the same
time. I hope and pray it will be a success and that whatever happens it will
materially hasten the end of the war.

My old friends, the 6 Battalion, had nearly a platoon wiped out on the Cassino front a little while ago.

1.5.44   The circles are getting smaller! Yesterday Tony was at conferences at Brigade and battalion H.Q. As a result we have to send into the line a M.G. platoon and a mortar platoon under command 2 Group *pro tem*. Tonight the recces start and I am going up to Trocchio with Coutts, who is having his H.Q. up there. Eventually I expect we will have the complete Group in, but when or how is not known. Thank God there is a moon tonight.

3.5.44   The trip up to the mortar position in front of Trocchio was very interesting and the Hun left us alone. The moon was kind to us again, but even Coutts lost his bearings a bit and mistook Porchia for Trocchio. We are taking over from the 21 Indian Brigade, the Support Battalion being the 5 Mahrattas. I was struck by their efficiency, cleanliness, and the platoon commander's grasp of the whole lay-out. The mortar position was spotless to a degree, everything being in first class order. He took us up to an observation post in a house, and from what one could see the area would in normal times be delightful, full of vines, and very well cultivated. Nightingales were singing lustily in the moonlight, most incongruous against the sound of Vickers firing just above us. The snag of the whole area, of course, is that it is completely overlooked by M. Cairo, and this prohibits any daylight movement. Enemy shells were falling in an infantry locality ahead of us, and according to the Indian officer, the whole area gets stonked on occasions. Tonight Coutts, Roy and one platoon of mortars and M.G.s go up to take over. At the moment they are under command of 2 Group but I don't think it will be long before we are all there.

4.5.44   Day by day little titbits of information are received, ersatz or otherwise – it is left entirely to the recipient's imagination. The latest thing is the mention of D-Day and talk of a big aerial bombardment on D.1. Today Dusty heard something about moves of A & B Echelon vehicles on different days, and about rations to be carried. The bonds of absolute security have to be broken to some extent in order that the necessary preparations can be made. The roads at the moment in this area are just a mass of heavy dust-flying traffic. Our Brigade has been practising river crossing and, in fact, did a scheme the other night. Various units are moving up to the line and back again in what appears to be a crazy system of reliefs, and which, in fact, is all part of the plan, and allows the maximum number of troops to get acquainted with the ground. When? – is the big question. I give it at least another fortnight. In the meantime, we

have gone into khaki drill, and I have been packing away a lot of my
winter clothing.

6.5.44   There are so many troops and H.Q.s coming into the area that a
            house was out of the question, and so we selected a site to dig
out H.Q. Tonight Val has gone up with a party so as to get an early start on
the job tomorrow. Tomorrow morning Traise and I go up to take up
residence. On the night of 8/9 two more M.G. platoons and the other
mortar platoon go into position. Things are beginning to take shape.

7.5.44   So tonight I am living on the green lower eastern slopes of
            Trocchio. I am in a dug-out, which is quite pleasant really,
although small. I can just get my bed in, and to the right of my head is a
little recess to take a Don.5. At the moment Dulcie's and Nicolas' photos
are there.

Tony was officially able to give me the gen today and most of my
surmises were correct. That is on the Divisional level anyway. What the
bigger picture is I don't know, but I am attending a briefing conference
tomorrow. D-day is not far off, apparently. We are crossing the Garigliano on a two Brigade front just south of Cassino; what a party it will be!

9.5.44   D-day is the 11th May, so we have been pretty busy just lately.
            The last two nights have been hectic. The chief impressions of
these nightly jaunts are fireflies, nebelwerfers, the fresh smell of new
green, so English and nostalgic, nightingales, and moonlight; the intricate
network of tracks leading to and from the dell 'Ascencioni'; the Monastery and M. Cairo seem to look right down on top of you.

Last night was rather tragic. There was more shelling and mortaring
than usual, and Fus. Willett of B company, a three-ton driver, got hit and
killed. We were walking up a lane to see the 3 Group M.G. platoons when
we found this truck in the lane. Tony and I got the poor fellow into the
jeep and took him to the RAP*, but he died in my arms whilst Tony had
gone to get a stretcher. I had to get a fifteen-hundred-weight to fetch him
from RAP and arrange for his three-tonner to be got out before daylight.
One tyre had been punctured by the mortar bomb. It was 0210 before I got
in, and got to bed, but I didn't sleep awfully well. I was up again at 0730
so, anyway, there wasn't much time.

11.5.44   Today is D-day for operation 'HONKER', the vast spring of-
            fensive by the Eighth and Fifth Armies in Italy. It is a beautiful
day with a breeze and bit of fleecy cloud, making it pleasantly cool. On the
lower slopes of Trocchio the martins and woodlarks and greenfinches add

---

*Regimental Aid Post.

their songs to a very summery background. Even the jolly blackcap helps. The poppies, the grass, the vines, are all gently waving in the breeze. Except for the occasional gunfire and enemy shells, the atmosphere is very peaceful, almost leisurely in fact. But it is only so because all preparations have been made. The assaulting Battalions are in their assembly areas. The boats have been assembled, the guns, at least 750 for this division alone, are all in position, awaiting zero hour. Four platoons (two of 2 Group, two of 1 Group) of 4.2 mortars and seven platoons of M.M.G.s are supporting the attack with barrages and concentrations. The other platoons, mostly of 3 Group, are waiting to pass through 10 Brigade with 12 Brigade. H hour is 2300, when counter-battery and counter-mortar fire is brought down for approximately forty-five minutes. At W hour the first boats cross the Garigliano with 1/6 Surrey on the right, followed by 2 Beds. & Herts. on the left. These Battalions are supported by an enormous barrage. On our right the 2 Polish Corps is attacking behind Monastery Hill, linking up on Route 6 with 4 Division, thus cutting off Cassino. 28 Brigade is crossing the Garigliano on left of 10 Brigade, on their left 8 Indian Division. The total number of guns must be in the region of 1,600.

Tony and I have been up every night completing details for the M.G. and mortar tasks, the assembling of vehicles, and many other operational and administrative details. There is not much left now. A letter from G.O.C. M.E. and G.O.C. Eighth Army is to be read to all concerned. Alexander states that we have the privilege of striking the enemy first, and that we have a terrific superiority in tanks, guns, and aircraft. So it does not coincide with the Second Front as we anticipated. What the Fifth Army is doing, I'm not sure, but I guess an offensive in the Beachhead. There is a landing deception plan. At the earliest possible moment after the barrage, our task is to get mortar and M.G. platoons across to support the infantry. So this time tomorrow, God knows where I'll be. 10 Brigade, after consolidating its objectives, swings round facing Cassino and in due course will have the task of mopping up. The Brigadier says this will be done slowly and inexorably. By morning D+1 the Polish Corps should be established on Monastery Hill. It's vital that they should be because of the observation it affords. The planning and thought has been of the best, and never before have I known such care to be taken over an operation. The security measures and cover plan have been excellent too, and I hope we create some surprise.

Tonight, then, hell will be let loose in the Liri valley, and men will die, killed by shell and mortar fire, blown up on mines, sniped, shattered by nebelwerfer fire. It will be a hard battle and possibly a prolonged one. We

have big reserves and there will be no let-up. God grant that victory will
be ours. God grant that the casualties in killed and wounded are as light as
can possibly be. God give strength to our dear ones who, tomorrow, when
they hear of the offensive, will have the strain of waiting; and God give us
peace of mind in all the horror about to come.

Since writing the last few pages, some hours have elapsed. This afternoon I visited Roy Gibson at his H.Q. forward of Trocchio. I had to walk
most of the way because of observation from the Monastery. So ruined is
it now that it looks like a very ancient castle. The walk down the dell
'Ascencioni; was one of the most beautiful I've had for a long time. It is a
partially dried-up wadi now made into a good surface track by the R.E.s.
Dulcie would have loved this part as the flowers were really delightful,
and I found a magnificent orchid which, to me, looked like a Lady Orchid;
wild gladioli were profuse, and nightingales and greenfinches were singing. Tonight this same track will be a mass of men and vehicles. I couldn't
believe that it was the eve of a great battle. Even the Germans were quiet,
though at lunch-time they nearly shelled an area near to Group H.Q. No,
this wood tonight might have been in Sussex, and Trocchio from the west
side is much greener and rather like a Scottish hill in summer. From the
Monastery the Hun looks down on all this.

15.5.44   Much has happened since I last wrote. Luckily, I have kept
          War Diary notes, so I can piece the grim battle together fairly
well. Considering the tremendous opposition, it has gone well, and still is.
But, as Alexander said, it will doubtless be prolonged. It seems to have
gone on unceasingly and we are all bloody tired with the lack of sleep and
the noise. I may as well copy my battle notes as I simply cannot think
clearly enough to put it into good order:-

11.5.44:

2300. H. Hour. The guns roar. It is a magnificent spectacle. The whole
of the sky and all the mountains are lit up by the biggest barrage of the
war. It gives me a great feeling. It has to be experienced to be
believed.

Over Trocchio came the red glow of the shell bursts. The 4.2 mortars
and M.G.s are all blazing away. In the combined Group H.Q. and
C.M.O., telephones are ringing and wirelesses buzzing. The sand-
bagged room rocks to the blast of the guns. It is deafening. Everyone
is feeling right on top and very excited.

1300. Terrific interference on W/T.

12.5.44:

All lines gone with shell fire and trucks. Heavy enemy shelling starts.

The roar of the guns goes on. Lines awful but men out on them all the time. Chaps nodding to sleep in their arms. 1/6 Surreys across river. Having a hell of a time on Pt. 36. The men manning the ferries having a bloody time, many killed and wounded and equipment shot up. Very heavy nebelwerfer and shell fire.

0345. Line to C company O.K. Company of 1/6 Surrey forward of Pt. 36. 2 Beds. & Herts. held on start line. The barrage held for them. No communication with A company. D company asked to shoot in front of Beds.

0520. Beds. forming up on start line. Hold up due to loss of boats in getting across. The morning is very misty, a blessing, and the smell of cordite hangs over everything. A & C companies carried out concentrations and barrages O.K. 10 Brigade out of action ready to go forward. The M.G.s fired nearly 300,000 rounds in their barrages.

0700. A company firing on earlier tasks, mostly nebelwerfers which are causing hell at the crossing places. A lot of casualties waiting to get back. Some W/T communication going now.

0900. 6 Surreys on Pt. 63 out of touch and cut off. A & C companies prepared to put down defensive fire north of 19 grid line to repel counter-attack on Pt. 36.

0920. Class 30 bridge up. Well done. The sappers have suffered.

1230. Tried to get a bit of sleep but with the planes going overhead and the continuous roar of the guns, it wasn't awfully successful. Fight very bitter and 28 Brigade cut to hell, and forced back. Minefields slow up Beds. & Surreys considerably and caused many casualties. Medium artillery engaging tanks on Pt. 63. Thirty prisoners taken. Information vague but another counter-attack expected on division's right flank. C.M.O.* very busy all the time bringing down counter mortar fire.

C company harassing fire on Route 6 area. Understand that the Indian div. now has a bridge up and a squadron of tanks across and most of their infantry.

1400. It's a horrible feeling not knowing exactly what is happening but it's such a bitter struggle that confusion is inevitable. Communication has been bad throughout so far, often the case where an obstacle like a river has to be crossed. Then again Trocchio screens the outstations to a certain extent.

1430. Regiment of tanks across, Indian division. Beds. digging in till

---

*Counter mortar officer.

tonight. 3 platoon in very unhealthy area by track leading down to bridge, a lot of nebelwerfer; thank God they are dug in well.

1455. Ian Cockburn wounded and Jack Ormston too. Another bridge put up, the first one hit by shell fire.

1630. Plan now is to hold small bridgehead firmly, get the bridge going, pass tanks and 12 Brigade through.

2030. 12 Brigade in area. Pipes of 6 Black Watch – a lovely sound. Poles had bloody fighting. Tank battle going on. Boche believed to be forming up for counter-attack. Altogether a day of great tension and bitter fighting, and 10 Brigade has done bloody well to hang on so grimly. It will have a tremendous effect on the outcome.

13.5.44

0725. Night spent in getting battalion up over river. Great difficulty experienced because of mortar and shell fire and snipers. Squadron Lancers across and morale gone up. Managed to get a little sleep last night. Lovely morning, cornbuntings singing and a feeling that things are going better. D.C.L.I.* putting in an attack on Pt. 63, supported by tanks, guns, mortars, M.G.s.

1000. 12 Brigade attacking BLUE supported by heavy artillery fire. I went round to Roy's H.Q. and found all was well. Our forward observation officers have had the worst time, and most of them are badly shaken. J. Dixon's wireless let him down badly. Jimmy Scott luckier and quite calm, as usual.

1200. BLUE captured by 12 Brigade. Heavy mortaring and shelling in all forward areas.

1600. News very heartening. 12 Brigade have done very well and so have 2 D.C.L.I. Both BLUE and Pt. 63 taken. George Strutt and Denis Wood are both over river making recces for their positions. One party of 65 Huns gave up. Army film unit at 9 & 4 platoons.

1830. A great atmosphere prevails. The prisoners are coming in and it is good to see such large batches again. They are certainly getting some stick and how they stand up to our fire, God only knows. A lot of them look very young. Dive bombing started and Spitfires are after them. Denis dive-bombed, mortared and shelled on his recce, and very shaken. He says it is absolutely bloody over there. He'd never seen so many casualties; it is one big hell.

We are the lower jaw of the pincer that is trying to encircle Cassino. The Poles are the upper jaw. The Hun knows how desperate his plight

---

*Devon & Cornwall Light Infantry.

would be if we could close those jaws and he is fighting accordingly, and with his best troops. The Poles have suffered heavily and are being counter-attacked relentlessly. They captured Pt. 593 and Pt. 569 but were later pushed off. The French have captured Cerasola, and are making good headway towards Apollinari. Castelforte has fallen to the Americans. It is a tremendous battle and you can feel the excitement in the air. The Italians are very excited, the women taking especial interest in the prisoners of war. We have been lucky under Trocchio, the enemy's counter-battery being our chief worry.

1900. 10 & 12 Brigades staying put consolidating. George Strutt got his M.G. platoon into action in D.C.L.I. area, a grand piece of work made in bloody circumstances. Sgt. Watson did well, salvaging kit out of a blazing carrier. Prisoners still coming in and the total is about 250 for the division. One B company prisoner of war escort wounded.

I cannot go on with all my timings. Yesterday was another day of heavy fighting; 12 Brigade attacked RED and captured most of it. 38 Brigade moved up to left of 12 Brigade, and 19 New Zealand Regiment relieved 17 Lancers. Tony visited George over the river and found all was O.K. In the morning heavy counter-attacks came in from the Cassino direction against 10 & 12 Brigades. The attack petered out, smashed by A company mortars and M.G.s., everything we had got. A lot of enemy killed and taken prisoner. In the afternoon I visited all platoons this side of the river and found them in good fettle, 3 platoon being somewhat shaken. Mortar bombs are still falling in the area. They had bad luck with a premature bomb which killed one R.E., and wounded five others, two of A company, two of B company and another R.E. I also went up into Jimmy's observation post and the battle area was an amazing sight, most of it smoked out because of the screens covering the bridges and Monastery Hill. We were doing some bombing and I could see our tanks. This observation post was in a house on the colourful slopes of Trocchio. Many things have happened today, including letters from Dulcie and Percy.* The main thing is we are all bloody tired now. Oh, for a good sleep.

16.5.44   Yesterday I covered quite a large part of the area this side of the river, making a recce for a new mortar position. In the end we landed up quite near Cassino station. It was very deserted, very shelled, stark, and graves all over the place. We went forward of the 3 Group's M.G.s and 3" mortar position of the 4th Recce Regt. As far as I

---

*Brother.

could see there was nothing that could possibly be called a 4.2 area. It was so 'bare arse', and overlooked immediately by the Monastery. We were glad to come away from this land of the dead. For the first time I went along the railway cutting ahead of Denis's platoon. It was a mass of vehicles, some ditched, some burned, and dead bodies don't improve the picture. I hear that 4 Division are definitely staying to mop up Cassino, and so for the moment, except for George, none of our platoons are going over the Garigliano, as we can do our tasks from here. Incidentally, George Strutt has again been wounded slightly; he has shown great leadership. In a fierce counter-attack on the 16th his platoon did great execution. Roy has put him up for an award. Another fierce counter-attack came in yesterday from Cassino and on the 2 R.F. and 2 D.C.L.I., but it was promptly despatched with. Our mortars and M.G.s are doing good work. Our company programme seems to have had its effect to a large extent. Last night there was an air raid in the vicinity, so we are definitely upsetting the Boche. Today 78 Division attacked on our left and have done very well, as far as we know. It is their intention to join on Route 6 with the Poles, but I don't know when that final phase is scheduled. The French have captured Esperia, S. Giorgio a Liri, and Anconia; the Indians have taken Pignataro, and we are bringing great pressure on to Route 6 west of Cassino. The Hun knows what this means and is fighting hard. We are killing a lot of them and I think the next few days will show the result of our labours and sacrifices. 28 Brigade badly cut up, have gone back to Alifito to rest and reorganise. Tonight we are supporting another attack by the Beds. & Herts. on the Masse di Liri and Matimola area.

17.5.44   A memorable and exciting day. It started off with the joint attack by 78 Division and 2 Polish Corps, which was preceded by a three-hour artillery concentration. The Poles had been fighting in the hills, and were unable to get down to Route 6. The 78 Division did very well, a 3,000 yard advance, thus almost outflanking the Cairo massif. Then 12 Brigade attacked and cut Route 6, which was bloody good. Later still 10 Brigade attacked to cut the railway and Route 6 near Cassino. The whole thing worked like clockwork and the Hun is in a very difficult position. The opinion is that he wants to get out, must do so, in fact, if he wants to fight again. Hence his fierce opposition to our attempts to seal him off. Even now his way out is precarious and can only be across the hills. The whole Liri offensive has pivoted on 4 Division, who have been battling at the enemy's most sensitive spot. And now we are cracking him. The prisoners I saw today bear witness to the strain we are imposing upon him.

This afternoon for the first time I went across the Garigliano, and the horror and chaos was appalling. We missed Amazon bridge and went over Blackwater. The river Garigliano was surprisingly fast-flowing and full, and of a queer deep blue colour. On either side were rich fields of wheat. All the bridges are heavily smoke screened and an acrid smell hangs everywhere. The ground is covered with shell holes, knocked-out vehicles and tanks, some burnt to a skeleton, and much equipment, German and British, and ammunition. The stench of war was worse than I've ever known, and parties of men were digging graves and burying the many dead. Never have I seen so many graves; never have I seen so much German equipment. After a somewhat hesitant bit of map reading and an eye for mines, I found George Strutt in his German dug-out with Sgt. Watson and others of his H.Q. He said, 'You'd better come in, he has a fixed line on this road with a 210mm.' I promptly took his advice. His platoon had done great work, killing fifteen Huns in one counter-attack, and capturing twenty on another occasion. Thank God for the German thoroughness in his defence, for we had used them fully and our casualties had been light. George's face was swollen badly with a shrapnel wound. He sets a fine example and is a born leader. I hope he gets his reward. They had a bloody time coming over on the 13th. Three of their carriers were destroyed by shellfire. The road at that stage, and the area of the bridge, were littered with dead and wounded, and many bodies burnt to death in their vehicles.

Never have I seen such a 'perfect' example of a battlefield. Let the warmongers come and see this; let them see the dead and dying; the bodies covered with a little earth in the ditches, the filth, the smell of decay. Oh God, it's just too bloody horrible, and I don't know how men stand it. George said many Germans were wandering about half crazy, half dazed with the terrific punishment we dealt out to them. Yes, they are suffering now, really hard.

We came back via the pitted, war-torn road over another 78 Division bridge – Congo – and thus did the complete circuit round Trocchio, which looked calm and beautiful from the west of Garigliano. The enemy started shelling the road soon after we left. The Monastery was getting plastered again by us. I suppose this will go down as one of the most famous battlefields of the war. To General Alexander goes the credit of overcoming such a formidable line.

As we were coming back we saw a lot of the 6 Armoured Division and 78 Division moving up into action, a fine and inspiring sight. When I got back to Group H.Q. I learnt that tomorrow, the 18th May, our Brigade attacks Cassino with the 6 Surreys and 2 D.C.L.I., supported by two squadrons of N.Z. tanks and assisted by the 1 Guards Brigade, who have, during the offensive, been playing a holding role in the outskirts of Cassino.

Corps has had information by interception that the Cassino garrison will try and get out tonight. We have accordingly laid on a terrific harassing programme with artillery, mortars and M.G.s, and 10 and 12 Brigades are acting as 'stops' on Route 6 and the Mairi Route. We will have a difficult task.

At about 1130 tonight I went out of this H.Q. to relieve nature and found, to my surprise, that it was practically as light as day. I had heard planes overhead but had assumed they were ours. It was about three seconds before I was assured they were Huns. The air was filled with a horrible whistling sound. I got down behind the sandbags outside the door just as the explosions, all very near, occurred. I could feel the blast even behind the sandbags. Hundreds of planes lit up the sky and then the A/A was at it. Another lot came down, nearer this time, and shrapnel was flying all over the place. Give me shelling any time rather than this! God help the Germans in a 2,000 ton raid. This was most unusual for the Hun, and rather confirmed that he hoped to get out of Cassino. This was a clever distraction to keep our gunfire down. Still I think it will have the effect of making us even more alert. There were no casualties, but some bloody near misses. The same was happening on the Canadian and French sectors, so today has been pretty war-like, and not as restful as one might wish!

It will be interesting to see what he does try tonight. We want to get as many of the bastards as possible, but it is not our intention to attack the Monastery itself tomorrow. That can wait and will fall in due course. It has so far been a well-planned and well-directed battle. Every step forward has been well thought out, and well prepared, with no undue haste, and with a goodly force and maximum support. It has been worth it. It has saved lives. It has been merciless on the Boche; he has been strained to the utmost. Now I think we shall see results. The hard crust has been broken, and a strong force is passing through with plenty of ammo. We in 4 Division who have played such a big part in breaking the Gustav Line, now stay to clear Cassino.

18.5.44   It is a great and memorable day. Cassino has fallen and the Gustav Line has been completely broken. We were not able to close the gap entirely by joining hands with the Poles on Route 6, and so a lot of the Parachutists were able to get away. Hence the fury with which they fought against both Poles and 4 Division. By keeping the jaws apart they were able to thin out to a large extent. Nevertheless, they have suffered terrific casualties. But the day is ours and a great victory has been won. Last night we received an operation order for the attack on Cassino in which we were to take part. It was to be supported by two squadrons of N.Z. tanks. But when the infantry probed the outskirts they found little opposition, and many Germans gave themselves up. There was some sniping and some machine gunning, but this was soon overcome, and in due course the place was mopped up. Some casualties were caused by time bombs left by the Hun. Later we learnt that the Polish flag was flying over the Monastery. It was very fitting that this should be so, for the Poles have suffered dearly. Georgi, the Polish liaison officer, told me that the hills behind the Monastery were absolutely indescribable. Hundreds of dead lay all over the hillsides, Americans, French, N. Zealanders, and now Poles. The Germans were dug in in steel emplacements and they would not give up.

I went down into Cassino at about 1100 and they were still mopping up. It was a phantom town, stark and horrible, the epitome of war. I went straight down Route 6 with its green fields and lovely trees on either side. On approaching the Rapido bridge, the green stopped. All the trees were naked, stark and leafless. The bridges we had managed to get up were almost totally wrecked. Route 6 dwindled into a 'sheep track' which wound its way through shell craters, bomb craters, and the gaunt remains of houses.

All the way up this track was a mass of kit, blankets, bits of clothing, boots, steel helmets. The whole of the area in front of the town was a ghastly marsh, caused by the lack of drainage and the bombs and shells which had blown everything to pieces. All the craters have filled with water, which stank horribly and were very often a watery grave. Down this grim avenue were many bodies, which had been untouched for weeks, a grim spectacle. The town itself was a shattered wilderness of rubble. I cannot describe the destruction. I looked up at the Monastery, a mass of jutting rubble. Every single tree on the shell-shattered mountain face below the Monastery was stark and naked. The warmongers should see the place, they should leave it as it is as a warning to all future Dictators, to all future generations. I saw some German prisoners coming back; they looked like ghosts. The town has been heavily mined and booby-trapped, so a complete inspection was not advisable. The stench was horrible and I cannot imagine anyone coming back to live there. It is hard to imagine a few months ago, this was a beautiful town. It has made an indelible mark on my memory.

Tonight all is quiet and the battle is over. 10 Brigade is going back to Alifi area to rest, and tomorrow I go off at 0600 hours on a recce. It is a very beautiful spot, not far from Alvignano. How long we shall be out I do now know, but I expect we shall rejoin the battle again in due course. It doesn't seem possible that only a week ago the battle was about to start. It has gone well, but dear God, there have been great sacrifices. And so for some sleep, and then await future events.

22.5.44   Two things happened yesterday. The Army Commander came and visited us and thanked us for our share in the crossing of the Rapido, and the taking of Cassino. He shook hands with us all and spoke to the chaps and generally left a very popular impression. He said that he hoped we should be through the Hitler Line soon, and that the army plan would not have been possible if we had not been able to establish a bridgehead over the Rapido. What our future is likely to be he did not indicate, but I should imagine that the idea is to break the Hitler Line with the Divisions now attacking it, and we will be passed through in the same way as 78 Division were passed through us over the Garigliano. The Armoured Division may, of course, be sufficient, but anyhow we are hoping for at least a week here in this peaceful seclusion.

The other main event was that we moved our H.Q. as we were beginning to get bothered by our neighbours. We are now in a beautiful vineyard floored with poppies and daisies and entirely on our own. it is very peaceful. Tomorrow we all go to Division for an address by the Division Commander, so more gen may be forthcoming then. In bed, with one's head against the pillow, you can hear the guns up at the front, some fifty miles away now. Early this morning the enemy seemed to be making a bombing raid somewhere, pretty heavy too. How good it is to be out of it all. I understand the fighting is still very fierce.

29.5.44   The last two days in our new H.Q. in the Alifi area, have been very busy. We learnt yesterday that the battalion was to reorganise as soon as possible and it would concentrate at the first possible opportunity. This we do on Wednesday. The selection of the new mortar company will bring a whole heap of difficulties of its own. This morning I went on another recce, this time to a range east of Alifi, and there were better prospects of a 4.2 shoot. Tomorrow I go on a Battalion signal scheme, acting as mortar Company Commander in the absence of Coutts who is in hospital with a bad knee. It is a good opportunity to find out about the new W/T lay-out, especially as I shall be Company Commander in the very near future.

3.6.44   The last few days have been extremely busy but to me very happy ones. One thing has followed another in such quick succession that rest has been out of the question. On the 30th, I took part in a Brigade signal exercise which was quite successful and brought out many points. I came back not to the old camp but to the new Battalion concentration area southwest of S. Polito, where the reorganisation on to the new establishment was to take place.

The next day was spent entirely on a conference at Battalion H.Q., discussing personnel, and that was a hell of a lengthy business. 1st June saw the C.O., Tony and myself doing a recce for a mortar exercise for the General, on which we spent the whole morning, only to learn in the afternoon that the Division was moving into action again forthwith and we with it. We were given till 5th June to be ready, so, what with M.T., equipment, personnel, nominal roles, etc., we've been moving ever since. Today we are seeing daylight out of all the changes of personnel, vehicles, stores and nominal roles, and are more or less O.K. My final selection is fixed and I don't think I shall have any heart burnings or difficult cases to deal with. The new company consists of four platoons with a pretty big H.Q. There are about 233 officers and men in the company and fifty-four vehicles. I am extremely happy to be in command again; what a world of difference it is after being a second-in-command to an unsatisfactory war establishment like a Support Group.

I have had no mail for about five days now, and I have only managed to write one letter to Dulcie. Already my advance party has gone up to the front, and soon we ourselves will be there. I must confess that throughout I have been very lucky in my officers and men, and there is no reason why the company shouldn't be the best Heavy Mortar Company in the British Army. I doubt whether there is one with more experience. It now really becomes the Division mortar company, and my half companies will be sub-allotted to Brigades as the situation demands. Coutts is my second-in-command, Graham and Bob my chief mortar officers, John Worthington my signal officer, and I have twelve platoon officers, so I have quite a lot to keep my eye on. But I feel very happy and very lucky.

4.6.44   Our reorganisation is now practically complete. Last night I held a company conference, in which we thrashed everything out, and it all ended very satisfactorily. This morning I talked to the whole company, put them in the picture, and told them the sort of company I wanted, and what was expected of us. Then at Battalion I learnt that we were moving up to a concentration area near Acre on Tuesday. The Division has already gone. It looks like more action.

The news continues to be good. This morning we saw great armadas of bombers going over, a fine sight in the early morning sun. I think the Eighth and Fifth Armies have joined up again on Route 6. I hope to hear the news tonight.

Dulcie has at last received some of my missing letters. It is so good to hear from her.

5.6.44   And so at last Rome is ours. What wonderful news, and how heartening after all these months of fighting. Hitler ordered his troops to withdraw northwest of the capital, and the latest reports say we are thirty miles beyond Rome.

Tomorrow we move to the Arce area, and we are ready for battle. I understand the Division has already started to move beyond that. I look forward to this journey, which should be full of interest. It is good to know that 4 Division played such a magnificent part in the battle for Rome by breaking through the long prepared Gustav Line. Now we are rested and re-equipped and on top of this the Battalion has had a complete reorganisation. It has done well to have effected it so quickly.

Dulcie has at last guessed that I am no longer in the Fifth Army. To me it is a new phase of the war. It is a complete change of scenery, and somehow I am very thankful that it should be so.

6.6.44   We wake up, we wash in the warm Italian sun; there is an air of excitement; we are on the move again; new scenes lie ahead of us, new tasks; we are in high spirits and look forward to our journey northwards. Then we have breakfast in the cool farmyard building. Everything is clean and neat and to our liking. We have porridge and fried bread and eggs. Then Traise comes and says the Second Front has been opened. I do not believe him; but yes, Graham has heard it on the wireless. It is true. Somehow it all seems part of the day. Somehow it ought to have happened now, it is so rational. I wonder what Dulcie is thinking and doing and seeing. Childishly I am proud of my prophecy that it would start in June. I wonder what it will mean to us. Perhaps a longer ride to the north, because it may affect the Italian theatre considerably. We pack up ready to go. Yes, a new phase has begun. We feel we are on the road to home.

9.6.44   The last two days have been somewhat hectic. Yesterday we had an appalling convoy journey from Valmontoni to the old Division H.Q. area at Cocilli. We started off at about 1400 hours and although we only had about ten to fifteen miles to go, we didn't arrive until about 2200 hours. Demolitions and bad traffic control were the main troubles, but it was most wearisome. The Hun had certainly done everything in his power to make things very delayed. Trees blown down and bridges blown, craters and mines, and, of course when I arrived, there were despatch riders and messages from the platoons waiting for action on my part. I managed to make decisions on most of them, but it was a horrible business trying to catch up like that.

16.6.44   After passing through Rome, aggravatingly in the dark, we are camped in treeless meadows by the Tiber; somehow it reminds me vividly of places in England. The sunburnt hay, the song of the cornbunting, the larks, the drowsiness, and the smell of the grass, are all just the same. I heard today that we move on the 19th to an area somewhere north of Viterbo. So we are gradually moving up to the line again. The advance continues but resistance is stiffening and demolitions are delaying us. There is apparently a new German defence line called the Gothic Line, which runs from the mountains north of Pisa across the mountains south of Rimini. It certainly should be a very strong natural defence line but how many Divisions the Boche are willing to put there must be determined, I suppose, by operations elsewhere.

Terrible fighting seems to be going on in the Cherbourg peninsula; the men there must be undergoing tremendous hardships and casualties must be high. God, what a waste it all is, and yet it seems beyond men to see the futility of it.

22.6.44   Yesterday, after a wet night, we moved and so the last twenty-four hours have been somewhat hectic, to say the least of it. Yesterday the rain stopped, thank God. I received a note from the C.O. that we were relieving 78 Division between 30th June and 3rd July, and so we started to prepare a training programme for nine days. That and many other things had to be done yesterday and we planned a scheme for today.

It is very English here in the early morning because of the dawn chorus – cuckoo, nightingales, blackcaps, thrushes, wrens, and others. There are large hawks nesting in the ravine – what an ideal bird-watching ground it would have been for me in peacetime. Even the woodlarks join in making the surroundings perfect.

But our plans were cut short in the middle of last night. A message arrived (waking me, curse it) saying that a half company was to move with 28 Brigade today, going into line on the night 22/23. We pass the start point at 1230 hours this morning, so things have been moving pretty much since then. However, I managed to finish a letter to Dulcie. We go up to an area south of Lake Trasimeno, which is slap in the middle of Italy. The rest of the Division move 23-25 June. So we don't get much time to ourselves, but the time passes. Even now as I write the vehicles are warming up, and there is great activity. I hate these quick moves but in a way they are better than long suspended ones.

23.6.44   I suppose we arrived at our concentration area at about 1800 hours, but we were buggered up by a R.E. unit which had blocked the entrance. This caused a hell of a delay and was most infuriating. By the time we did pull off the tracks were in a frightful condition and we had several bogged vehicles. It was strange to be with the guns again, which were blazing away, and a battle seemed to be raging at Chiusi. However, we got them all in round a rather lovely picturesque farmhouse, and then settled down to cook an evening meal.

Then we had a message from Hugh saying he wanted to see us in the light if possible, but it took some time to get everything ready, and although we set off in reasonable light, the road congestion and the mud prevented us from getting there in daylight. However, we got there, west of Lake Chiusi, and went straight in to the Kensingtons' mortar commander. That took a long time but we got to his H.Q., in a house, and arranged for the relief. I had an argument with their Group commander, whom I had met before and strongly disliked.

At about 0130 hours we returned slowly and precariously in the dark and on the very bad roads, but only as far as Hugh's H.Q., where I decided to stay till first light. I slept for a couple of hours with my head on a table, and at 0430 hours set off back to the company. That was a hell of a ride back, and the platoons which had been sent for sometime ago were a long way off relieving the Kensingtons. Eventually the 'first light' relief was completed at 1030 hours, just about what I expected and bloody good at that. I came back to my sunset brick farm, had breakfast, a wash, and finally went to bed in one of the rooms of the farm. They were quite nice people, a big family of nine, and when they started arguing with Jimmy, our interpreter, about a pot that had disappeared, I had to intervene by showing them my photo of Nicolas, and that made them all smiles. She then showed me a photo of her first son, in the Air Force, now missing, fifteen pounds at birth and eight days to arrive! We laughed like hell at that.

This afternoon I went out to the platoons and Bob, and found they had both fired on observed targets, and were all happy. An attack was being made in the morning by 78 Division on our right, and 28 Brigade, and we were supporting the latter. I returned tired but reasonably happy, called at Battalion after supper and learnt that 12 Brigade wanted a platoon, so I arranged for 14 to go. I was thankful to get to bed. But before I went off to sleep I had the joy of being able to read a letter from Dulcie. It had been a pretty hectic twenty-four hours but everything now seemed on an even keel.

26.6.44   Today has been another busy and hectic day. In the afternoon I went up to see Bob, who was expecting to move, and then on to Jimmy, who had moved during the day near La Villa. The road from

Variano to La Villa was very much under observation and being shelled. We went right into La Villa (John W. misread his map!) and found that we could go no further because of mines. We turned round and went back a few hundred yards, when I found the platoon concealed in an olive grove. They were in action and ready to support an attack on Gioiella. We had not been there very long before La Villa was stonked good and proper, and the road, and the ridge on the other side where some tanks were moving. The Control Post was in a farmstead just on the hill, and to get to it you had to go through a 'mousehole' leading in from a cowstall in which was a bloated dead cow, horrible sight. There were several graves in La Villa, and it has been costly. We bided our time waiting for the shells to pack up. We misjudged it, for we had hardly gone fifty yards when bang, a shell landed on the corner just ahead. And then the stonking started again properly. We dived out of the truck and took cover between the truck and the bank. Several fell near and shrapnel was whizzing. Again we waited for a lull, and this time we were lucky. We nipped in and I got the old bus going like hell up to Variano. 10 Brigade were moving up and it was some time before we got to H.Q., what with infantry, carriers, and what not on the roads. Bobby Gore was wounded today in the right shoulder; I lost a Sgt. in a stupid truck accident at H.Q. The bloody thing went over a bank. Ah well, it's just one of those things.

30.6.44   The last two days have been extremely busy. On the night 28/ 29 Jimmy pulled back to a line apparently running from Variano to Petriguano. This means that yesterday was a day of sudden moves for everyone. It was a grand sight to see the dust of the advancing columns on both sides of Lake Chuisi, and on the west side of Trasimeno. We had hoped for a complete breakthrough but there is another line around Valiano. Last night I visited Bob across country in the Utility and had a hell of a job getting back on the narrow tracks against tank and carrier convoys. We did it in the end, and soon after we got to H.Q. the Hun started an attack, machine gunning and bombing all around. The roads being white would show up very easily in the moonlight. It seems to be a favourite trick of his when he is withdrawing. I think he aims at keeping our guns quiet.

Today has been a sad one for D company. This morning 15 platoon, who were sheltering in a house ready to move forward, received a direct hit from a heavy gun and Cpl. Macintosh, Fus. Hudson and Cpl. Osbourne were killed outright, and five others wounded. That was a heavy blow. 14 platoon had one casualty, Gorman the cook, and 13 platoon had their M.P.O.A. wrecked. So it has been a heavy day. I went up to 15 platoon soon after it happened and there lay the blanketed dead, terrible to see in the bright sunlight. Oh God, how it seems to go on and on, this war. Just nearby, under the trees, were some white ducklings preening their feathers in the sun and making a very summery picture.

2.7.44   A new month and an old war; and a tiring one. Yesterday I was able to get round the Right Half (of my company) who, by the end of the day had come just outside Pizzuolo, and had been able to get a little rest. Graham went forward to Valiano and both his platoons did likewise. In the morning I tried to sort out 15 platoon, helping them with the odd men, etc., and in the afternoon I went with John W. up the Petriguano road to look for a new H.Q. but the Hun thought otherwise and stopped us with shells. One very close blew rubble into my face. Then back to Bob who had also had heavy shelling, having his jeep hit. Last night more aerial attention, followed by a disturbed night being called to the set by Battalion with orders for Bob who had reverted to my command during the day. Also a call from Graham with a situation report. He thought the Boche had gone and asked for the Arezzi maps – and a goose we had cooked for him! Now I am off to look for a new H.Q. up near Graham. Ah well, it's a sleepless sort of life.

3.7.44   When John W. and I got to Valiano yesterday we found that Brigade had moved and, in fact, we didn't fetch up with Graham until we got almost to a place called Foriano della Chiana. It had been a big move forward and we started to look out for a new H.Q. Immediately I had my eye on an area which I had spotted from the map, and this we decided upon. On seeing 15 platoon we went there to brew up, and the Italians kindly provided us with eggs, so we had a good tiffin. All the Italians were in a most welcoming mood, shaking hands, offering wine, and generally jolly pleased to be rid of the Hun. An advance is very exciting; you look on the map; you know your objectives; suddenly there is a surge forward, and what was once a coloured piece of paper soon becomes the living country, green, brown, and changing. And when you arrive you soon take the new area for granted. In places the Hun has left all his signs out; German papers litter the farms, and in some cases half-prepared meals are found. Denis was telling me his platoon had Danish butter for two days! Bob and his lads were over on the right and I didn't see anything of them all yesterday.

5.7.44   On the night of the 3rd we moved again, this time to a big white house east of Marciano. It was a terribly hot night, and the following morning I found I had the collywobbles and was not at all well. John Dixon has been reported as missing since 3rd July 2000 hours, and he is still missing. This is a blow. I was unable to contact the Left Half yesterday owing to the state of the roads, a thunderstorm making things hopeless. They are north of a place called Monte S. Savino, but demolitions have made it a cross-country journey. Both platoons have been doing a lot of shooting. In the afternoon I went out with Tony to contact the Right Half, who are moving with 28 Brigade along the road west of the Canali Maetro della Chianci; a better route altogether with demolitions that are fairly easily overcome. I saw both 12 and 13 platoons but they have both moved again now.

My great worry today is that John Dixon is still missing. He was taking a 21 set to 15 platoon and hasn't been seen since. I hope to God he turns up. I am just going up myself with Tony, and I expect I shall have to move the H.Q. forward again, probably on Bob's axis.

7.7.44   The last forty-eight hours have been hectic. All the platoons have been in action spread over a front something like 10,000 yards, which takes a bit of covering with most lateral roads blown, and travelling is bloody awful in the dust. John Dixon hasn't turned up, and I have now had to post him as missing. I feel that he is a prisoner. A great tragedy came with the death in action of Clifford Hill; he was such a cheery chap, so young and intelligent. He was one of the first officers I met on joining the Battalion. Yesterday morning I went up with Bob to see 13 platoon, who had had some casualties the day before. They were behind a great house, so typically Italian, the old-fashioned drawing room picture of an Italian house. It was a place called Doma, east of Civitella, and the Boche spotted them getting in a firing. However, they were cheerful enough and seemed to have quietened down. 12 platoon last night had heavy shelling but no casualties. In the afternoon we recced a new H.Q., and went on the 15 platoon, where we saw Graham. They were in a queer place above the village of Oliveto, and the C.O. had browned Jimmy off a bit by not using them to the best.

10.7.44   Nicolas is two today – from Dulcie's anecdotes and descriptions to me he seems older; I hope I am home for his third birthday.

The war has changed these last few days. We have over-reached ourselves, for the Division, after hard mobile fighting, pushed forward into the well-prepared and good defensive position west of Arezzo, south of the River Arno. The country is thick and corrugated and in our haste we pushed forward some salients which have since turned into 'bloody noses'. Casualties have been heavy and further progress is just not on. Enemy artillery is strong and well consolidated, and in fact it is a bloody nuisance for he seems to have observation all round, and so our intentions have changed. The Division is now to hold here whilst an attack is made elsewhere by other Divisions. Thank God! At last the men can get some rest; but not much, for I still have to keep three platoons in action, and only some of the men can come out at a time, and then not for long, as we don't expect this phase to last for more than a week. I have been busy this last day or so arranging to get as many chaps out as possible. And today I wrote my first letter to Dulcie in seven days. They are all in need of a rest and showing the strain. 12 platoon have to go back tonight to relieve 13; such a short time they have had, but it can't be helped. There is a lot of shelling and on some roads we are only allowed to go at ten m.p.h. because of the dust. It is a nasty feeling going round a bend at that speed, knowing it gets heavily shelled.

So this little book begun in the Cassino offensive comes to an end in the Chuisi valley. It is a long way from Cassino. It is a good step towards home. Many things have happened since then and are due to happen. There is a great air of optimism that the war is nearly over; pray God that it comes true.

15.7.44   The attack by the 1 Guards Brigade and the N.Z. Division duly went in last night, supported by strong artillery fire and a demonstration by 10 and 12 Brigades, in which D company took part. 12 platoon were unlucky in that just before they were due to start, one of the mortars had a direct him from a spandau. The crew had just left after carrying out some defensive fire. Mortars and bombs were wrecked. The attack, as far as I know, has gone well, but I believe the tanks are having difficulty in getting forward. The Boche were still shelling quite heavily, and on my way back from 13 platoon this morning I had a very narrow escape on a cross roads on Route 73. Some heavy shells burst about twenty to thirty yards away, and the road which had been all right on the way up became a mass of craters.

We have got to change our unit number of 53 to 64; white on a black background – very sombre after what we have been used to. I wonder what bright staff officer thought that one out!

16.7.44   The war seems to be changing again, and sudden moves will again become the order of the day as the enemy goes back. Already the infantry are pushing forward, having lost contact, and we are standing waiting to be called forward in support. It looks as though I shall still have both Half Companies in. It's all a damn nuisance whatever happens. It is a hot sleepy Sunday, and not the sort of day to play war. It is strangely quiet after the previous day's shelling, and I do hope the Boche has gone right back to the Gothic Line. At the moment there is no news about Arezzo.

Last night I went up to visit Jimmy again (how I hate these ghostly and alarming night visits) and found them all O.K. A lot of shells and mortar bombs kept falling round us, and I must confess I should suffer very much from claustrophobia if I was in their place. Oh, to sleep and forget the bloody war.

18.7.44   This morning I was up early and moved up in advance of my H.Q., who were to be guided up later. It was a pleasant ride so early in the morning traffic, no dust. We went through the battered villages of S. Pancrazio, Bodia Aquasio, Capaimoli, Pogi, where we stopped and looked at a possible place, and then on to Buemi, where we found what were a few days ago some delightful villas, but most of them had been made disgustingly filthy by the Hun, who had only left yesterday. It is very sad to go into a beautiful house to find all the glass broken, everything ransacked, litter and filth all over the floor. It is especially sad to see all the children's toys lying littered and broken on the floor.

21.7.44   With the Japanese Cabinet resigning and an attempt on the life of Hitler by his own officers, one could easily be tempted to optimistic wishful thinking. But it pays, I find, to control such tantalising thoughts, for they accumulate at an alarming rate and the blow of disappointment is greater than ever. Still, things are going well here and in Russia. Leghorn and Ancona are just steps forward and Florence should be next on the list. For the moment we are held up beyond Montevardi. Of course, we are all hoping that there will be a landing behind the Gothic Line as a slogging match through the hills is to us most undesirable. But our commitments may not allow this. Churchill has said that big forces will become available for the Far East this year and I think that is every soldier's dread – to think that he may be sent to Burma or some such bloody place. This is especially so with all soldiers who have seen a bit of fighting. I'm very much afraid, though, that some of us are bound to go, but how they will work it out, God knows.

It really is incredible how browned-off, how imprisoned, we all feel now. This unnatural life, this life where one lives on one's nerves, is so apt to get you down. We are for ever asking – 'How much longer?' This unorderly life, with all its chaos, its dirt, its misery, is beginning to tell on our minds. It's all so shoddy, meaningless, often so petty, and lives upon lives are being consumed by the insatiable demands of war. Oh for a gentle home, with furniture, curtains and books, a fire and a wife for company. But it goes on and we have to go on with it.

We had no more shells yesterday – touch wood – but as a result of the day before, one of our chaps went away with shell shock. The house is clean again, but very rubbly outside. We were very lucky.

I hear that 46 Division is somewhere in the Orvieto area, so perhaps it won't be long before I see John again. We are all wondering what happens when we get to Florence.

22.7.44   Progress is slow against determined enemy resistance, terrific demolitions and extensive minefields. Our forward infantry are up to about Giovanni and 28 Brigade have now taken over the advance from 10 Brigade. So far, I have had no orders that the Right Half will revert to 28 Brigade, and Bob and his party are back with me at company H.Q. So, for the first time for about a month, we are out of action, although we are still very liable to be called upon, of course. Life is very dreary, and there seems nothing to look forward to, despite the many rumours and the queer events in Germany. Even so, I think a hell of a lot will have to happen inside and out of Germany before we take notice, or any different course of action from that planned. To maintain pressure now is the surest way of effecting a collapse. The dusty roads are terrible to be on these days; I fear the dust is the cause of a lot of tummy troubles.

Everyone is asking what is going to happen now that we have reached this stage of the Italian Campaign. Rumours are rife. One of them is a particularly interesting 'latrinogram', in that it states that 46 Divisions are taking over from us in ten days. If so, what happens to 4 Division; do we go with 46 or what? For myself, I should like a rest, and a bit of leave, going to Florence or Rome, staying in some good hotel and doing a bit of shopping for Dulcie. I haven't heard from my beloved just lately, and it is a bit worrying with this flying bomb business, which seems more serious than was first thought.

25.7.44   The last two days have been hectic again. John W. and I set off early yesterday morning on one of our H.Q. sorties. It was quite a pleasant ride really through Mercatali, Montivarchi, and up through the weird down-like and yet cliff-broken country that seems to typify the Arno valley. The day was terrible. Eventually we reached the charming village of Cavriglia, which was to give us so much trouble and so much good shelter. We found most excellent and comfortable billets in the Rectory or its Italian equivalent, a large cool airy building adjoining the Church, and after John had tried out a bit of Italian and French on the Padre, we found ourselves most hospitably received and our mess was the dining room. We were given several good bedrooms, the wall of the one Graham and I slept in being a gaudy ecclesiastical red, including the cover to the 'Pope's' bed, as Graham, who slept in it, had christened it. They were certainly not short of food or wine, and a good orchard gave us tomatoes and pears. So far so good, and I went to see Coutts to get the low-down about the platoons.

In the afternoon I went down to see the Assistant Provost Marshal about a small matter of chickens and having smoothed that over came back to H.Q. all smiles, only to be met by Bob, who said, 'Something dreadful has happened.' It transpired that a platoon, which had been in a billet opposite to us the night before, had done a certain amount of looting. The C.O. happened to be at H.Q. at the time and I was so browned-off that I put the case to him forthwith. We went over to see the house and it certainly was in a chaotic state. The Platoon Commander was sent for and the C.O. put him under arrest. So the day was turning out bright and sunny! Then, on top of it all, came the tactical side and I had to go to Coutts to arrange about 15 platoon establishing an observation post. On the very exposed route we were shelled to blazes and nasty bits of shrapnel came whizzing over the jeep. By this time my head was aching somewhat at the changed course of events. Of course, the incident was reported to the Assistant Provost Marshal (whom I had just left, on very good terms!) and in the evening he came up to take a statement from the Italians. It was all very annoying and I am one of those people who take things frightfully seriously, worrying like an old woman.

This afternoon I visited 12 and 13 platoons in their rather pleasant villa, with a blue kitchen and a nice verandah. On my return I had to try John's batman for refusing to obey an order, a court martial offence of course, and then, to top matters, Tony came in to say that the Right Half were to come under command 12 Brigade at once, and would proceed tonight to a concentration area right away to our left, south of Dudda, the idea being a flanking move by the Brigade. And so it goes on, and will go on, I suppose, until the war is over.

1.8.44   A good day! The Germans have withdrawn quite a way and our forward troops are on the Florence map, about eight miles from the place, while the New Zealanders on our left are even nearer. All the platoons have come out of action and are concentrated well up, ready to move forward again in support of the advance which is continuing. Bob has seen Florence for some high ground near Mignana, and with any luck another forty-eight hours should see us there.

Then I had two more letters from Dulcie, and just now John* called in

---

*Brother.

to see me, which was a very pleasant surprise. He had great difficulty in finding me and the roads were very choked, so he couldn't stay long as he had to get back to Division, where he was to collect an officer. They are still 150 miles away down near Trasimeno somewhere, and their fate is not decided. He rather thinks they may be going to 5 Corps. So who and when we will be relieved by, I don't know; in fact, the General has sent a letter out today about suppressing the rumours of apparent moves. John has enjoyed his travels but I believe is very glad to be back to a bit of greenery, after the barren heat of Palestine and Egypt. So much has happened to both of us since we last saw each other, that we were a bit tongue-tied with all that we would have liked to have said if we could have remembered it all. But over a glass of chianti we gave each other a brief outline of each other's doings. The time seems to have passed quickly and it's difficult to think that nearly five months have elapsed since we last saw each other.

2.8.44   We had a rather interesting personal message from the C-in-C, in which, amongst other things, he stated that extensive re-grouping was nearing completion to bring about the final collapse of the enemy. 'It is my intention to proceed with the second and perhaps final stage of the destruction of the German armed forces in Italy.' This significant message is not to be read out to the troops till tomorrow!

3.8.44   A day of dusty rides but in an atmosphere of excitement as our troops draw nearer to Florence, the Black Watch being only about three miles off the city. In the morning we went up the delightful valley to Poggio anci Croce to see 14 and 15 platoons, and found them in a good heart after a trying day or so. They were to stay put until called forward again, so I hope they may get a bit of time off now. An early lunch and then off to see Bob through Strada, where heavy fighting had taken place yesterday. It was the usual scene of destruction and desolation, with the women returning in tears to their ruined homes. We saw Jimmy and Tommy, who were cheerful enough after a bloody day yesterday, when 12 did very well to get into action and recover their vehicles which had been hit by shellfire on one of the most exposed roads I've seen. 10 Brigade are moving up to relieve 12 Brigade, much to the disgust of Elgy, who will hear nothing of it and already the Black Watch with their pipes are ready to go into Florence. I don't think it will be an easy matter to relieve them at this interesting juncture, especially after the heavy fighting they have seen lately. We came back to H.Q. against a heavy stream of traffic, resolved to move ourselves tomorrow.

5.8.44   The last two days have been filled with those crowded wartime experiences, no separate one of which can be properly assimilated. First, early yesterday morning, I moved off with John W. to find our new H.Q. on the lateral road S. Pola-Strada. We had to wait for a bridge to be put up and we had to go very gingerly because of mines. We did get one place but were turned out by Division, who were coming there. Later we heard a truck had blown itself up on a mine in this area, so we weren't sorry about that. Then we seemed to strike a patch of dead horses and humans, but did find a good place on top of the hill, Pt. 281, near the village of S. Stefano. Then Graham got on the air to say he was moving and had booked a magnificent place for us. Before going to it, however, I went to Bob and on to 13, who were themselves esconced in an enormous building, The Germans had looted everything.

Got back to H.Q. and saw an enormous building on the next ridge, and decided to recce it. Found it a bit shelled and looted but got the Italians to clean out some rooms, and here we are. Five people were killed in the room next to me by one of our shells. They are buried in the garden. A thunderstorm developed and we were glad of the shelter; then a glorious moon came up over the hills we had fought over – lovely scene, so peaceful. I was woken up in the middle of the night to find Graham had not returned since 1900 hours. I had a message in the morning to say he had been wounded near Balatu, also his operator Patience. I went round with Coutts to see what had happened, and found he had been evacuated to Grevi 8 Casualty Clearing Station; he was cheerful and wounds were in leg. He said tonight that Patience was very poorly, poor fellow. I arranged for Peter to take over and went to Ruffola to see 14 and 15. Had my first good view of Florence today in better visibility.

And so it has gone on, one thing on top of another, and no time to think about things much. I have been inclined to quick irritability all day but things are cooling off now. Two letters from Dulcie to read quietly in a minute, and a sad one from George, who has, I'm afraid, finished his life with the battalion, having got an ulcerated stomach. So D company have lost two of their best officers, but Denis came back today, which helped a bit.

9.8.44   We are being relieved by 1 Division. As usual, it all happened in quick time. We got a message early yesterday morning saying 12 Brigade were being relieved, and the Right Half were to go with it to the Foligno area. That is south of Perugia, west of Lake Trasimeno, and I understand a nice part of Italy. So Bob and I dashed off to make all arrangements, and they came out last night, being very fortunate not to have suffered casualties in some very heavy shelling which wounded a platoon commander and the company commander of the 2/7 Middlesex, who are taking over from us. The Left Half have been helping to clear the high ground in the loop of the Arno, and have done good work. Today the ground is clear and the platoons have been taken out of action. 10 Brigade are being relieved tomorrow and, with any luck, we shall be on our way to Foligno then.

I hope we are given a good rest, and I hope to be able to visit Rome and perhaps buy Dulcie a thing or two. No-one seems to know what the big strategic picture is just now; there are apparently many troops south of us and after Alexander's message, something must be afoot.

17.8.44   The last few days, in Foligno, have mainly been taken up in petty administrative problems connected with leave parties, leave allotments, etc., and conferences. Today, however, something of an interest did come our way in the form of an address by the Army Commander. He congratulated us on our fighting in the last three months; he reviewed the situation as it stood today, which he called good, and then went on to the future of the Eighth Army. He said it had never been stronger, in all eighteen Divisions! It was poised for a great new battle, which he said might be the last major battle of the Eighth. After our past efforts, he said he would give us as much time as he could afford to rest, re-equip, absorb reinforcements and train, before this battle in which we would take part.

The Russians are all out for Berlin, the Western Front for the west of Germany. We must look to Vienna, he said. Perhaps we could finish it this year, for that is what we all want. So, in about another fortnight, perhaps we shall see our future more clearly. The last battle! I wonder! May it be so.

23.8.44   Yesterday I had a very interesting day going with Tony and Jimmy to see Peter Gorst at the battalion rest camp, Piediluco, which is a little village on the side of a delightful lake – Lake Piediluco, in fact – because it's shaped like a foot, which it is, remarkable to relate. We went down past Tuori to Spoleto, where we turned off, and climbed up very high, getting a magnificent view of the plains; then over a saddle and down a winding mountainous road into an enormous valley, which, with its delightful river – Neva – made it very fertile. It was very hot and we stopped and parked ourselves under a tree by the river and had egg and tomato sandwiches – lovely! Then in the heat of midday we travelled right down this valley until we were almost to Terni, when we turned left up the hillside again, and soon down again with Piediluco stretched out before us. It was a lovely scene, the water a deep blue with the hills rising on all sides, and the sun burning down fiercely. Many little boats were on the lake, being navigated by soldiers on holiday. They all looked very brown and fit.

We eventually got to the Scuola which houses the Battalion rest camp, and were ushered into a house next door, a lovely villa, very cool, with shutters and tracelike curtains. This was Peter roughing it! He was thoroughly enjoying himself running this show, and said he didn't want to be a soldier any more! George Strutt looked fitter than I've ever seen him, and I suppose he should with his favourite sport at hand and plenty of senoritas to enjoy it with. Peter proffered us some very nice 'Spumenti' which I liked, but the afternoon is not the best time for a drink. I came away with a lot for the mess, though. Tony and Jimmy went off for a bathe, and I stayed and talked to Peter, who was really happy doing his job. After a quick tea we had to go, and made our way round the lake, hoping to get to Terni that way, although the road was collapsing. We got to Marinori, and saw what is, I believe, the highest waterfall in Europe, a truly lovely sight, which the Germans had improved by blowing the lock gates! There was a perpetual rainbow made by the sun striking the spume. The beautiful curtains effect of the falling water was indescribably lovely, and the great power behind it, awe inspiring. I'm glad I saw it.

The road was *'nienti buono'* and we had to come back, passing underneath the waterfall on our way to Terni.

Today is a great day for France for after four years of domination Paris has at last been freed, and by Frenchmen. The total liberation of France should not be far off now.

30.8.44   For the last three days I have been in Rome on leave with four other officers of the company. We go back tomorrow, but as yet have heard or seen nothing about the big push up the east coast, although we have been advancing in that sector. Bulgaria has asked for terms, and apparently wants to assume the status of a neutral state. She will be lucky if she gets off as lightly as that. So the whole of the Balkan front is rapidly crumbling, and, when the Russians link up with the N.L.A. in Yugoslavia, it should not be long (with an offensive from us) before the whole of Italy is cleared. In France the Americans are over the Marne, and we have strong bridgeheads over the Seine. Marseilles and Toulon have both fallen, and an attack on Brest is in progress. That has been the victorious military background to these few days in Rome. The news is as startling as it is exciting.

1.9.44   The news at the moment is terrific. Last night we were ten miles from the Belgian frontier, Amiens had been captured and the Hun in N. France was retreating in complete disorder, utterly demoralised. Since D-Day something like 400,000 men have been killed or captured. The Russians were in Bucharest and if the Gothic Line has been breached then I think the Germans will be finished on their southern front altogether. It really is quite stupendous, unbelievable when one looks at our position this time last year. May it continue thus. Have heard that John Dixon is a prisoner of war.

3.9.44   Five years of war and today we are not much more than ten miles from the German border. A lot has happened since the day I attended the Service in Souk Ahras a year ago. Since then the tide has turned indeed. And again today a simple Service amongst the olive trees near the camp, surely our last war anniversary.

I had a conference at Battalion. It was much as I had expected. Things were on the move again, and it seemed likely that we should move on the 5th to a concentration area south west of Faro on the Adriatic coast, to be ready no doubt to fulfil our very mobile role. This involved many cancellations and recalls from leave, etc., but I hope by tomorrow night to have the whole company ready to move. I think there is heavy fighting in the Gothic Line.

But in Belgium we are on the Moselle, and God grant that it will soon all be over. We have reached a tense phase in the war.

4.9.44   The news is simply colossal. Brussels has been liberated and we are not far from the Dutch frontier. Nancy has been reached, and we are into the Gothic Line and soon Rimini should be ours. Hostilities between Russia and Finland ceased at 0800 hours, and I really wouldn't be a German today for anything.

9.9.44   It is appropriate that I should make an entry today for it is a year ago today that we landed at Salerno. A year in Italy. A long year indeed and a hard one.

On the 6th we completed our loading and at 2005 hours left the Spello camp to feed in behind A company. It was one of the few convoys I've been in where headlights have been allowed, and we sped along, at times immensely fast. It was a goodly sight to see all the lights sparkling on the road as you looked down on the convoy from some high mountain road. I was very disappointed at not being able to study the country, which in parts was very mountainous with deep ravines which looked extremely interesting. The half moon coming up over the dark hills made it a lovely night for travel. The lack of colour which makes a jeep journey so absorbing was offset by the soft moonlight, which made strange towns we passed through quiet and ghostly. Not a soul was about and we passed on unhindered and unheralded. The battle was far away still.

We arrived at our concentration area south of a place called Monterado, and just a mile north west of a place called Ripe at the ungodly hour of 0330. The usual business of getting a night convoy into its harbour area ensued and a rainstorm didn't help matters. I tried to rest a bit in my Utility but gave it up as a bad job. During the morning Traise put my bed down by a haystack and, after a wash and shave, I did rest a bit, only to be disturbed by messages from the Orderly Room, one of which called me to a conference at 1330 hours. I cursed.

At the conference I learned that I was to take my company to a concentration area near a place called Tomba di Pesaro. 4 Division was to come under command Canadian Corps and its likely task would be to pass through 5 Canadian Division, who were making the crossing of the river Mariano, or if that failed, to make it ourselves, not very enviable tasks, either of them. From here I had my first view of the Adriatic.

We left at 0300 hours, going a roundabout route before we started making any headway. We got through Corinaldo, and were going nicely towards Orciano when, at a road junction, we were stopped by Military Police and told the roads were impassable to traffic, and 4 Division had been ordered off the road. So we had breakfast on the roadside, then lunch, and bedded down in various nearby farms.

At Tommy's farm a great harvesting day was in progress, with all the families helping with the threshing, and the women busy preparing a great meal for all concerned. It was a pleasant scene and very reminiscent of England. I went to bed in pyjamas hoping that we wouldn't be called till morning. But at 1230 we were told we were to be on the road at 1330 ready to move again. The third night ruined! So once again we set off – it was a lovely night – and went straight down to the coast, and from some way off we had a lovely view of the moon and Orion shining across the Adriatic. We went up by the sea through Faro and Pesaro and got to our dispersal point at daybreak. The whole of the area was battle-scarred and smelt. Not one house was standing on the lateral road; grim fighting here all right. Now we could hear the guns and see their flashes – oh, too familiar sound. We turned north through Tomba di Pesaro. Tanks littered the ground and the villages were totally wrecked. We saw many Hun turret emplacements, fierce-looking affairs that must have caused a lot of trouble. We were in the Gothic Line and it was pretty grim, no half-heartedness about the war here. So on to our harbour area via a circuituous route. It is the same undulating type of country. We are behind the grim areas and all day our planes have been going over bombing. The Hun A/A has been very heavy, and we have dug slit trenches. So here we are and we wait to know our fate. The Boche are fighting like mad and have been reinforced. We can almost see Rimini. I am in a tent again and my first job after breakfast was a complete wash and change of clothing, which was an absolute joy. May 9th September next year see us out of this business and may Providence be kind tonight and give us a night's rest before we go up into the line.

10.9.44   We were granted a complete night's rest but the Boche spoilt it by sending over his planes, and I was woken by the roar of our A/A which was considerable. It is most unpleasant lying in bed in a tent when an air raid is in progress. One feels so exposed and naked, not only to bombs but to A/A shrapnel. Once I got out to see the direction of things, but it was so cold that I soon nipped back again. I slept on and woke up to a lovely Sunday morning with the sun shining into my tent, and the cocks crowing and Church bells ringing. I shaved with the sun warming my back – lovely. Our planes were already going over in 'sixes' but no news has come in as to whether the big attack has been made.

The Padre gave us a Holy Communion Service, which was well attended; the last possibly we shall be able to have for some time. We are all a bit on edge waiting to see what is required of us. It is much better to know the worst.

We have all made up for lost sleep, and I had a lovely experience yesterday afternoon. I had been sleeping soundly, and waking up at 1630 hours, I espied on my table *four* letters from Dulcie and the newspapers. It was as though a fairy godmother had put them there in my sleep. Included in Dulcie's letters was a sea letter which had some delightful pictures of Nicolas. Incredible how he has grown up in the last year.

11.9.44   Things are beginning to clarify themselves at last. Both Bob and Peter, my Half Company commanders, have been to 28 and 12 Brigades respectively for a conference, and the picture as it stands now is that the big attack takes place on the night 13/14, when, from what I can gather, the whole Italian front goes into action. Our 'do' is to pass through the Canadians who are attacking the high ground around Coriano. Ever since we have been here the Boche has bombed continuously and all day we hear the roar of planes and exploding bombs. Already I have sent chaps off to recce harbour south of Misano, and in a day or so I shall have to move my H.Q. I feel somehow that it is going to be a particularly tough battle, but if the weather holds I think we'll break him all right. Pray God that it is our last major battle.

15.9.44   The company has seen a lot of action mostly around Coriano in the last forty-eight hours. On the night of the 13th Bert Brittain

Propaganda shot over by the Germans in Italy.

Propaganda shot over by the Germans in Italy.

WHY HASTEN THE END OF THE WAR?

What interests us is to get definite results and avoid World War III, which the communists as well as the capitalist Jews are already preparing.

It may take a few years more. No matter. With England barred from the continent since this war began, a new European life is getting stronger and better every year. In the Far East the Japs are installing themselves more definitely from year to year. England, with her forty millions having a terrible drain of blood on all fronts, is getting more and more indebted to the States every day that passes.

The Island is under continuous bombardment by the "hellhounds"

Time is working for us. We are in no hurry.

We want a definite peace for a long period and no Jewish World War III.

Kr - 023 - 7-44

Propaganda shot over by the Germans in Italy.

and his O.P.A. were wounded when they were with a forward company of the Black Watch preparing to establish an observation post. Their carrier had broken down and they had gone ahead on foot. They came in to a terrific concentration of shell and mortar fire and heavy casualties were suffered by the infantry. All those I have spoken to so far say it is far worse than Cassino, and after yesterday, when I first went over the battleground to see 14 platoon, who had done brilliantly to get so far up into action north of Coriano, and who did some fine counter mortar and defensive shoots, this view seemed to be confirmed. Despite the terrible night that they had had (Sgt. Lamb said it was the worst shellfire they had experienced since Salerno), they were very cheerful, but I had to make two efforts to get there because of heavy shelling on the ridge above which we had to cross. It really is the most bare country and coming over the ridge west of Misano one got a perfect panorama of the whole battle from the coast to miles inland. Each valley and ridge (one has to go across country as the roads are *non est*) is a scene of utter desolation; each ridge is a Cassino in itself to be contested. Our losses in men and tanks and vehicles, etc., have been heavy but it was good to see the prisoners coming in batches of fifty or so.

Last night 12 platoon, going into action northwest of Coriano (which is now a shell of a place), came under heavy fire and Peter Gorst and one Fusilier were wounded. Two officers in two days is very high and leaves us pretty short. They are not badly wounded, however. 15 platoon is in the most desolate place, a shell-torn valley with many knocked-out tanks and ruined farms. They were heavily shelled getting in last night but escaped casualties. They were just behind a bit of a farm under which the Boche had dug great dug-outs; in one lay a dead German. It was most smelly and warlike.

In the evening I went up with Bob to visit 12 and 13 platoons, who were both in position between Coriano and the river Mariano. I think I can say without exaggeration that Coriano is the most shelled place I have seen in Italy, with the exception of Cassino. But Coriano had not been bombed at all (presumably to keep the roads open) and it was just one hell of a mess with dead bodies, bullocks, kit and rubble all over the place, making a horrible smell. Soon after we got through the Boche started shelling again. The chaps were O.K., despite the bloodiness of the previous night. They were digging hard when we arrived, as were the infantry, very wisely.

We were a bit delayed coming back by hitching the jeep onto a Tank bridge, and waiting for the shelling to quieten a bit, and it was dark by the time I reached camp, where I had a chicken dinner, the hens being looted by yours truly from 14 platoon position! These journeys are a bit of a strain, and each time I return safely I say a little prayer to myself.

19.9.44   Last night was, I think, one of the noisiest of the campaign. We must have sent thousands and thousands of shells into the Rimini Gap, and the fighting is most severe. But we have advanced to within a mile or so to the southwest of Rimini, which is excellent, and in a day or so might see us through. I slept against a bank last night and had my bed dug in for safety, and even though sleep was well nigh impossible, I did feel secure. It was a fine night and at first the whole sky was lit up by gun flashes, until six or seven searchlights at moon brightness were switched on behind the guns to light the way for the infantry. It had a lovely effect against the velvet starry sky. But the noise was terrific, and when the 5.5s just behind us opened up, I coiled up. Thank God no casualties so far, except two vehicles. I am exchanging my Utility for Swill's jeep, which will make me much more mobile.

21.9.44   Yesterday the battle was going extremely well with lots of prisoners coming in. All today masses of armour was moving up and the roads were a great heaving of vehicles which, with the nasty wind, threw up an unpleasant spume of dust. We heard that the Army Commander had ordered the armour to break through to F. Morecchia by nightfall, as rain was on the way. In the afternoon I went over again to look for a new H.Q. and so great was the conglomeration of troops and vehicles that I had difficulty in finding a field even. But I got a place in the end, near the platoons. I made arrangements to leave early this morning, but it was not to be. Soon after 2100 last night it clouded over and rain fell hard and continued most of the night. This morning we are completely immobilised, although the rain has stopped and with any luck we might be able to get away late in the day. It is a great pity that the weather should have turned against us at this juncture – but generally speaking the weather hasn't been a friend to us in this war. So for the moment we stay in our vineyard slope. There are masses of grapes all around us, and we hardly ever think of eating them. Tons of them have been ruined.

It is now afternoon and there isn't a hope in hell of our getting out of here today as the rain has continued. What a tragedy for the old 8th Army and how the Boche must be clapping his hands. To have fought through this bloody country and to have reached the Plain only to be stopped by bad weather is indeed bitter irony. But the news is good, and I understand we are in Rimini and across the river Morecchia and going for another crossing on the left.

Most of the prisoners say that Germany is finished; some give her six, some eight weeks. They all seem to fight until things are pretty sticky, when they gladly give themselves up. Those I have seen are a pretty mixed and dirty lot. When asked what they thought the V.2 was, one replied, 'A lot of rubber boats which are going to circle round England and wipe her off the map.' A remark which reflects the feelings of the German soldier about their new weapons!?

The news on the other front seems good, with the latest airborne landing in Holland going well, the Americans fighting on German soil, and the Russians making an all-out offensive along most of their front. Why the devil doesn't he pack it in, I don't know. I wish he would!

23.9.44   It seems, although we have not heard officially, that we are coming out into reserve again. The weather cleared again yesterday and we dried out. The New Zealanders and 28 Brigade got across the Morecchia and straddled Route 9. The ground still made it impossible to move my H.Q. over the Mariano, but I got round in my jeep in the afternoon. Then came this extraordinary codeword 'Beeswax', which meant that after 1830 no 4 Division transport was allowed on the roads, so that 5 Canadian Armoured Division might pass through. So we accommodate ourselves to the circumstances.

I received a new pipe today from Dulcie. It is an enormous Parker which Traise calls a 'Codger's pipe'! The main topic of interest of late has been the proposals for Releases from the Forces, which is based on service and age, each two months of service counting an additional year. At the end of the year I shall have had fifty-four months of service, which, with my age, makes me in the fifty-sevens' category. Of course, the plan has yet to be accepted but I think generally it has been well received.

The leave proposals are almost rosy. Under the main scheme you get two months' leave with full pay and allowances, gratuity and clothing, plus an additional day on full pay for every month's service overseas. It should give chaps enough time to get re-orientated into civilian life, to refresh themselves about their particular profession, and generally look round to get the lie of the land. It's pleasant to think on these things, but I wish those Germans would have the sense to see that they are beaten. They are making a horrible legacy for themselves.

28.9.44   Still no move orders and patiently we wait news of what is to happen to us. Our troops are nearing Saviguano and the New Zealanders are well up the coast, but there is no sign of a real breakthrough. The tank going is not as easy as we had hoped because of the numerous ditches and dykes.

The chief world news of late has been the epic stand of 1 Airborne division at Arnhem, where for nine days in a small pocket, without relief and with little food and water, they have held against powerful attacks, and been constantly under murderous artillery and mortar fire. The British 2nd Army were unable to relieve them and on the night of the 26th September(?) they were withdrawn over the Rhine: 2,000 out of about 8,000 got back under the most difficult circumstances. How easy it is to imagine what hell that nine days must have been, how grim, stark and horrible.

30.9.44   We have at last had some news as to our future and it is that 4 Division will be prepared to relieve 56 Division on the night 3/4 October, at twenty-four hours notice to move from 0600 hours 2nd October. So, weather permitting, it looks as though we shall be at it again soon. 56 Division are advancing along the axis of Route 9.

2.10.44   Thirty years ago today a 'mewling brat'! Never again in my life do I want to celebrate my birthday in such miserable circumstances that is my lot today. We are still in our hillside camp. I shall know the skyline of that battered village by heart soon if we stay here much longer. I woke this morning to the patter of the rain on the tent. By the time I had got up it was pouring in torrents. It has poured so torrentially since that I have had to wait till I got to bed tonight before I could write this. It is the only dry place – and that, only just. I have had to remove one puddle already. It is now 2100 hours and still raining. my tent is a drippin sodden mass of canvas. The floor of the tent is a slippery sheet of curly mud. The table, on which we eat, is sodden, and we sit gloomily on wet chairs in macs and hats, whilst the water drips into our tea and on our plates. Some drops on to the candle, causing it to fizz and nearly go out. This evening we sat thus enjoying a tot of whisky and talking of better things, of 'happier returns'! But we were not unduly depressed. We found room to laugh. After all, we had tobacco to smoke; something to drink and eat; we had a bed; we weren't in the line, and we had companionship. I said to Coutts, 'I wonder what our wives would say if they saw this?' He said, 'Mine would weep with tears of pity.' I was less dramatic and said, 'Mine would be shocked.' The almost empty rivers are now raging torrents, the roads in places feet deep in water; many diversions have been washed away.

5.10.44   The 3rd was a beautiful sunny day and we dried out quickly. Our normal life continued and we were just waiting for new orders about the Division's move. Sitting quietly talking to Coutts in the tent in the evening, we were interrupted by an operator saying that a very important message was coming in from 2 N.F. We waited expectantly, if a little pessimistically. In due course the Intelligence Sergeant arrived with it. It was to say that D company was to come under command 46 Division forthwith and the company was to be prepared to move off at first light. Later I got an order saying that I was to report to H.Q. 46 Division at 0600 hours on the 4th. A pretty fast ball. I immediately summoned a conference at Peter's place, giving my plan and sorting out all the snags that were bound to arise with a move at such short notice. Luckily it was a brilliant moonlit night, and that helped considerably. I got back at about 1100 hours and got up at the ungodly hour of 0300. At 0400 I set off with the Half company and platoon commanders, leaving Coutts to bring up the convoy.

As we got into Rimini the sky was just beginning to get light, and it made a glorious blue and gold effect on the calm Adriatic. We crossed the Morecchia, and forked left for Santarcangelo. I sped along with my jeep convoy because Jimmy had delayed us at the start. We got to 46 Division just on 0600. They were about three miles south west of Santarcangelo, between the river Rubicon and Morecchia. I went in expecting to find John,* only to learn that he was now liaison officer at 128 Brigade. I was glad to hear then that the whole convoy was to come under command 128 Brigade and that I was to report there forthwith.

About the first person I saw was John, whom I had got out of bed by sending a message from Division. He gave us breakfast and then started the business of finding out what was wanted of us. In the end it meant taking over from a platoon of the 9 Manchs., and making room for two more platoons. John, meanwhile, made a recce for our H.Q. I went up the smelly track to Mantalbaro with Bob and found a place for one platoon in a farm nearby a very dead horse. We still had no move order to get the company up from the Coriano area. I went off to see what John had found us. The whole area was liable to be shelled and I went off down the main road, having rejected John's choice, to find something else in the opposite direction. I found a house which the 46 Recce were just leaving, and took over. But little did I know that the area had been allotted to the 60th, and, of course, as soon as we had got settled they came along and said we would have to vacate. Of course, I got this information when I returned to Brigade but, nevertheless, we did stay for one night.

Then I got a move order and sent that over to Coutts, went back to my H.Q. and arranged guides, and had more wrangling with the 60th. It

*Brother.

seemed that they would be coming so I set off to have another look at John's area, got warned by an R.E. about mines in one, and just missed heavy shelling in another, so came back determined not to go there at any price. The company arrived after dark and by some miracle everyone got to their allotted place, rations were distributed, we had a meal, and then to bed, glorious bed.

This morning I was up at 0600 hours and after breakfast went off to see Brigade and the platoons. Later in the morning it transpired that I had to leave my H.Q. and John came to tell me the sad news. However, as luck would have it, we found another farm near Brigade and I am duly installed here tonight, trusting in God that we don't get shelled. Some have fallen close already.

7.10.44   So once again we support the crossing of a river obstacle and this time the Rubiconi Fiumione. At the Brigade conference the plan was set for an attack to go in last night but it was cancelled for twenty-four hours. It rained very heavily in the evening and I was very glad the attack had been postponed. Nevertheless, the Boche seemed to suspect something, for last night was very noisy and the whole area was heavily shelled. John Scott in his observation post got rather badly wounded in both shoulders, right forearm, left wrist and right leg. His wrist wound was bad.

It has been rather extraordinary to be working so closely with John, and it's the first time we have been really like it in the same battle.

8.10.44   During the night the weather changed and by morning it was raining hard, and has continued to do so during the day. To-night it is pouring in torrents. Nevertheless, the attack went well and the Brigade got their objective – Montegallo. This morning we fired a lot at Boche attempting to pull out and altogether in the twenty-four hours we have fired some 2,500 bombs. All the platoons were shelled but no casualties were sustained, except by some R.E.s on Jimmy's line. This afternoon a counter-attack came but we stopped it all right.

And so on this wet October Sunday, as we fight on the edge of the Po valley, there looms up the possibility, nay the probability, of another winter campaign, another winter of cold, wet, snow, of war and misery. As I write I hear guns and the patter of rain. Pray God that it will not be so; our homes are still very far away.

14.10.44   'Short stretches of furious activity and long stretches of bore-dom' is how someone described war. It's pretty true, I suppose, for even though one may be out of action for a short time, it seems longer, and in that time one is apt to become so broody and introspective. The separate masculine existence becomes more pronounced and the physical and mental longing for one's wife, and one's home, becomes bitterly acute. There is a horrible feeling of wastage, of life going by unfulfilled, soulless. And the mind broods on past happinesses, now so horribly frustrated. And, of course, one looks into the future and asks, what is freedom, what is happiness? Freedom of want and fear is not freedom – somehow our society is so complex, so bound up in red tape – may probably be more so in the future – that I am not sure that we won't be shackled by our own artificial devices. The daily trip to the soulless office, the petty officialdom, the whole salaried life – can that give us all happiness, even though we know that the food and shelter of one's family depends on it? War seems to imprison the soul – is it so easily released in peace? I know we must work, and I know life is nothing without work, for that I believe is where true happiness lies. I know, too, the inter-dependence of persons, bodies, and nations, and it is in this conception the mind wants to give of its utmost. It depends on the particular mind, whether it is satisfied with the confines of a narrow routine. But I expect my thoughts are very one-sided and ill-balanced – the war and its (sub) conscious strain no doubt makes one very warped in one's outlook. I suddenly realised how 'inwardly' I have been living when I went for a short walk on the grassy olive-strewn hillside about our farm. It would have been dangerous to do this before because of shells, and suddenly realising I was all right no doubt had its effect too.

But I remember actually standing and admiring the grass and the little, rather autumn-touched flowers, the weirdly old and venerable shapes of the olives trees. Yes, I could look at all this without being afraid. I could look out to the east to the blue Adriatic, and once when I looked up at the lovely afternoon sun, I saw a great string of birds, flying from east to west, possibly migrating. I hadn't been in this receptive mood for a long time, not only receptive but reciprocal. I could see the beauty of it all. The land itself had still its intensive beauty, despite the shell holes, the muddy roads, the filthy ditches, broken walls and shelled houses, the whole symmetry of which had been ravaged by the wanton acts of man. From the hillside I could see that it was only man who had lost his symmetry – it wasn't God. The fight of good against evil – I suppose it has been rightly called that – but how strange that man cannot live amicably, how incredible that the very gift that makes us different from animals – the power of thought – should have been so misused, so often misused, that the world of men is where it is today. Is it too much to hope that after this terrible struggle, we shall use this gift in the light of God, and bring peace for ever?

15.10.44   The bells of the Church in this little village of Canonica ring out – the war has passed by, leaving the land ravaged and homeless. But at least it has gone and one can imagine the people offering up their thanks.

There has been lack of news – at least about what we are likely to do – I expect they are waiting to see how things go before committing us. From south of Cesena to the coast the Germans are in force and are taking some shifting. In fact, all across Italy resistance is strong.

It was a joy to hear of the liberation of Athens, that long-starved city, and that food had been taken in by air. Riga has been taken by the Russians and Belgrade is invested by Tito and the Red Army and should be free soon. On the Western Front things have slowed up considerably.

19.10.44   For three hours I looked for an H.Q. but every house was occupied, except a very dilapidated one which had suffered from our own shelling and was marked 'Reserved for Medical'. Reserved or not, I took it as a last resort and am still in it. Upstairs it had one and a bit rooms. We are in the bit; that is, John W. and I. In one corner there is a great gnashing hole, through which can be seen the rubble and beams of the demolished part of the house. The end wall of the room was extremely cracked and rickety and the Italians had put up three supports. I was a bit wary of sleeping in it as it was not proof against fire, and even our own guns made the place shake like hell, and stuff fall off the ceiling. Downstairs was only room enough for the men. However, it was at least reasonably clean and very 'airy', so I took the chance. During the night, in my somewhat wakeful sleep, there were so many guns in the area and bits of plaster kept falling on me that I thought it was raining! By the afternoon the rest of H.Q. had arrived and soon we were making the best of a bad job. Plenty of Flit and a good sweep make a world of difference to an Italian household.

21.10.44   And so D company is participating in yet another river battle. This time it is for the bridgehead across the river Savio at Cesena. Yesterday the Royal Fusiliers got over and made a small bridgehead which they held against fierce resistance and intense shelling and mortaring. It was not possible to evacuate wounded or prisoners, and no food got across last night. 12 and 13 platoons moved forward to positions behind the ridge south of Point Abbadessi and have since carried out many tasks. Yesterday I went up to see them. The views out to the plain were magnificent, so incredibly flat after all this hill fighting we have done. The Boche had good observation on us from the twin peaks west of Bertriobo and he stonked the nasty hairpin bends on M. Romano, causing quite a few casualties. Bob moved yesterday to north of Celincadia, and I moved to a farm just south of it this morning, on a steep reverse slope. Last night the Royal West Kents and the Black Watch went over to extend the bridgehead, which they did to some extent. They were heavily counter-attacked by infantry and tanks, and supplies were very difficult today.

George Hulme went over with the R.W.K.s with an 18 set party, wading in up to their chests. We have not been able to contact him all day, but it is hoped a bridge will be completed tonight, and Bobby might get across with a carrier to relieve him. It must be hell over there. 10 Brigade have moved up just behind us, and no doubt will soon be going in. And tonight we are cursed by rain which will make things hell.

24.10.44   The epic battle of the Cesena bridgehead ended today when we put in 10 Brigade and pushed on for about five miles. This morning a bridge was completed and tanks and infantry have been going across all day. On the 22nd everything was bogged down by the heavy rain and the supply parties suffered heavy casualties that night getting stuff across. We still had no contact with George, although we knew he was not wounded. Yesterday we managed to get a 22 set across to him on a tank and got through satisfactorily. He immediately brought to bear a great weight of fire over the left flank, which was exposed. On that day I moved into Cesena following Bob who had gone in the day before with Brigade. We found a wonderful billet, and it was quite incredible after all these hovels we have been used to, to be in a strong, clean residential house again. This morning the gunners and ourselves put down a barrage in support of the Surreys who were going through 12 Brigade. At about 0430 this morning it started, and the sound of the barrage in the town turned it into some incredible 'symphony of guns'. It was a wonderful hunting ground for the composer. The double basses, the drums, the violins, the horns, all were there. It was macabre. But we got through and well on to Bertriori. Tonight the Left Half platoons are across and ready to go into action. I shall soon be over. How far is he going to withdraw, I wonder?

The Right Half came out for a well-earned rest in billets in Cesena. Today we saw George for the first time after what he called five days of hell; he looked as though he had been in hell. But more of that anon.

25.10.44   The Boche has pulled his main forces right away from the Savio line, and today 10 Brigade made good progress against slight opposition, many mines and booby traps. The cratered roads are perhaps the biggest hindrance to our advance, and, of course, blown bridges.

The high ground village of Bertrioro had been taken and the advance was continuing. I found an H.Q. in this area and decided to move in this afternoon. Once again we are in a small farmhouse but a clean one, which is a good thing as it was a great pity to leave our last home in Cesena. Still, it is no good getting settled in these days. Denis, nearby, has just come in to say that three cases of typhus are in a barn near his farm, not too happy for them. When I look at the filth and rubble and general conditions the civilians live in, I wonder disease isn't rife.

27.10.44   It has rained solidly for forty-eight hours, and as a result our small bridgeheads over the F. Ronco were counter-attacked by tanks, and we were pushed back this side of the river, the 2 D.C.L.I. suffering fairly heavily. The weather has been persistently against us just when we have wanted it fine. It was the same over the Fuimicino and then the Savio.

And so we are before the F. Ronco, which in the last two days has risen very considerably, and is at least 150 to 200 feet wide and flowing very fast. The fields about are just one sodden mass of water, so it looks as though we may be here for some time. Apparently one German prisoner has brought the story back that Kesselring has been given twelve days to get the German Army out of Italy. I wonder how that rumour started. He was still shelling last night and today anyway! But the Russians and Yugoslav effort in the Balkans must be worrying for them.

31.10.44   Things have got moving a bit more today with an improvement in the weather, although heavy rain has fallen on the last two nights, making side roads horrible. 14 platoon moved into action west of Forlimpoli today, only a thousand yards or so east of the river. During the day the Surreys got across the river and are consolidating their gains. It is hoped to erect a bridge tonight over the Ronco at Route 9. 14 platoon are carrying out a heavy harassing programme and 15 platoon, who are moving in tonight north of Route 9, may join in, but anyway will be on call by the Surreys at first light. The country is flat but close, and cover from fire is only provided by digging and by houses, not very big at that.

3.11.44   The last three days have been busy and not pleasant. On the 1st November the Bedfords reinforced the Surreys across the Ronco, and Tommy, Tony H. and Steve went over with them as L.O.s and O.P.O. At that time there was a pontoon bridge across the river, but in its usual evil way in the evening the weather broke and it rained hard all night and continued for most of yesterday. The Ronco ran amok and the bridge was swept away. However, we managed to get supplies over by ropes, etc., and casualties were evacuated over an aqueduct on the 10 Indian (now 46 Div.) front.

I had recced a hill farm near 14 platoon for a new H.Q., and yesterday during the pouring rain we moved in. The room I had chosen for John W. and myself was flooded, there being a shell hole in the roof; we are always spoiling billets for ourselves! However, we soon remedied that with some tarpaulin and buckets, and got a fire going. It is now a delightful room which we use for a mess and office, our bedroom being separate and upstairs. By evening we were comfortably settled in and Denis came to dinner. Then Peter called with the intention of going to 15 platoon with me. But that was not to be, for shortly afterwards the Boche started a tremendous stonk and shells and shrapnel were flying in all directions, making life very unhealthy. It lasted for about three hours and Peter slipped away in a quiet spell back to Brigade. John W. and I waited up till 2300 hours before retiring to our upstairs bedroom.

I slept well but occasionally was woken by shells, guns, and a M.G. battle that seemed to be going on across the river. We are not much more than a mile from the river ourselves, and everything is very audible in this flat country. We are west of Forlimpoli, which itself got shelled heavily last night. The only damage we could find this morning was on my jeep. My new windscreen, which I had gone to such bother to have put in, had a nice big hole in it, despite the fact that it had been parked against the wall.

7.11.44   Tonight we start another attack on Forli. All day the medium and fighter bombers have been over softening up. The Right Half are over the Ronco and in action south of the aerodrome. So now the whole company is in. We were over there this morning and from 14 we walked to 13 and 12 platoons.

9.11.44   So for the last twenty-four hours the war has been raging round Forli airport, and to the southwest of it. Tonight sees the airport ours and on our left flank S. Martino in Strada taken by 128 Brigade, and all along the resistance has been grim. It has not been without casualties, and we suffered when a shell hit the 2 Hamps. H.Q. Dibble, who recently joined us from the Middlesex, and Bob were both wounded, and have been evacuated; Valgren, ex-signal officer of 1 Group, lost a leg and later died, poor fellow. A. Hamps. company commander was killed. The whole thing was a great tragedy, especially as they had not been committed into the battle as yet. The company has fired since last night the best part of 1,000 bombs, and they are still at it. We had some very close shells last night, which woke me up, and another shell at the fated Italian farm just down the road killed four gunners. Sleep has been very much lacking of late, and that and the noise is, I find, apt to make one very depressed. The noise goes on all the time – guns, shells, mortars, M.G.s and during the day the continuous sound of planes bombing and machine gunning. As I write now I can hear our guns and the whine of German shells as they go overhead or across the river. I did that same walk to 15 platoon this afternoon, and the new shell craters don't improve matters. We got there O.K. but just as we came away the rebels opened up and we dashed back into the farm.

10.11.44   A strangely quiet night indicated that something was afoot, and, sure enough, the Boche were pulling out beyond Forli. Today Forli is ours and we are already beyond it, and probably over the Montano as I write this. I had a busy but interesting morning. I set off early in the morning mist to see exactly what was happening to the platoons and, of course, found them all packed up ready to move. I then went on to MANNEQUIN, a crossroad south of Forli, and saw Hobby and got 13 platoon location. They were at TRAGEDIAN on the outskirts of Forli, and once again we experienced the clapping crowds. I'm sure they all admired my very new duffle coat which I was wearing.

The platoon was in a nice area, from which we could see the F. Montano, which the F. Rabbi joins higher up, a river which had already been crossed by 46 Division. Patrolling was going on and there were occasional bursts of M.G. fire. These sudden advances are incredible, like a sudden release, that brings all the civilians out, not unnaturally as they had been living in cellars all this time to escape the shelling. But there is a new atmosphere; the enemy has gone, the war has passed, and they have new visitors, perhaps more friendly than the last.

11.11.44   The night before last saw heavy rain, but it cleared by morning, with a cold crisp wind blowing. There was snow on the hills, making a lovely scene in the sunlight. The outskirts of Forli had not been promising for an H.Q. because of the heavy shelling, and so I went up again to see John W.'s place, and generally to get the atmosphere of the surrounds again. In the end I decided to come up, and sent back a W/T message to that effect. We then proceeded back to our 'tiffin', getting held up in traffic jams on the way. However, I was back in Forli at 2.00 p.m., and the rest of the H.Q. very soon after. I went into Forli proper to see Peter Gorst again, and 14 and 15 platoons. The town is very empty as there is a lot of shelling, and Peter is installed in a cellar. So nearly the whole company is now in Forli or its surrounds, and yesterday we fired about 1,000 bombs from these positions.

We are in a block of flats, on the ground floor, rather cold with their stone floors. It was uncannily quiet to start with yesterday evening, but I had not long been in bed when, crash – shells and mortar bombs fell around, a most uncomfortable feeling, with bits and pieces hitting the walls. I lay awake trying to orientate myself to the various sounds, enemy guns, our guns and mortars, most difficult in a town. We are only about 600 yards from the Boche here with the F. Montano luckily between us. Our room is graced by some of the most magnificent chrysanthemums I've ever seen; great big ones.

I got to sleep eventually, rather lightly. When the sun did come up I heard a wren singing away, a very friendly and happy sound. It was a cold frosty morning, but the sun poured in through our glassless window, making a shadow of the iron bars and curtains on the far wall.

It wasn't long before the fighters came over machine-gunning and bombing, so close that they had started their dive long before they reached us. Today we fired over 1,500 bombs and the task of replenishment from Cesena has been a heavy one. Tonight our drivers are still at it, and I hope to have a further 1,800 dumped by tomorrow morning. One of our targets was 'Enemy retreating in confusion, their Commander being wounded'. We got this by wireless intercept.

13.11.44   The last two days have been very busy ones, with hard fighting and good progress being made. In the last four days the company, chiefly the Left Half, have fired over 5,000 bombs, half of the total being fired on the night 11/12. Tonight our troops are not much more than a mile from the loop of the Montano north of Route 9. 46 Division to the south are also over, and I saw John* today, whose Brigade H.Q. is quite near my own. 15 platoon moved out of Forli yesterday to an area called Clettini, and during the night had trouble from their left flank south of the river with spandaus, shelling and mortaring. Still, they had an egg each for breakfast today. The Hun had left their farm in haste and the ammunition carts with oxen all yoked were still there, as was a motor cycle, which we are now using.

John W. and I made our first trip out to the northwest of Forli to see 15 platoon, and the whole area was smashed and battle-scarred, and with an eye to a future H.Q. there didn't seem to be much in that line worth having. The weather has been good for these last days but it is raining tonight, which may slow us down somewhat. Their chronic lack of transport must be a great hindrance to the Boche – they have oxen and horses to tow some of their guns. Yet they are conducting their retreat extremely well and show no signs of breaking. How browned-off they must be.

---

*Brother.

16.11.44   12 Brigade, having fought extremely well up to the line northwest of Forli, was taken out on the 14th and 28 Brigade took
over.

That night was our last in Forli, for the Right Half went in just east of
the Montari – and consequently yesterday morning I moved my H.Q.
about two miles north of Forli on the roadside by the Canchi di Rivaldino.

18.11.44   During the last two days the fog of war has been well-nigh
complete, with numerous plans and alterations coming out for
the continued advance across the Montari, and the lesser obstacles. Today, however, a final decision seems to have been made, which involved
the whole of the company, Peter being under command 10 Brigade, and
Bob in support. I have not seen the operation order yet but I think it will
be a big attack, and by tomorrow morning we shall be deployed ready to
do what they ask of us. It will be a hard fight, this advance to Faenza and
the F. Lamone, but if the weather stays like it is, frosty and sunny, with
the terrific artillery support, things should have a chance of success.

Rumours are rife just now about going to Palestine and then to England,
but I think something must be afoot, even if it is only that we are coming
out of the line. I say this because the C.O. thought (he probably knows)
that we should be out in a week, and I don't suppose he would say so if
there weren't good grounds for his doing so. But even supposing it is true,
what lies ahead is the question that is uppermost in our minds.

20.11.44   And now things have crystallised. We attack tomorrow morning at 0200 hours, a Corps attack, with its objective Faenza.
Everything is ready, and we wait. The talc is marked with all the objectives; what grim things will take place in these little areas so blandly
marked up. It is a big attack and tomorrow a big air support programme
has been laid on, but it will be a hard battle for all that. All the mortars
have been well dug in or otherwise protected, and fire charts arranged.
This phase of preparing for a battle is a queer one. You dash about in your
jeep, getting the 'gen' and eventually make the arrangements that immediately concern you, and somehow it all comes out and the battle starts. And
so from one battle to another.

22.11.44   Our efforts to get across the Cosina on the morning of the 21st
failed. Our infantry encountered a very deep minefield and
mud, and although one company did get across, the heavy mortar and
shellfire and tank opposition made it impossible for them to stay, with so
little across and with no support, so they were accordingly withdrawn,
having suffered fairly heavy casualties. Our neighbours did make some
progress towards the river but no advance was made over it. But it was to

be expected, the Hun is a good soldier and he doesn't let chaps get over an obstacle like that without desperate opposition. However, new plans were made straightaway. The heavy bombing from the mediums went in as planned and it was a goodly sight and sound. The same thing has been happening today in perfect weather, and as I write this the guns roar out as another attack goes in across the Cosina. Let us hope we have better luck this time.

Yesterday we had some casualties on 14 platoon's line when it suffered direct hits from nebelwerfers, and set a lot of our bombs alight. Very gallantly, several of the men immediately set about putting the fire out when a bomb exploded, wounding two of them. How grateful we will be to come out for a rest.

24.11.44   This time the attack in conjunction with John's* Division was a success. After fierce fighting for the first bridgehead, in which we held firm against strong counter-attacks, we resumed the advance, supported by tanks. This morning sees us practically up to the F. Lamoni, the other side of which lies Faenza. The Right Half did some good work in supporting the attack, and they were stonked in no uncertain way.

There is a general end-of-term feeling, no doubt engendered by the dry, sunny weather, and the satisfaction of another obstacle crossed, but most of all by the fact that things are happening to the Division, and we don't expect to be here long. We are all asking where we are going, and no-one can give us the answer, or those who can don't! Deductions are made from every small sign, and so it goes on. Unless it's England it doesn't matter except that we are out of the firing line.

25.11.44   This morning saw John W. and myself up Route 9, which was a mass of heaving transport, and over the river Cosina to see Peter at 10 Brigade. The news was good for our troops had reached the Lamoni on a wide front and were still exerting pressure. I had hoped Peter would have some information about being relieved, but, on the contrary, the talk was of moving 15 platoon forward. Anyhow, we went up the depressing and shell-torn side road to see Steve, and found him and his platoon esconced in what was apparently a school. Soon after we arrived it started to rain and that, coupled with the shelling and general dreariness of the whole scene, made us very depressed. Knowing that we were likely to come out soon, we didn't want the platoon to go forward again one little bit.

---

*Brother.

Imagine my pleasant surprise then when I heard on return to company H.Q. that Peter and 15 platoon would be at the Ritz by the evening. Today at last would see the whole company out of the line for the first time in two hard months. So tonight sees them all in Forli, and my H.Q. joins them tomorrow, the first time we will have been altogether since Foligno days. Now I wonder how soon before we are off to 'fresh fields and pastures new'. Let's hope we are there for Christmas.

28.11.44 The last 48 hours have seen a mass of fleeting impressions – rush, sleeplessness and changing scenes. We left Forli on the 27th in a drizzle which developed, as we moved down Route 9 through Cesena, Santarcangelo and Rimini, into a downpour, which didn't cease.

After Ronco we had headlights, and I shall never forget the view through the windscreen of the rain beating into the jeep, and the two plumes of water thrown up by the forward wheels. Sometimes, when we went between an avenue of trees, the dead leaves would float down in the lamp-lit rain. Luckily, I was in Peter's jeep and kept fairly dry. It was a long journey, most of it done in the dark, but the roads were good.

It was still raining when we arrived and we then had to set about finding billets for all. After some time this was done and we had a high breakfast at about 2 o'clock. Coutts had found a good billet for us, the home of a high-class surveyor and his family of three rather attractive daughters. It was a good home and the electric light worked.

29.11.44 At a conference in Atri I learnt that all our kit had to be packed and away by tomorrow, so it hasn't been too easy a life today. We stay here till 4th December, when we entrain from Ortona to Taranto, where at some future date we embark for Palestine. This continual moving of bodies and kit is a most depressing business, and it will be a long time before it is finished with. However, it has always been like that, and always will be in the Army. I have had three letters from Dulcie, and Peter has got two turkeys, some cabbage, celery and potatoes for dinner tonight.

1.12.44 Atri, 1,300 feet high, seems to be permanently in a cloud at this time of the year, and the last few days have seen us working in a sort of misty rain, most depressing and uncomfortable. We have now handed in all our heaters and lighting equipment, so the long nights are spent by candlelight, and it's so raw cold that I usually go to bed as soon as work permits. We are now beginning to get out of the wood, and the next day or so will see us ready for the next stage of this rather tiresome journey. We apparently stage at Taranto for a few days before embarking for the Middle East – the land of 'Red Tape'. Yesterday afternoon the whole of the transport of the Battalion, with all its stores, moved off to Pescara to be handed over to another unit, and at the top of the hill on the outside of the town, I watched it go. They have done us good service and since the forming of this company we have fired some 30,000 bombs with that equipment. I only wished to myself it was the last time, and that such things were going for good. But we shall get some more in the Middle East and another lot no doubt when we come back to whatever theatre we are destined for. Thank God it is not the Far East.

5.12.44   One gets so used to looking ahead in the Army that when things happen which have been pending for some days it all seems to take place much as you expected, and nothing is new, except perhaps one's ever-changing immediate environment. And accordingly the last day at Atri came about and ended. It was an unexpectedly beautiful day and on the way to breakfast I took a walk to the south side of the town, and the view of the sunrise on the distant snow-clad mountains was a memorable sight.

The foreground was made up of the steep, jagged, and green valleys that typify Atri, and looming behind were the great mountains. We bided the morning in the warm sun, and after an early dinner the R.A.S.C. transport arrived and we made ready to move off. The convoy set off at about 1600 hours, taking it slowly down the whaleback curving road to Route 16, giving us another fine glimpse of the astounding geology of the place. Then on to Pescara with the men singing in the back of my vehicle and shouting to all the senoritas. Then inland a bit during one of the most wonderful sunsets I've ever seen, glorious changing colours over the hills reflecting themselves in the mirror of the truck, and lighting the country in an incredible manner. So on to Ortona over winding roads in the dark and missing the scenery. The entraining went really well and I was glad that I had sent Tony ahead as all the officers' valises were well installed in Box waggon No. 35 by the time we arrived. I have never before travelled overnight in what amounted to a cattle truck, and with fifteen officers I expected it to be pretty grim. But once we had unrolled our beds and snuggled down, we weren't too uncomfortable, a bit hard on the hips but we had expected that. It was warm, too, and I slept, but with what a creaking and groaning, knocking and banging, that pulsated through your body, the wheels seemed to scrunch at your hips. But we got used to it and as the speed increased the row seemed to lessen.

7.12.44   So through this monotonous countryside of olive trees and flatroofed farms – a red, stony land – we arrived at Taranto at about 2100 hours on the 5th. There was a blaze of light from the railways, and many ships in the harbour, a very unaccustomed sight. Not for a long time have I seen the pleasant sight of lights shining across the sea.

So far so good, but the ordeal was to come as, of course, by the law of averages it should. We had to detrain on the line, carry our bedding about 300 yards to some waiting lorries, which were for luggage only. When the business of loading all this kit up was done, we formed up and marched five miles to Robertson Camp near Taranto. Thank God it was moonlight and not raining, but it was a weary business after a trying journey, and my legs felt queer. We got there about midnight, threw off our equipment and went for a meal of M. & V. and tea. Next began the business of unloading all the baggage lorries and finding personal kit and bedding, no easy task in such a jumble. There were no tents for the men but they were very good and bedded down in the open with no fuss or nonsense. I got to bed very thankfully at about 0330 and slept till 0900, waking up to the feeling of warm sun and a view of old lovely olive trees. It was a decidedly warmer clime down here. The day was spent in sorting out kit, erecting bivvies, and getting more sleep. It was pleasant to know that a part of our long journey was over.

We will be here for about a week, and it gives the chaps a chance to get out a bit and visit Taranto. In the evening I went for a stroll with Coutts, enjoying the scene of camp fires of the Indians.

10.12.44   How easy it is nowadays for incidents and events in other lands to have repercussions that affect one directly. Yesterday we were in an idle mood of preparing to embark in a few days' time for a rest in Palestine; we were enjoying ourselves in Taranto, building ourselves up, as it were, for an even greater orgy of pleasure – and to that end we were putting up very stoically with the rigours of transit tent life. Then – last night, after a thunderstorm and heavy rain, in which our tents became flooded and our beds looked like Bailey bridges, came the blow. In brief, it was to the effect that we were to send parties back to Pescara, re-take over our kit and vehicles from 5 Division and concentrate in the Taranto area, ready to sail to an unknown destination. And so not only did we have to reverse all our emotions but put into reverse all the programme that we have just carried out, except that, thank God, our kit and vehicles will be brought to Taranto and save us that beastly train journey. But what a mouthful to be told at 0215 in the morning.

We had been reading, very scrappily because of lack of papers and wireless, of the trouble in Greece, and noted that some well-known units had gone there, some by sea, some by air, but we were not quite aware how serious the situation had become. And what a situation – we liberate

Greece – aided very largely, I admit, by the action of Russian in the Balkan countries – we send supplies – we uphold a certain government to maintain law and order – and then Greek fights Greek, politics again. Now to strengthen the government position we start fighting the guerillas, for that is what they are really, however they may be formed. It is a crazy world and one had to be very elastically minded to cope with these ever-changing situations. It wouldn't be so bad if we had beaten the Germans, but all these things are cogs in the wheels, and the consequent extra commitments are just what the Boche wants.

I went to O Group at 28 Brigade today and they are standing ready to fly to Athens, or if the situation doesn't remain as urgent, go by sea as a complete Brigade H.Q. We cannot fly because of our weapons and vehicles, and so we wait till all our kit arrives to prepare ourselves in as short a time as possible. The men didn't seem to mind the change at all.

To me this all reflects the shape of things to come, where in all these once conquered countries the people who lived and suffered there together with the guerillas and underground organisation have decided a political future which has often been the direct opposite of the governments of those countries as constituted in London. There is the inevitable hatred and ill-feeling, when once freed of the German occupation these governments return to take office and begin to run the country as they think fit, backed usually by London. Who is in the right? It is a complex and unenviable problem, which I think will take many years to solve. It has happened in several countries already, where no doubt the picture of 'liberation' is by no means as rosy as the press likes to paint it. It is an ironical task for the British soldier who wants to get on and beat the Hun, to be embroiled into these civil strifes, especially as it is playing so much into the hands of the Germans. It is a bitter thought that many have lost their lives by the very arms we supplied these countries to help rid them of the enemy. The best help we could get from them would be a change of heart – not a resort to arms to hinder our main task.

14.12.44   And now the circle has almost turned full wheel. I must recapitulate the last few whirlwind days, in which premonitions, preparations, changing plans, waiting, ended finally in a tumultuous climax, out of which the first calm had just made itself felt. December 11th was a day out of tents and mud, spent idly and pleasantly in Taranto, and included a cinema, lunch, tea, dinner and a ride back to camp in the jeep of a neighbouring Greek Unit! Pleasantly tired, on Tuesday, after a march we returned hoping for sleep and eats, but I found I was on a conference at 1400 hours, and there were signs that all was not as it should be. The Bren guns were being unpacked for instance, the Padre and M.O. were sorting their kits and suchlike. At the conference it transpired that 28 Brigade had flown to Greece that morning, and that 12 and 10 Brigades had embarked for the same place today. The C.O. was away at the time but he had passed a message to say that it was five to one we should be embarking on the morrow. We should go without vehicles and weapons, go, in fact, as infantry! And as we had to march down to Tosi pier at Taranto if we did go, and prepare Deck and Hold baggage, and decide what was left behind with the rear party to be put in the vehicles when they turned up – there was some quick thinking to be done and action taken.

It was almost too much – this waiting, and uncertainty – God, I was tired too by now, and the idea of marching in full kit about seven miles without a good sleep just made my brain reel.

Then came yesterday – 13th December – embarkation day; and it came at about 0530 hours when I was woken up with some messages, one saying I was on a conference at 0800 hours. So I got up and made final arrangements for the transporting of kit, etc. At the conference I learnt we were embarking on the *Cameronian* of the Anchor Line, and were to be ready to move off by 1000. Later we were told we were leaving the camp at 1130 hours

So on that wet and muggy morning we formed up in battle order and marched down to Tosi Pier, where, after a certain delay but not as long as one usually expects on these occasions, we got onto an Italian lighter, together with our Deck Baggage and made off under the swing bridge to the *Cameronian*.

Today has seen a little uncertainty about where we are sailing, and finishing and loading, more good meals, and news that the rebels are going all out to take Athens before more reinforcements arrive. I wonder if I have left the shores of Italy for good.

15.12.44   We left Taranto harbour at 1600 hours yesterday and my last view of Italy was of a sun setting in heavy rain clouds, and over the misty mountains were occasional gaps of an incredible turquoise sky, not unusual in rainy weather. After a practice Boat Stations, we had tea, and in the comfort of the lounge afterwards I read some articles about the Dumbarton Oaks Conference. The news after dinner said fighting had broken out in Athens with the rebels shelling the place, but a game of Solo soon made us forget that. This morning we hear of a general strike in Greece which, of course, all adds to the melting pot. The food situation will no doubt be a source of worry, and I have heard that we are on half rations, but how true that is I don't know.

Greece

16.12.44   It is almost impossible, with the usual military vicissitudes, to
            assimilate or analyse a day like today. It is so easy to say we
landed in Greece, that it was a beautiful sunny day, that the panorama of
Faliron Bay was superb, and leave it at that. But somehow the experience
demands more than that, and yet to make a pen picture of it is an over-
whelming task, which takes much patience.

   A dull windy early morning saw us somewhere off the east coast of
Greece with clouds hanging low over the barren and rocky islands and
hills on the mainland. By the time the clouds had gone and the sun was
shining on a deep blue sea, we must have been well into the Gulf of
Samnikos, for it did not seem long before Piraeus, Athens and the surrounding heights came into view, a truly magnificent spectacle of a lovely
city nestling under mighty barren hills wreathed in clouds. The hills
encompassed us, and the blue sea and sky made a setting the like of which
I have never seen before. The contrast of the great stony mountains, of
city and sea, gave it all such a dreamlike quality. To starboard we could
see a stretch of green under the Imittos mountains, a great whaleback of a
ridge, and there too lay the aerodrome, crowded with aircraft. Next our
gaze was cast on the Acropolis, on a hill overlooking the city, which I
have heard about so often and know so little. Dad would have loved this,
with his knowledge of Greek history and the language. Suffice it to say I
am very glad I have seen such an imposing scene. Then on the port side
was Piraeus, a lot of which is in the hands of E.L.A.S., and the absence of
people, together with the peculiar hollow look of the houses built on a
rocky prominence, made it look like a city of the dead. This part fasci-
nated me a lot, and to some extent reminded me of Constantine in N.
Africa, except, of course, that the buildings were smaller; perhaps it was

the colour. Then further to the west lay the island of Salamis. Truly a magnificent waterfront, which surely can have no equal the world over. It was, for me, unforgettable, and the cliché 'The cradle of civilization' came very naturally. It was, in fact, difficult to believe, especially after the comfort of the ship, that we were here not as holidaymakers but to uphold the principles of our mode of civilization.

Other liners lay off the harbour disembarking troops on to the landing craft, which made off as soon as they were loaded in various directions. Many aircraft were flying around, and the ships and aeroplanes all added to the contrast against this ancient scene. We could hear some shelling and M.G. fire in the town somewhere, but it was of a sporadic nature and not very alarming.

We waited eagerly to know what was expected of us in this peculiar political war against the E.L.A.S. forces. We learnt our fate after an early lunch. It was to the effect that we would take over the defence of the aerodrome from 10 Brigade, disembarking straightaway. This seemed a most reasonable task for a M.G. Battalion without its proper weapons, and we were quite light-hearted at the thought. The aerodrome was the Kalamaki 'drome just south of Athens proper and, of course, very essential to us.

So the Battalion disembarked on to a smaller craft in the bright early afternoon sun, and it wasn't long before we were making our way to the beach on the right of Faliron Bay, where, after a little navigational difficulty of hooking up, we debouched on to the sacred soil of Greece, in full war paint!

We formed up into companies by the main road, waiting for transport to take us to the aerodrome. A few children were about, and some older people, peculiar dark-skinned individuals. A lot of evacuees were being brought off some island or other where E.L.A.S. prisoners were going to be camped. There were a few small pine trees and, of course, the peculiar names on houses, etc., made us realise what a problem the language would be. The different architecture and the stony soil were other impressions at this juncture. It was all quite peaceful, odd soldiers walking about with rifles and tommy guns, and some shelling on the hillside above the harbour.

We embussed and moved off to Kalamaki airfield, where we moved into tents on some waste land amongst houses surrounding the 'drome. D company had no operational role, which was good. We were in reserve. The sun went down and it got very cold, and we did our best with two blankets, groundsheets, and a twenty-four hour pack, a great blow after our food on board. I wrote these notes on the stony Greek soil on my blankets and a candle on my steel helmet for light. Nearly everyone was brewing up his packet of tea, and the smell of rosemary wood fires will, I think, always remind me of this, my first day in Greece.

It was so cold, and I got in between the blankets, but it was no good. I wouldn't have been able to sleep – and then, great joy, our valises arrived in the baggage, and it wasn't long before Benning and I had my bed up with the usual quota of blankets.

17.12.44   I gather that Field Marshal Alexander has given E.L.A.S. forces till 25th December to stop this business, after which he will strike and strike hard. The E.L.A.S. forces are military elements of the E.A.M. Government, which is very left wing. The bulk of the population consider them as hooligans and rebels rather than a political party. It has been proved conclusively, however, that the arms which we supplied to these guerillas, as we did with Zervas and E.O.K.A. forces, were partly set aside and hidden for the day, i.e. when the Germans fled the country and they could, by force if necessary, set up a *de facto* government, leaving their political opponents stone cold. For seven years now the Greeks have had no say in the politics of their country, what with the Metaxists, and the Germans; and Churchill's policy of getting the country going so that the people can elect a government is obviously very right. And the great welcome given to our troops here seems to uphold him, too.

The E.L.A.S. say they will make peace and withdraw from Piraeus and Athens if we disband the Greek Mountain Brigade and the Sacred Battalion, and send them to their homes. They, of course, stipulate that we will have nothing to do with the politics of the country, but only exercise our authority in a military sense! That, of course, would only be putting off the evil day. From what I've seen in the prisoner of war camps, they are a lot of ruffians, and the country would be ill-advised not to be rid of such an unscrupulous lot. It will be interesting to see how they react when they see we are not going to be gulled by them.

20.12.44   We are gradually getting to grips with our new life in Greece. Denis is back with us, and Hobby has gone out under command C company to the northwest of the airport. We still have our prison guard commitments, and the scene at these places is really quite fantastic – people of all types, some in uniform, more in shabby dark civilian clothing; officers, men, women, some walking hands behind back, up and down in serious discussion. It is reminiscent of old campaigns long forgotten. The small camp has protected personnel, women, children and Sisters of Mercy and suchlike. Still there is no sign of a ceasefire in this incredible situation.

I hear of demonstrations in Trafalgar Square to stop fighting the E.L.A.S. and the challenge might have serious repercussions. I should have thought this would have been a case where the United Nations would have declared a strong positive policy – but it seems that independent action is being taken by us because Greece is in our 'sphere of influence'. All this is grist for the Axis mill, and tends to split rather than unite the Allies. If E.L.A.S. is allowed to control the country, taking advantage of its weak condition, the sufferings of the people will be indescribable. The food situation is critical and if we condoned an E.L.A.S. Government established by force of arms, how could we be sure that a fair distribution of our supplies would be carried out. Some classes would be bound to suffer.

We have cleared most of the city but the R.A.F. H.Q. seems to have been captured by E.L.A.S. and most of the personnel taken prisoner. Tony Hutton goes as liaison officer to fetch a Greek battalion of the National Guard who were to take over some of our positions. Last night we went to a film in Faliron, everyone taking his rifle or pistol!

21.12.44   For the first few days of our sojourn in Greece we had as a mess a room of a battered windowless house, which we tried to make draught-proof by using bivouacs. Nearly every day a cold north wind has been blowing, making our existence pretty gloomy. Yesterday, when it seemed to me that our present commitments would perhaps mean a somewhat longer stay in this present area, I asked Bob Hutton to see if he could find another mess, more like home, in one of the other houses that bordered our tented camp. The idea bore fruit, for soon he was escorting me into a lovely little house, complete with furniture, windows, curtains, rugs, the owners of which were most charming, and insisted that we used their dining room and crockery for a mess, and their sitting room for an anteroom. It was a bit of an invasion but they would not hear of anything like us refusing what they had to offer. Madame could speak English, which was a great help, and it appalled us, when talking about using their kitchen for cooking, she said it did not matter as they had nothing to cook; she was at that moment boiling grass for their meal, which she said, sardonically, only took twenty minutes anyway. So I told her she must share our food, and she even tried to refuse, saying we were soldiers and needed it, whilst they, as civilians, did not.

It was quite incredible and horrible to find in this lovely house, very English with its nursery (there were two children, one of whom, the little boy of eleven, could also speak English), and its chiming clocks, its beautiful carpets and curtains, table cloths, ashtrays and glass, and even a maid, and perhaps best of all, the lovely vases of flowers – to find all this amidst starvation.

For four months they had no bread, and as we had read, people died in the streets of Athens, died of starvation. The Germans would stretch out bread and butter to the children, only to snatch it away before they could get it, or they who show them a bowl of food and, instead of giving it to them, fling it on the ground. Poor creatures, they were so hungry, they would tear it up with the dirt all over it. At first no-one would work for the Germans but when so many people died the blackmail worked and some got food that way. Relief came at the instigation of Great Britain from the Red Cross, and they say the Germans only took a small percentage for themselves of these supplies. Without that I doubt whether the Greek Nation would be surviving today. Money, of course, was worthless, and if you were lucky enough to get a cabbage or something, you would spend all day counting the money out to pay for it. When we arrived we were amazed to hear that three cauliflowers cost thirty shillings or five cigarettes.

They are eternally grateful to the British for all this military aid we have given, for our supplies, for our general sympathy. They have a great admiration for us, and when we left these shores in 1941 everyone was weeping. Now they feel ashamed of the E.L.A.S. who, after all we have done for the country, turn their weapons against us, because we know that it is not the will of the people that they should be in power.

Not long ago elections were held in many institutions and public services in Athens, and not in one case did the E.A.M. or K.K.E. get a majority. Sensing how the wind would blow in a properly constituted election, the E.A.M. set up a *de facto* government by force of arms. The great majority of the Greek Nation do not consider these men as Greeks but as outcasts, brigands, communists, who they say must, and will, be eliminated, perhaps by politics rather than arms.

I broached the question of Russia and, of course, they cannot help associating the troubles in their own country with the Russian regime. In fact, they think that if we, as a Nation, give in to E.A.M., then Greece will at once come under the control of Russia through the communists. They want a democratic government, and the friend said that he thinks once the various parties get a chance to express themselves, they will vote for the return of the King, whose status, since the troubles, has gone up in leaps and bounds. That may or may not be, but it is an interesting view, especially as you hear often that the Royalists are very few and far between. Col. Zervas, of course, is an ardent Royalist, and very pro-British, as he well might be!

So now I have got the thing straight in my own mind, and that I know that the majority of the Greek Nation fully supports the actions taken by Churchill since the E.A.M. rising, I feel glad that we were given this task of assisting the Greeks purge their land of these undesirable elements.

23.12.44 The cold wind continues to blow, bringing with it a dull snowladen sky. It brings no cheer to a cheerless life of huddled prisoners, of scantily dressed and ill-nourished refugees, to a barren land and all the chaos of this political upheaval. Life seems to have lost all meaning, it is a wandering, a scavenging, a scrapping. We too are on very short rations, but in this land it seems a lot and we help the people of the house as much as possible. We hope to get our Christmas fare at a later date. By a bit of ingenuity we have managed to make up a Christmas stocking for the two children, sweets, chocolate, and so forth, and Bob Hutton has volunteered to be Father Christmas. I hope it makes them happy.

Hobby is still doing the same job of night patrols, and Denis yesterday took over a position to guard a bridge, so we are all committed now. The prisoner of war cage is the big worry. We have had escapes, trouble with a crowd of women, relatives of the men, which caused a shooting incident, and friction with members of the Prison Staff, who are a low grade, bullying, heartless lot. These chaps, who have probably never fired a shot in anger, make our men boil with wrath at the harsh and unnecessary treatment of these prisoners, many of them only suspects. It will do our cause a lot of harm if it is not stopped, and prolong the suffering of the people. Tony Hutton, who has been away helping to form a battalion of the National Guard, says that the refugee problem is pitiable. This is especially so, as we sent leaflets over telling the people to get away from the E.L.A.S. positions, and presumably thinking they would be bombed, they came flocking out to find we had no arrangements for receiving and dealing with them. So they had to go back.

25.12.44 *Christmas Day*. It really is quite amazing! I could never have seen myself sitting down at this table in a pleasant Greek home, with three little Greek children playing around full of Christmas excitement. On the sideboard stand bottles of champagne, oranges, tangerines, flowers, and our wireless is playing Dvořák. Tonight we have a dinner party of about seventeen, including our Greek friends. The servants are wondering about the problem of seating. Outside it is brilliantly sunny and very windy, a cold wind, and in the distance the hills are covered in snow.

It could quite easily be a Christmas Day in England; the sounds and sights are very similar, it is only the background on which it is painted

Mme. Pappa's children, Athens, December 1944.

which is different. Yes, the wind blows hard up the valleys, over the rocky
bare mountains, bringing with it a dense pall of snow cloud, and whipping
up clouds of dust off the aerodrome.

Our peculiar task continued and yesterday some of the company officers
had to go and supervise the distribution of food to the neighbouring population. It was quite orderly, however, and everything went off in a peaceful
manner. In the morning I went to a Carol Service held by Padre Squires, all
dressed up in Greek Orthodox robes, which rather startled me. The Service
was held in the small Church of Hellenico, a pleasing edifice shaped like a
Maltese Cross. We had some good carols which I enjoyed singing.

For the first time in my life I slept in a tent on Christmas Eve; it was a
bitterly cold night but warm enough in bed. Yes, it is all very strange and
difficult to understand. There still seems no likelihood of a major improvement in the situation, and, indeed, I understand that a battle is now
going on between Zervas and E.L.A.S. forces.

It was proposed yesterday that the prisoners move to a new camp, and all arrangements were made when, at the last moment, it was cancelled. It is an unpleasant task, this guarding of political prisoners, many of them, some women, entirely innocent. They are very crowded, have only tents and one blanket each, and things are just not as they should be. It is a hateful business for the Geordies, who are very kind people, but the administration is nothing to do with us, unfortunately. I wonder if next Christmas I will be seeing two little Greek girls with ribbon bows on their pigtails!

27.12.44   It was the best Christmas since 1940, and the most homely. Our guests and their children made it so. I shall never forget that table with its small and friendly atmosphere. It seemed inevitable that family photo albums, and what photos we had, should be produced. In the end I had to give Madame one of Nicolas in his pixy hood, and I am getting one of her daughter Nicky (or its Greek equivalent). Nicky is a sweet doll-like little girl, very quick and very quiet. The children were very happy with their presents. They finished their dinner with some difficulty, not having eaten so much for a long time, and, as the adults put it, 'their stomachs having gone all small'. Many toasts were given, in which Bob excelled himself. Bob is a man who is very sensitive and has a heart of gold. He did excellently. They produced for us some lovely almonds and vermouth, carefully saved for such an occasion.

Boxing Day brought news of Churchill, Eden, Alexander and Macmillan in Athens for talks; and the attempts to blow up Scobie's H.Q. We also took over the guard at the new prisoner of war camp, a depressing business of lines of dirty ill-nourished civilians being herded from one pen to another. Still, they get fed well there. Hobby took over his windswept hill and I went up to see him. It was a hell of a place and the 'tactics' of our higher commanders were, to say the least of it, not exactly appreciated.

John Scott turned up from Italy after an unpleasant journey which ended in his landing craft being shelled, causing casualties. Poor John looked frozen and lost; I felt very sorry for him. However, he cheered up later. After a mess meeting, in which we had settled some minor points and decided on New Year's Eve jollifications, a blow at the heart came from the Orderly Room, when I was told on the 'phone that we had to move today to B company's area in the middle of the windswept aerodrome, bang on top of battalion H.Q. That shook us to the roots! We went to bed full of gloom, to be woken at about midnight by a lot of firing, and yells of 'Alarm'. E.L.A.S. had put in a small diversionary attack. We hustled out of bed and 'stood to', a most disturbing process. However, the trouble died down and after an hour or so we got the stand down; thank God, I said, as I went back to bed.

This morning I spent rushing about all round the aerodrome defences with Tony, as we now have a Mobile Reserve role. It was a very sad business having to leave our delightful home, with its kind people, for a marquee tent, but the house is at our service to go to when we like to write letters, etc., and to get out of the wind for a bit occasionally.

29.12.44 So we have settled down to the windswept aerodrome, our tents being pitched near some ramshackle hangers. Fortunately, the weather has been kindly, and the wind less fierce, and that, coupled with the discovery of one of our oil stoves, has made us reasonably comfortable. One thing, we have a better view of the bay and the changing lights on the islands and coast. Yesterday was spent in getting an organisation for my three platoons going, and in the afternoon, after seeing Mr. Churchill's colossal plane leave the 'drome, I went round the defences with the platoon commanders.

There seems to have been no agreement at the conference between the E.L.A.S. and the Royalists, except in that a Regency should be set up. Fighting is continuing, and last night E.L.A.S. made an attack on the Bedfs. I was given a line on the set-up by a military liaison officer the other day. He said that the E.L.A.S. resistance during the days of the German occupation was only token, presumably so that we should maintain our supply of arms. When Italy collapsed, the G.O.C. of the Pinerole Division, who is very pro-British, immediately offered his division to fight with E.L.A.S. against the Germans. They agreed and arranged for a rendezvous where they immediately stripped the Italian division of all its arms, clothing, vehicles, and sent it naked into the hills. The E.A.M./E.L.A.S. engineered the mutinies in the Greek troops in Egypt, and we had to clear them of all Communists and other left wing merchants. As a result, the Greek forces, as reorganised by London, were very much Royalist. Then came Papendreou and his conference, to which E.A.M. sent six delegates, who signed all that was asked. E.A.M. in the meantime had been offered a sort of underground organisation by K.K.E., the communists, which they quickly accepted, with the result that K.K.E. soon had all the say in E.A.M. Although E.A.M./ E.L.A.S. had agreed to disarm at Papandreou's conference, they, in fact, did not do so, unless we disarmed the MT. Brigade and the Sacred Battalion, which of course was impossible as they are an integral part of the Allied Forces, and, anyway, it would have been playing into their hands. Scobie had to refuse therefore. E.A.M. next day said they would stop fighting if they could keep an E.L.A.S. division of equal strength to the Greek Forces. And so it goes on – a position in which a large force, armed by us, controlled by an extreme political party, wants to assume the government of a country, which has been struck down, has no regular army, is suffering from starvation, and has not yet been able to choose a government by election. The majority of the Greeks are staunch right, even Royalist, and very anti-communistic. It is fear that prevents the K.K.E. from stopping the fight, because they will not get into power by the wish of the people.

1.1.45   There was a rumour yesterday that the E.L.A.S. war had come to an end, but it was found to be false. But now that the King of the Hellenes has agreed to a Regent, who will, of course, be Archbishop Damaskinos, there ought to be some hope of an early settlement. He is a man who rises above party policies and is admired by all. Whether E.L.A.S. will cease hostilities and hand in their arms under the Regent remains to be seen. I personally think it may take some time yet, some jockeying by E.A.M. for a reconciliation of the terms as demanded by General Scobie. The King says he will not come back to Greece unless he is summoned. I gather that a lot of the Greek people would like him back, but I think it would not be wise at the moment.

Anyway, it is good to know that the food supplies are improving, and, in fact, in those areas which have been cleared, the people are doing well and have a good ration.

I went to see my friends – the Pappas – yesterday to wish them a Happy New Year. With the flour Madame had received she had made her first bread for a long time, and she insisted on giving us a loaf, and all the refusals in the world would not move her. Before we arrived at the house before Christmas they had been fifteen days without anything, and when I pointed out what a lot they had to make up she still would not hear of it, and, indeed, we also had a lovely cake made for us for New Year's Eve. It was impossible to be ungracious for this was their way of showing their gratitude, and a very Christian way too.

Bob Hutton did us really well last night – soup, turkey, steak, roast potatoes, peas, carrots, apple tart, pineapple slices, and coffee, and, of course, a liberal supply of drink. It was a goodly happy gathering and a lot of us stayed to see the old year out, just before we had an invasion by the Sergeants, and, of course, there was a good set-to for 'Auld Lang Syne'. Yes, it is difficult to believe another year is upon us; God grant that we shall see our families before it is out.

4.1.45   These last few days have brought little change. More of Athens
has been cleared – in fact, I should say most of it – but fighting
still goes on. Damaskinos has asked General Plastiras to form a new
government and that I presume he is trying to do at the time of writing.
We have taken many E.L.A.S. prisoners lately, and I can hardly feel that
their morale will be very high, especially if they are turned out of Athens.
We must persevere to obtain conditions in Greece where the people can
elect a government of the majority. If we do not persist, then we are
allowing the very symptoms that bred Hitler in Germany.

During the day I interest myself by visits to the liaison officers I have
provided with the Greek National Guard battalions. I have four of them
out, and it is a regular manhunt to trace them down in their haunts in
Athens. I spent about three hours with Bobby and George last time. Their
platoons occupied a hill position overlooking the 'drome, and they are up
all night. It was half moon as we climbed over the rocky ground, and we
could see gun flashes and very bright lights, and the outline of mountains.

9.1.45   General Scobie has drawn up new terms for a truce, but as yet
there seems no sign of a definite armistice. We are in Thebes,
about thirty-five miles north of Athens. I had a platoon ready to go there
but it wasn't required.

Information about our future is *non-est*, although it is reported that the
General has said that this is not to count as our rest! I should hope not. It
looks as though we should stay here until hostilities cease, but what would
happen after that depends on many things.

14.1.45   I had a very interesting day yesterday visiting Jimmy. We set
off at 0800 hours in a crisp sunny atmosphere. Thank goodness
there was no wind. Once through Athens and its busy crowds, we went
through the suburb of Dhafni and then started the climb on the Aigaleos
mountains, whose rocky stone gives little fertility, but there were little
patches of grass, and an old village characterised by that odd square-
shaped architecture. Soon we were given the glorious view of the Kolpis
Elevsinos – almost a lake it looks, so well surrounded is it by the hilly
land and the island of Salamis stretching out beyond the Gulf; beautiful in
the early sun were the Parnis and Patnas mountains to the north and west
respectively. On a good road we passed Elevsis and then went northwards
through Máridra. The olives stopped soon after we began to climb over
the Patnas mountains, whose slopes again were pretty barren except for
shrubs and occasional belts of pines, and here and there a little farm or
village which must have had a very thin time. The road was now rapidly
deteriorating and from now till the end of the journey was the worst

feature of the whole business, a continual bumping and banging. And so I really wasn't surprised when we reached the rather more fertile basin that supports the community of Oinoi, an ugly flat-roofed village, that we had sprung a puncture. We had reached an area called Káza Karni at the beginning of the Pastra group of hills. Troops of the Greek Mountain Brigade were there, stopping and searching civilians and their vehicles. In the sun we wandered over the hill waiting for the tyre to be mended. I found a flower like a crocus blooming, very lovely, spreading its petals in the warmth. At the other side of the road was a stream and occasional pocket of snow which had not yet melted.

At last all was ready and we started our climb through the barren hills to the village of Erithrai, which was built on the lower slopes of the north side. These mountains are bare and bleak and are quickly deforested of any timber by neighbouring villages. Donkeys with loads of sticks and carts full of wood were common sights here; whole mountain sides have been stripped of timber, I suppose the only source of warmth to be had. Now the road straightened and we made for Thebes, over a plateau of downlandish country, where the grey crows changed to the ubiquitous magpie. Here the land was ploughed a little, and larks and finches and cornbuntings were to be seen. Ahead lay the Ptóon mountains, snow covered and showing up splendidly against the lesser hills in the foreground.

There was no time to stop in Thebes, and soon we were changing direction westwards through Piri. And then began that horrible stretch of road, which detracted from the interesting surrounds and remained like it till we got to Levádhia. The road runs to the north of the Elikon group of mountains; in fact, it hugs their northern edge, and at the same time is the southern extremity of a very fertile basin which, before it was drained, was Lake Kopnis. So here one gets trees, grass and streams. At the water's edge were thousands of coots, and many other small birds were in evidence.

Finally we arrived at Levádhia, which like all the other towns, is built up on the side of the mountains, whose precipices and rockfaces tower up menacingly. In this town there were a Brigade H.Q., a battalion of the Royal West Kents, some gunners, and 12 platoon, and on the surface one would have thought, as in Italy, that the situation was normal, and no enemy within miles. But such was not the case as George and Co. were quick to tell us when we found them billetted in what had at one time been a brothel! No, in this medieval Greek town was a story of murder, fear, and atrocity, all at the hands of the K.K.E., whose stronghold in the hills and top houses of the town they called 'The Little Stalingrad'. The situation is quite fantastic and smacks of storyland.

These guerillas amount to nothing more than a murder gang who will stop at nothing. The normal townspeople dare not show their approval of the entry of British troops; they hate to talk with them or have them in their houses because K.K.E. will note it all and bring revenge in the form of murder and pillage. Persons who are found helping us are put in the 'Book', as it is called, and when the opportunity occurs these brigades will strike. It is a difficult situation to cope with (the Germans found that too!) for the culprits are so elusive. Arms and other supplies are carefully concealed, mostly in the mountains, and searches normally provide little evidence. Normal civilians cannot or dare not to do much in the way of informing for they know what would happen to them if they did. They dread us leaving the place now because of the murder that will be committed. The K.K.E. will fight on even if E.L.A.S. as such makes peace. They are well stocked with food and supplies, and little did we know when we were supplying them that it was their own power they were thinking of. They killed some Germans, certainly, but only because they like killing; it was nothing to do with freeing their country, for they now think we are just as much a menace. Yes, these men are Andartes by nature – it has no specific purpose – it's a way of living. It is an internal problem which, when Greece is stronger, will best be dealt with by Greeks, and happily too. There must be many scores to be wiped out.

In such a short visit it was difficult to grasp such a situation. With the sun shining on the mountain stream that runs through the town, and wagtails calling, my brain was reeling as we set off home.

15.1.45   It was an unhappy day for us yesterday. A tragic occurrence took place at the prisoner of war cage which we are guarding, when one of our trucks being placed to light up the wire at night went over a mine. These mines had been laid by the Germans as part of their defence against a possible Allied landing in Greece. The driver, Fusilier Bray from Cornwall, was terribly injured, poor fellow, and lost a leg and a thumb. He was very brave and I am happy to say is still alive and showing every sign of pulling through. It upset us all for he was a good fellow, strong and cheerful, quite young and typically Cornish. It was grim irony, too, that he should have come so far after landing on the Salerno beaches and then be maimed on prison guard duties in Greece. The incident excited the prisoners and we had more attempted escapes during the night, which resulted in two of them being wounded by sentries. That prisoner of war cage has really been a headache and the sooner we get shot of it the better.

The truce started at 0001 hours today, and so if E.L.A.S. abide by the terms, we may soon be released of this commitment.

19.1.45 We had very good news – that we were moving into billets, and here we are, very comfortably disposed, just off the Leofros Surgrin, and about a mile from Athens. As a company H.Q., from being the worst off, I think we are now the best, and our proximity to Athens is another advantage. We have an attractive mess, and the kindness and generosity of these Greek people surpasses anything I have ever known. If only some of those cantankerous politicians at home could come here and see for themselves the gratitude the people feel, the happiness it has brought them to be spared the gangster law of K.K.E. Goodness, how easily people are gulled if they do not know the facts of the case. It has taught me a lesson how always to take with a large pinch of salt the sonorous announcements of our M.P.s. Seeing is certainly believing.

22.1.45 Our new life in New Smirni is becoming a very comfortable one, and we should like to stay here for the rest of the war! The electric light works and to be woken up by your batman as he brings you morning cup of tea and turns on the light gives you a great sense of wonder and gratitude. In the evening, perhaps over a cognac or some retsina, or some Turkish coffee and a tangerine, we discuss the situation, past, present and future, in a mixture of bad English and French. They are full of gratitude for what we have done; want us to stay, as they think the K.K.E. will return when we go. When I point out that we want to get home to our wives, and that they have a National Army, they shrug their shoulders. Madame is very anxious about the future, just as she was in the past.

I had heard that 46 division were coming, and yesterday I got John's* location and went to find him, which I did on the coast in Glifadha. He thinks he is here for three months but doesn't know for sure. He came to dinner the other evening. I heard that they may be relieving us, but there is no sign of that and we have battalion cadres going on till 12th February. May life continue in such a pleasant manner.

28.1.45 After a morning of not very exacting work, an afternoon devoted to entertainment, life is '*bon*', and we hope to stay in these pleasant billets until we leave Greece. What chance there is of that no-one seems to know, but I must confess I am not awfully keen on going to Palestine. I would prefer to stay here and rest. Much depends on the outcome of the massive Russian offensive, which in the last fortnight has swallowed up E. Prussia, Silesia, reached Breslau, and crossed the Oder,

---

*Brother.

by-passed Posen, only a few miles from Danzig, and at one point is only 100 miles from Berlin. The Germans now have three major powers fighting on German soil; it seems incredible to me that they do not ask for an armistice. Is it their fanaticism, or is it fear of what an unconditional surrender means, or are they just putting off the evil day? Anyhow, the Russian advance is stupendous, and although we have become rather wary of wishful thinking after five years of war, hope and general morale must, I am sure, be pretty high in Allied Countries. Conversely, the Boche must be feeling a little sick with the capital of E. Prussia directly threatened and with E. Prussia itself cut off from land communication with Germany proper. *Their* refugee problem must be quite acute!

Things seem to be settling down very well in Athens now, although the talks between Damaskinos and E.A.M. have yet to be held. I have just been reading Hebbe Percy's interesting report on Levádhia. It seems that we have been of great assistance in these outlying parts too, but the snag seems to be the difficulty of finding arms hidden by E.L.A.S. and K.K.E., and one wonders what will happen when we depart. However, by then the Greek National Guard will no doubt have things well in hand. There is no love lost between them and K.K.E.

15 platoon goes up there tomorrow to relieve 12 platoon who come back with their Brigade. Tommy and John are going and now I expect George and Ralph will start to paint Athens 'bright red'!

Many of the Greek hostages and our prisoners have now returned, and I saw some of the hostages one afternoon in Athens. They were up on a balcony, looking down on a shouting crowd of hostage relatives. It was a memorable scene – the dirty, bearded, dishevelled and ill-clad hostages gesticulating to the frenzied crowd below, who were wanting to know the fate of relatives. I don't suppose it could happen in England. The British prisoners said they had all their stuff taken off them, and were marched into the hills, but supplies came by plane, and these they were allowed to keep.

30.1.45   John called last night to say he was going to Argos today, which is down on the coast of the Peleponnese. Rumour has it that we are going to Palestine after all, but nothing official yet. John said 139 Brigade were coming back to this area.

Tony Hutton, who is now a liaison officer (temporarily) with L.F. & M.L., spent the day with one of the M.P.s visiting the country – Lawson – Labour. Lawson, in true Parliamentary manner, said he could see only two sound things about the situation in Greece – the Acropolis and Tommy Atkins!

He admitted how badly the whole affair had been represented in the Press, and when asked when Shinwell and Gallagher were coming here, he said – 'Perhaps it wouldn't be wise.' He had received a message from a paratrooper for Mr. Gallagher but said he would have to take a 4.5 pistol if he was ever brave enough to pass it on! He had held a press conference, which went off very happily except for one Greek journalist writing for an American newspaper, who said the British were sticking their noses too far into the Greek Government. Such is democracy that we have to let things like that go by.

He went to battalion and talked to some of the men, promised to make enquiries, etc. I'm glad someone has brought to his notice the disparity between leave from the Western Front and the Italian Front.

4.2.45   And may it be my last wedding anniversary spent without Dulcie. It has been a warm, sunny day, and there has been a very English Sunday atmosphere – altogether very pleasant. I attended a Church Service in the little Church of Hellenico and we sang some good old favourites like 'Eternal Father', 'Greenland's Icy Mountains' and 'Abide With Me'.

I have paid my first visit to the Acropolis and wandered over the various Temples – the Parthenon, the Wingless Victory and the Erechtheion, which has the Basket-Bearing Maidens. The whole thing is quite over-powering and the general setting lovely.

The peace conference between E.L.A.S. and the Government of Damaskinos is reputed to be going well – it will be interesting to see the outcome, and whether all parties come to some agreement. I don't know how long they reckon to keep British troops here, but nearly every report from villages say that things are running smoothly now, but there will be trouble directly we leave.

I hear that the division in Palestine is being relieved by a division in Italy, and it seems unlikely that we shall go there. We are being relieved of our guards here but I do not know what it portends.

11.2.45   A beautiful day, with the chiffchaff singing, and canaries, too, in their cages. A lot of blossom is coming out, almond especially, and I have seen carnations too. There is very definite Sunday atmosphere in Greece, quite distinct and unmistakable. It is very pleasant and leisurely, a day for a stroll by the sea and a visit to friends. I visited Madame this morning for the first time for some days, and partook of some of their own retsina – but had to refuse some of her spinach roll. I met there a Mrs. C. Stangos, an elderly, sad-looking woman and a widow. She spoke English well and was highly intelligent. She said, speaking about the Greek situation – 'We Greeks are funny people; we can do wonders out of nothing and then suddenly we will ruin all that we have done.' Then added – 'After a time we will forget all about the war, and another will start.' She thought it an inevitable outcome of the war that there should be a swing to the left. She asked me to call on her next Wednesday and meet her family.

It seems that it is very likely that we shall be in Greece for some time yet; the Divisional Commander said he hoped we should all be here by 15th March. The common rumour, of course, is that we are going home preparatory to the Western Front. I must say I would prefer that to another summer in these climes, even, I think, though it involved another farewell from home.

Stalin, Roosevelt and Churchill have been in conference for some days now in the Black Sea area. The first communiqué was just to say that plans for the final defeat of Germany had been agreed upon, and the conference was now concentrating on arrangements for a permanent peace and the occupation of Germany. Meanwhile, with the Russians now along the east bank of most of the Oder, with constant pressure from all other fronts, and with heavy air assault, the Germans have still shown no sign of capitulation.

The Government have put forth tentative suggestions that a formal armistice may never come about and because of this they may, on their own account (with the United Nations), have to announce that the war as such is over, and mopping operations are in progress. The date decided upon would be the day for celebrations, etc., and would be the legal Armistice Day. It seems on the face of it a most unsatisfactory way of concluding the greatest conflict in the history of man, rather an anticlimax, in fact, but I suppose it may be necessary under the circumstances.

14.2.45   This afternoon I was fortunate enough to witness a memorable and historic scene. I had noticed during the late morning that many flags had appeared on the buildings in New Smyrna but my office clerk gave me no satisfactory reason for it.

After lunch I went to the Officers' club to get a haircut and noticed on the way a large crowd gathering outside the Palace. There was bunting on the tramway and flags, both British and Greek, hanging from the windows of the Palace. In the brilliant sunshine the scene was very colourful. On the way back I mingled with the crowd. Soon Dan Hinson came along and I learned that all was in aid of Mr. Churchill, who was coming to Athens on his way back from the Crimea Conference. So I waited to see what was going to happen. The crowd increased and so did the tension. Officials were hastily putting up a tannoy system and many officers and other dignitaries began to gather on the steps of the Palace. The whole face of the Palace and the crowded court below was lit by the mellow afternoon sun, very fitting for such an occasion. An hour passed by and the shadow, thrown by the buildings of Constitution Square, moved slowly over the Palace itself as the sun sank lower in the sky. Some cars arrived and there was clapping, but it was a false alarm. Then overhead passed a great silver four-engined plane with six Lightnings as escort, and the crowd clapped as they looked upwards.

More waiting, more false alarms as other high officials, military and civil, arrived. The crowd called for Scobie, who answered with a wave of his hand. Then suddenly there was a looking, a shuffling, and shouting and clapping, as another group of flag-bedecked cars arrived. Military policemen ran hither and thither, opening car doors and directing them on. The familiar figure of Damaskinos were soon acclaimed by the crowd. Then out of all the confusion came Churchill and Eden, and a great applause. Soon Damaskinos and Churchill were standing side by side, Churchill taking off his hat to the crowd. A band struck up the National Anthem. The crowd called 'Chur-chill', 'Chur-chill', 'Chur-chill'. But it was Damaskinos who spoke first, a fine and picturesque figure he looked, and he spoke with a fine deep voice. How I wished I could have understood him. He was well applauded. Then Churchill spoke and I shall never forget his deep familiar voice as it rang out and echoed across Constitution Square. The main gist of it was that party strife should cease and that each man should do his duty in a new united Greece, whom the World would never forget, and move forward to take their place in a new Europe. He spoke a few sentences at a time, and then it was interpreted amidst the applause of the large crowd.

Then Mr. Eden spoke and he, too, was well received. It was the first time I have seen the Prime Minister and the Foreign Secretary in person, not to mention 'his Beatitude'. When Churchill mentioned with pride the part the Army had played in the liberation of Athens, there was a great call of 'Scobie', but he did not speak. This memorable occasion ended with the British and Greek National Anthems.

20.2.45   It has turned bitterly cold, a sharp snowy wind coming down from the north. It was very sudden after such a warm, even hot, spell, but apparently was expected by the populace, some of whom say it will continue for a fortnight. The Imittos mountains are covered with a thin layer of snow and are whiter than I've ever seen them. Light snow has fallen in the street but it melts away. I no longer hear the chiffchaff in this weather; in fact, all the birds have made themselves scarce. Thank God we are not in tents.

Peter Gorst ('Fanny') has joined us from Italy and is the same as ever, a little more doleful perhaps after his jaundice. He is, at the moment, on the horns of a dilemma, having been accepted for the Regular Army. He is not sure whether he wants the job or not, his chief worry seeming to be its effect on his 'holy matrimony' as he calls it. Via the U.K. leave personnel, some of whom have rejoined in Italy, he brings lurid stories of the many domestic upheavals caused by long separations of men from their wives. Apparently, a high proportion of the leave parties have, or are about to institute divorce proceedings. How much these stories are tinged with exaggeration is difficult to say, but I know there is much truth in it. It is a sad and tragic tale, for these marriage contretemps are eating into the very foundations of a strong and happy nation – i.e. family life. But has there been ever, in the history of man, such long and enforced separation, under conditions of extreme anxiety and strain? Have there ever been such vast movements of the population? Have there ever before been the terribly crowded and unnatural living conditions caused by bombing, etc.? The answer is definitely 'no'. It is inevitable that the effects of such tragic cases should be a decline in morals, and, if so, does it indicate a limit of endurance beyond which the social frame as we know it will break down? It is a big question, and I expect the situation has been noted with some alarm in high quarters. Shattered homes can be rebuilt, but to rebuild shattered homelife is another matter.

The plight of other countries, and especially those over-run by the Hun, is in this respect far worse than our own. For as well as the causes mentioned comes perhaps the worst – hunger. Hunger has driven people to desperation, and you get the case of a woman selling her body for a tin of bully beef, or biscuits, or chocolate. (I mention these things as they spring to mind readily; I do not mean to cast aspersions necessarily on British forces!) But it is the stark fact that such has been the trade of many women. A report the other day showed that within the radius of one mile from a certain square in Athens no less than 6,000 women were known to be professional or amateur prostitutes and, of course, most of them contracted disease.

24.2.45   The day, Dulcie's birthday, has marked a change in the weather. The grey driving snow cloud has given way to a lovely blue sky and the wind has almost gone. The night before last saw quite a heavy fall of snow and yesterday morning the ground was white. The children made full use of it whilst it lasted, and snow-balling was the order of the day. But by this morning it was all gone, except on the hills. Yesterday afternoon I went, with Denis and Jimmy, to the foot of Mt. Parnis, and even on the lower slopes drifts were very deep and difficult to negotiate. It was dull and visibility was bad, and the view of Athens was consequently marred. Denis took some photos which will be an interesting record. The soil out here is very rough and barren, and all I saw was a great herd of goats, shaggy and with great horns, and watching over them was a hardy goatherd, dressed in thick, ragged but picturesque garb. It was very cold there and we did not dally. It seems now that we are not moving till next weekend.

28.2.45   At a conference yesterday we were told that the battalion was moving to Khalkis over next weekend. One part is to leave Athens on the 2nd March, and the second, of which D company formed a part, is to leave on 5th March.

The terms of the truce are apparently being carried out with great expedition, almost too expeditiously it is thought in some quarters! There is a feeling that E.A.M. are only too anxious to comply with the terms, so that the need for the British Army to remain in Greece will no longer exist, and the sooner it departs, the sooner these ardent left-wing gentlemen can start their tricks again. However, whatever the reason, and it is easy to find reasons if you want them, the Division with the Greek National Guard units are now going to enter previously unoccupied territory, more in the role of a guardian angel than anything else it seems to me. The British in this new territory are not going to be billetted in towns but will remain in the country. The reason for this is that the country will be entirely under Greek rule, backed by the Greek National Guard. We are there to assist only if absolutely necessary. It has been the habit of Greek officials to approach the nearest British Commander in the event of any trouble, and if we are going to arbitrate in all these things, then the country will never stand on its own feet. And so the dumping of arms and the disbanding of E.L.A.S. goes on, and I so sincerely hope that all is well and nothing fishy is going on in those quarters.

We relieve a Brigade in Khalkis and if, as it seems, we have the place to ourselves and in reasonable billets, then we should be very happy. Our pockets will certainly be spared, and I'm sure it will do us a power of good to get out of our 'cinema-paved Athenian' rut.

Nevertheless, we are leaving a rear party with John W., so that we still have one foot in the 'immortal city', and thus provision is made for leave parties, etc. In view of the fact that the C.O. thinks we will be here for some time to come, this is an excellent arrangement, and I suppose it is

always possible that we may return *en masse*. The C.O. thinks we have
seen the last shot fired in Europe but for myself I am very wary of this!

6.3.45   The company is now safely esconced in Khalkis on the island
          of Eubboea. It was cold when we set off from Athens yesterday
morning with light snow on the mountains. Up to Thebes our route was
the same as the one I have tried to describe when going to Levádhia. A lot
of blossom had come out since I last travelled this road, and offset against
the pine trees and olive trees it made a lovely sight. I spotted many
anemones by the roadside and at one halt before Thebes found a lot of
speedwell and a flower like a kingcup. The road over the Pastra heights
was clear of snow but on the hills themselves the many drifts and patches
made a beautiful tracery effect. Then came the unknown part of the
journey, and for the most part the country was typical of these mountain
basins, fertile rolling downland, and hardly anything in the way of villages, or even hamlets on the wayside. Then came the climb of the Ktipás
range, the highest of which is 1,021m, a very beautiful and symmetrical
peak. These hills overlooked Eubboea and the gulf that separates it from
the mainland.

The view of this island from the top of the pass is unforgettable. It was
nearly three o'clock and the sun was behind us shining onto the island and
the sea. It was a glorious spectacle – first the deep blue sky, then a layer of
white misty cloud along the mountain tops, and below the snow line the
dark slopes leading down to the tongue of land on which lies Khalkis,
looking very inviting with its red and white buildings; all this set in a deep
blue sea, the many bays and natural harbours making a most fascinating
scene. Our descent to sea level from the hills made me realise that the
plateau was high up, hence no doubt its downland flora and fauna.

7.3.45   The war news is very good of late for the Russians have
          reached the Baltic coast between Danzig and Stettin, and have
captured Stargard which is only twenty miles from Stettin. Thus, their
right flank is considerably strengthened and they may now resume their
advance on Berlin. In the west the Americans have captured most of
battered Cologne, and the west banks of the Rhine from Cologne to
Nijmegen is almost completely in our hands. Another American Army has
made rapid strides towards Coblenz, and Churchill has been to Germany.
How much longer can they last out?

10.3.45   The last three days have been a period of mixed emotions, the
           most pleasant of which, I think, was Thursday when I took the
company for a march round the fertile basin that lies below the low rocky
hills to the east of Khalkis. The diligent husbandry which has yielded such

pleasing olive and vine groves, together with the blossoming fruit trees, gave the area a most luxurious appearance, almost startling against the bare hillsides.

Yesterday I went in a jeep through the village of Nea Artaki, on the coast road north of Khalkis, and there turned inland into the hills for a short way. We stopped and admired the view of the 1,021 feature and the blue Gulf. Down below us was a quaint little village with a small and simple church by a single olive tree. Hoodie crows and magpies were much in evidence, but best of all were a pair of ravens, which we watched on the craggy hillside opposite. They were making nuptial flights and chasing off a buzzard that was in their territory.

14.3.45   I was rather looking forward to going back to Athens, but I must confess that now the real spring weather seems to have set in, the changed plan of moving to Volos pleases me. It is a large sea town on the mainland, in a bay north of this island. It has a population of 50,000, and it seems we are to be the only British troops there, so life should be good.

17.3.45   The last few days have been concerned mostly with the move of the battalion to Volos. The battalion, less ourselves, left Khalkis today. We leave tomorrow, staging one night in the vicinity of Lamia. We go through the famous pass of Thermopylae and our journey takes us over some very rough mountain roads. Volos lies at the top of the Gulf of Pagasitikos, which is shaped like a horseshoe. A ring of mountains protects Volos from the north, the chief group of which are the Pilion mountains. I am told the scenery is very beautiful and I am looking forward to our journey, especially if the weather stays like it is, warm with clear skies and no wind. Volos is the sort of Marseilles of Greece, and there are no less than ninety-seven brothels there, and I expect we shall have trouble. Most of the battalion will be in barracks just outside the town, but I think messes and officers' billets will be in Volos itself.

21.3.45   The last three days have been somewhat hectic and much that I would have liked to record will have to go unrecorded. I did manage to get something down though during the journey, and in the harbouring area past Lamia.

My last view of Khalkis with the dark mountain beyond and Or Dhirfir rising up, snow-covered above all, was a calm, typically early morning scene. The zigzag road below me as I looked down had a fascination of its own, despite the fact that I have seen many of them now.

The mountain side was looking beautiful with a blue shrub in flower and occasionally a glorious splash of anemones. As we proceeded the day got warmer and sunnier, with blobs of cotton wool clouds anchored in a lovely sky, a blending of colour that symbolises the Greek scenery. It was really beautiful, the warmth, the new green of the crops, the superb blossom, the contours of the hills, grey of the rock, and the occasional scene of peasants and donkey, and all the time the bright sun. I saw many birds and flowers and would dearly have loved to stop and watch and inspect them, but that was not possible. Hawks, crows, cornbuntings, larks, finches, magpies – all were very much in evidence. Their presence made the journey even more exciting – as though I was going on holiday.

After lunch, and travelling through some of the fiercest and most beautiful mountain scenery I have ever known, we came down to the pass of Thermopylae.

The view from the top of the pass of the fertile Lamia plain, the meandering Sperklios river and the Gulf of Maliakos to the east, and Lamia itself, was really a bird's eye view. It was startling in its clarity and contrasting flatness against the mountain scene. We were on top of what seemed a great precipice and the road by which one descends this great steep mountain slope is quite fantastic, and unlike anything I have experienced before since I've been abroad. As far as I could see, it consisted of three great loops, each loop consisting of hundreds of smaller loops, making some of the most hazardous hairpin bends I have ever seen. Looking down one stretch it was as though rope had been thrown down the slope, and its coils lay twisting and turning to the bottom. And then someone had pulled it straight from the bottom right to Lamia. This straight road was striking for its contrasting straightness, and so steep was the mountain that it was impossible to see where the straight began. Small wonder that the Spartans decided to fight the Persians at this place!

22.3.45   Since our journey to Volos I have had great difficulty in catching up with my work, and the only part of the town that I know is the sea front, with its broken houses and view of sunken ships, and the horrible road with its depressing shops that lead to the barracks from the mess. But it is not difficult to see that Volos has nothing of intrinsic interest; it is a typical port but it could be improved if the people just took the trouble to have the gutters swept and the streets kept clean. I can see now that we do get something for paying our rates in England.

The day after our arrival we had the usual conference at battalion H.Q. and there we learnt of the numerous guards that were to be our task in Volos; of brothels, V.D.; and celebrations on the 25th – Liberation Day – and threats of violence by K.K.E.; of training; all the old things came up and somehow I felt utterly tired and fed up with it all. God, what a joy it will be to walk in an English village or town again and see the green of English fields.

It is lucky, therefore, that the battalion is in barracks and not in billets in the town, for control is simplified, and temptation is limited. And, if for no other reason than getting the men clear out of sight and mind, I am glad to say we have a mess away from the barracks. It is a big house on the sea front and I share a room with Coutts, which has windows facing east and south, so it is always sunny, and, of course, we have the sea. Our tin boxes have arrived from Italy, so we are now well set up for clothing again – just as summer is here!

24.3.45   Tomorrow is a great day of celebration in Greece – the anniversary of the country's liberation from the Turks. They have not been able to celebrate it for at least four years, and after the recent inter-party fracas it is highly probable that the excitement will be pretty terrific, needing only the usual Balkan spark to set things going in the prescribed manner! It has, in fact, already come to the ears of the I. Staff here that a band of 400 armed E.L.A.S. are in a nearby village waiting to cause trouble on this occasion.

By force of circumstances, it has fallen to my lot to take charge of a parade of the Fusiliers, which is forming part of a biggish body, including the R.N., Greek Navy, Greek Army, and Greek National Guard. The curious thing about this peace celebration is that all the Greeks are carrying ammunition and grenades! We are taking the precaution of having ten rounds on each man, but officers will go ex-pistol!

Yesterday afternoon, with the C.O., we visited the C.O. of the 6th Greek Battalion at his H.Q., a very attractive house, which had some lovely pictures. His Battalion Liaison Officer was a Scot, and they conversed in French. I cottoned on to some of it but it annoys me to be so bad at languages. The Greek C.O. was a good-looking fellow and seemed very efficient. We were invited to tea, which, as usual, was very weak, but somehow the setting was pleasant. '*La musique de la ville*' were to provide the band for the procession, so what that will be like God only knows.

Then we all set off to the Cathedral where the business starts with us lined up ready to do 'present arms' to various local British and Greek military and political authorities. Then comes a service, after which we do a march past. The whole thing has very amusing possibilities.

The great news has come today of the crossing of the lower Rhine by British troops. So far I have not heard any details. Is this, I wonder, the beginning of the last battle of the war against Germany?

26.3.45   The parade went off without a hitch and curiously enough without any political incidents. Timings were a bit off but that's not surprising in Greece. It meant, however, that we had to stand with the hot sun on our backs for over an hour outside the Cathedral, and it made me feel glad that the Greeks had liberated themselves from the Turks in the early part of the year! It was curious to stand there before masses of Greek civilians, and as I watched them I could not help feeling what sombre clothes are worn by civilians, the predominant colour being black or blue.

Behind an odd band we marched to the sea front, where we had another wait whilst a children's parade was finishing. And what masses of children, orphans, school children, girl guides, and what have you – hundreds and hundrds of them, all marching, all obviously inculcated with a sort of pseudo-military discipline; such regimentation is quite alarming.

Thousands of people thronged the sea front, and it was impossible to hear the band with all their clapping as we marched past the saluting base. I was thankful when it was over.

The news continues to be very good, with the bridgehead across the lower Rhine expanding after the capture of Wessel. It amazed us to hear Churchill had visited this place only yesterday. The 3rd U.S. Army has done one of its famous spurts and is reported not far from Frankfurt.

30.3.45   Yesterday afternoon I was out again on the slopes of Mt. Pilion, this time with Peter, Denis, Jimmy and Paddy, and with goodly intent to get to the summit of Pilion, we went by jeep through the villages of Alli Meriá and Portariá, and up to the spine, running practically due south of the final ridge, where we got out and started our climb. But this was my first visit to this wonderful mountain road with its fine views and spring glory. I dallied often, sometimes to stop to inspect some flower, or perhaps look through my binoculars at an eagle. Peter who was longing to exercise his limbs and who had already passed this way, was alway goading me on, for it was no short climb – from jeep-head sometimes takes three hours there and back.

Looking back, I am amazed that we ever got as far as we did; there was so much that was beautiful to see – 'to stand and stare'. It was no place for hurrying. Mentally I divided this short afternoon journey into three stages, the stages being marked by the changing flora of different altitudes.

The first stage began soon after we had got out of Volos – a bad, bumpy, and typical Greek road carried us out of the shopping centre that got dirtier as it reached the outskirts. Then the town ended and we started to climb. We had entered a cultivated spur, made vivid by its excellent husbandry, and the changing view that each of the many road turns gave you. Here was a land of olive trees and fruit trees, all of which were out in blossom, colours the like of which I have never seen before. On the bank and by the roadside were masses of those dark red anemones – glorious to see – and offsetting them were many plants of a bright yellow colour. From one bank a peasant girl threw a bunch of anemones into the jeep and they splattered all over us. The scenery remained the same, always attractive and fresh till we got past Portariá, from whence we had a goodly view of the other clinging town of Makrinitsa.

The second stage brought bushes, trees like oaks, trees covered with ivy, running streams from melting snow – so good to see a mountain stream running through a steep, richly covered gully – and more grass and undergrowth; very English despite the odd vine grove and the peasants and humble donkeys waiting. It brightened me up very much, for the wanton destruction of the houses in the village we had just passed had had a depressing effect. Yes, there was buoyancy here that made one look down at Voloswith a certain distaste – it looked cramped and without air.

How right then was it that we should find primroses here – delicate white petalled ones with a lovely indefinable scent, and especially beautiful were the anemones, not red this time but blue, amazingly blue, growing daintily in the grass under the bushes. It made me realise what a fatal mistake we were making to think we would get to the top today. There was too much to pass by.

Soon the twisting road, taking us higher and higher, brought us to the last stretch before the snow – short mountain shrubs and rock and, lovely to see, bracken. From a place on the road above here we could look down into the deep gorge-like valley, which lower down was carpeted by a great belt of olive trees and which, from this bird's eye view, had a crinkled-etching, unreal-like quality. High up was the grey village of Dhákia, that ill-fated village that had suffered hideously from the bestial Hun. For it was here that he lined up nearly all the male population and mowed them down with machine guns, their bodies falling down the steep slopes. In its sombre grey slate stone and in the dull afternoon light, it indeed looked a sad village.

Soon we had to get out and start walking on the steep bracken and rocky slopes. Here it was that I found crocus and other interesting flowers that I was unable to identify. We got to the edge of the spur by the snow line and, behold, our view was magnificent. To the northwest we could see Lake Voivús backed by great mountains, and looking down whence we

had come, and almost as though it were a large scale map, lay Volos Bay
and the Gulf of Pagasitikos, and beyond Eubboea with sunlit Dhirfir
standing gloriously above the misty cloud. The plain of Lamia and great
mountains to the south were plainly visible. It was dull, unfortunately,
with a slight sea mist in the air, but this did lend a softness to the mighty
scene of island, sea and mountain.

It was too cold to stay long so we started our journey back. Just before
we left I watched a lovely white harrier with black wing tips quartering
the ground. On the way back we picked some flowers for the mess. Yes, I
must visit this place again, this time starting early and taking food. To
hurry is sacrilege here.

1.4.45   The news is terrific at the moment, with places like Kassel,
            Paderborn, Munster being mentioned, and a great withdrawal
of the Germans from the Netherlands. A blackout of movement of the 21st
Army Group makes it difficult to see exactly what is happening there, but
they are moving very fast. The Russians have reached the borders of
Austria and in some places are over it. The news commentator said today,
'Signs that the German Nation is about to suffer its greatest military
disaster are multiplying!'

And so we have much to be thankful for on this Easter Sunday, for
never before in this long five and a half years of war has there been so
much genuine ground for hope of an end of at least the war in Europe.
With gratitude and humility we lift up our hearts this Easter. With sorrow
and reverence we remember those who have laid down their lives in this
great fight against evil.

5.4.45   At a conference yesterday the C.O. brought to our notice a
            letter that he had received about being prepared for Victory
Day. It also concerned suggested form of celebration for this event. Safety
of arms and vehicles was then discussed, and arrangements made. The
letter contained an opinion as to what may happen to personnel after the
defeat of Germany. It was possible that persons in the 25 group and over
might quickly be flown home for twenty-eight days leave prior to their
transfer to the Far East. That it would be at least three months before
demobilisation of the 1-24 groups began. It was also given as an opinion
that if the peace did not come by then we should be in Greece until June at
least. It was all a little disturbing to talk about. Victory and the further
prosecution of the war against Japan, all in the same breath. The idea of a
short leave in England and then straight out to the Far East appals me and
has lowered my morale considerably. I hate to think what Dulcie's reaction will be if this is in fact the scheme that will come into operation.

9.4.45   It seems unlikely that there will be a decisive surrender by the
Germans, for even though we are investing places like Bremen
and Hanover and Vienna they have shown no signs of taking such a step.
So it's a period of waiting and wondering when and how the so-called
armistice will come about. It is a phase too in which the abbreviation
B.L.A. has come to mean 'Burma looms ahead' to many soldiers! It is a
time when separation from those near and dear to you seems to weigh
more heavily than ever, for the future is still uncertain.

But with St. George's Day not far off, and a visit from Lt. Gen. Scobie
in the offing, we have plenty to do, and life is not really unpleasant. The
men are very fit and well, getting much sunshine and exercise, and most of
the sick list comprises injuries resulting from sport!

The Greek Government has resigned, the reason I do not know, but I
understand that Damaskinos has asked the C.-in-C. of the Greek Navy to
form a new government. I did hear a letter had been found which showed
that General Plastinas was in favour of the Italian invasion of Albania, but
this seems rather a tall story. I can only hope that the political situation
will at least be settled enough to enable the voters at the forthcoming
election to reflect by their votes the kind of government they want, and the
men they want to run it. Mutual trust must be established.

10.4.45   Today I walked some of the company to the low, olive-covered
slopes that lie to the northeast of Volos. I was lucky in my
choice of day for it could have been any April day in England, a gusty
wind, white clouds, sunshine, and none of that 'calm fierceness' that
characterise a warm day in the Middle East. It was splendid for walking,
and the air was exquisite. We had fun in twice crossing a mountain
stream, fresh and sparkling, reminding me of similar joys in the north of
England. The fresh green of barley and the new leaves of the vines, the
dark poppies, the whin and vetch, the daisies, all made the walk full of
interest. I saw wheatears and crows, and many other birds. Even the olives
did not seem quite as solemn and austere as usual. The banks of dried-up
gullies were covered in red anemones, and other flowers, making a very
delightful scene. We passed several peasants with their faithful 'mokes'
carrying their worldly goods. Sometimes it seemed that a walking olive
tree was coming down the path but it was only a moke completely covered
with olive prunings. We gave the usual salutation 'Klaramira' as we
passed odd farm houses and little houses set by themselves amongst the
olives, neat and clean one-storeyed affairs with no garden at all, giving an
odd, almost uninhabited appearance. Yet they looked very inviting and no
doubt were most cool in summer.

13.4.45   It is a sad thing to end this notebook by recording the death
           yesterday of President Roosevelt. He went to bed complaining
of a headache, and died soon after. It was always an incredible feat of will
that such a sick man should carry on with such a tremendous wartime task.
But he never let his disability hinder him; no man ever did more to better
Anglo-American relations, and he was a true friend of Great Britain. The
strain on him of a journey like that to Yalta for the Crimea Conference
must have been tremendous, and yet he never flinched. It is indeed a
tragedy that he did not live to see all the fruits of that meeting, although
he died knowing that Germany was as good as beaten, and that the
momentum of attack against Japan was increasing.

His troops are now across the Elbe in the Magdeburg area, and only
about sixty miles from Berlin. The loss of this great Statesman, this wise
Counsellor, is indeed a blow, at a time when inter-party friction, and no
doubt Nationalism, will be rearing their ugly heads. For he had a broad
worldly vision. Senator Truman has been sworn in for the remainder of
the term. Stalin and Churchill have both sent messages of heartfelt sympathy, and I believe Churchill had intended to go to America at once. But
late despatches from Europe made him, regretfully, change his mind, and
Mr. Eden has gone instead.

15.4.45   The great news came today, in a letter from Dulcie, that Denis*
           had been freed from the Germans. The exact circumstances of
his liberation were not yet known but the telegram said Ellen* would
receive further news and Denis would be returned home as soon as possible. What joy must be theirs today, after such a period of anguish and
separation. It is almost five years that Denis had been a prisoner in
German hands – that is longer than I've been in the Army. Their reunion
must seem like an answer to their faith and courage, to their refusal to
give in. It must have seemed an eternity.

And so life inexorably goes on. On this Sunday in Volos all the Greek
flags are hanging in the streets at half mast in respect for President
Roosevelt. The President is being buried today. Time is quite merciless.
Biologically we grow, we seed, we die, and from our seed others grow. Is
it like that – cold, impersonal, animal? Or is there some reason, some
higher ordinance, for this life on earth? I believe there is. This is the
operative word – I believe, I do not know. I know happiness, love,
sadness, anger, comfort, but surely these are the means to the end, not the
camouflaged purpose of existence. Man must reconcile himself to man. It

---

*Sister and brother-in-law.

is inevitable that inequalities must arise. Does it matter if we are not all kings? We want to live to the full, that is granted, but we must not be drowned in materlialistic oblivion. We must have faith that life is good, that life is worth living, but living virtuously and in the knowledge that part of the Christian faith is belief in the resurrection of the dead into the life everlasting. We are apt to be day-to-day sort of beings!

16.4.45   Major General Dudley Ward, D.S.O., seems to spell bad
           weather! It did at his party at Piedmonte d'alife after Cassino last year; it did for his battles in the Gothic line; it did again today when he came to say goodbye to the battalion, for he is leaving to take up a staff appointment in Field Marshal Alexander's H.Q. We were putting on the St. George's Day Parade for him, as he would have taken the salute. But last night after a cloudy, close day, a great wind sprang up, bringing rain which lasted till lunch-time. From a personal point of view I enjoyed the rain and the freshness and cleanliness; it had brought out so vividly the new green of spring, and it laid the filthy dust, which is so apt to be whipped up into miniature sandstorms. So our parade, with its 'march past in column' and its final 'advance in review order' was cancelled. He came round the barrack rooms instead, an unsatisfactory and unsoldierly business. I hope he liked the many pin-up girls!

19.4.45   Life in Volos is becoming extremely monotonous. We work in
           the mornings, and occasionally in the afternoons, but most afternoons are spent in recreation, which in my case amounts to sunbathing on my balcony with a book. I am very lazy; I really must go up to Mt. Pilion again, for after the rain I expect many new and interesting flowers will be out. In the evenings most of the officers seem to go out to dances or to the Club, etc. That bores me, even more than staying in and reading a book, and listening to the nine o'clock news. Sometimes, if I'm lucky, I get a good orchestral concert on the wireless, and that makes me grateful for my solitude. Then to bed, and more reading under the mosquito net (which we have unfortunately started again) by the light of two candles. I wake up very early and often sit out on the balcony in the sun waiting for my morning cup of tea to come up! A pair of jackdaws nesting in the chimney in the house opposite cause me some amusement. They are such fussy creatures. But for all that, times goes quickly, and it is good to be able to do some reading again.

President Truman has reiterated the 'Unconditional Surrender' policy agreed to by President Roosevelt, and the Germans still fight on desperately, despite everything. And everything just now amounts to a lot. The Ruhr has been cleared, so has a lot more of Holland; we are on the outskirts of Bremen, ten miles from Hamburg; Magdeburg is clear; Leipzig has been entered and is almost surrounded. Czechoslovakia has been reached and entered, and in the southern redoubt Nuremburg has been entered in stiff fighting. In Italy hard fighting is going on for Bologna, but Argenta south of Lake Carnacchia has been surrounded and the Eighth Army have broken through this gap to Tenara, a key focal point in the Italian campaign at the present time. Some of the hardest fighting is going on in Italy now. I often wonder if we will ever return there. I should like to go up through Italy to Venice, and then Vienna, on my way home! On top of all this, the Germans report a great battle west of the Oder where they say the Russians are making an all-out effort to reach Berlin. So far, no announcement has been made by the Russians.

21.4.45   Whilst we are practising for St. George's Day Parade, great things are happening on the battle fronts. I think most of us had a curious feeling of regret that we were not with the Eighth Army when we heard it had started another offensive. Curious, because had we been there, I'm sure we would have longed to be out of all the horror, waste and strain, that is war. And yet I suppose it does arouse many inherent emotions, normally latent in men. Out of them springs a great comradeship, truly giving it the quality of a crusade, which in fact it is – although that sounds like paper talk. And yet in battle the average English soldier is very calm and nonchalent about it all; perhaps this is the result of five years of it. They have about them the easy air of experts. They have certainly travelled many hard, dusty (and muddy) miles, these men.

And whilst Goebbels exhorts the Germans 'to trust in their lucky star, even if at the moment it is clouded over' – (does he mean Hitler?) – a report tonight says the Russians are only four miles from Berlin. It is also reported that Bologna has been captured by the Fifth and Eighth Armies.

Field Marshal Alexander is reported to have said that once the Greek Army is formed, consisting of three divisions, and some National Guard units, then all British troops will be withdrawn from Greece. For myself I shall not be sorry when that day comes – unless it is to go to Palestine, which in summer will be unbearably hot, for I feel that our task in Greece is well nigh over, and the sooner the Greek Nation have to look to their own people for their protection the better it will be for them. There is apparently much ill feeling between the Greek Army and the Greek National Guard, which, from a military point of view, would seem fairly natural, but, unfortunately, like everything else in Greece, the grievances are founded on politics. Never have I known a nation to be so easily divided on any matter, amazing at a time when complete co-operation by everyone is absolutely essential.

Father McRama said last night that a lot of the food coming into the country for the poor people is finding its way to the black market and being sold on the streets. And no poor person has any recourse to any Greek Medical Organisation. The doctors won't tend them.

24.4.45   St. George's Day went off very well. The parade was marred to a certain extent by a nasty wind which blew right into us. Luckily it was from a direction which didn't bring the dust. The Acting General was dead on time, most unusual, and so we had no hanging about. It was all over by 1140. Then came a session of drinking in two marquees that had been erected for the purpose, and I had the job of looking after the Commander of the 6th Greek battalion and his battalion liaison officer.

In the afternoon we had a crazy Sports meeting at which I tried to officiate – God knows why! It wasn't meant to be crazy but most of the soldiers were drunk, not to mention the officers. Chaps came riding on horseback and in carts; one humorous individual was dressed up as a coster. So, instead of it being a boring affair, a certain picturesqueness was added and there was much mirth and sweating. By the end my head was pretty hectic and I was glad to indulge in a nice cup of tea at H.Q. mess. A concert was laid on for the evening but I found this too much, knowing what was coming after that. So I slept instead and was much refreshed for the excellent Regimental dinner, during which, of course, we toasted 'The King, God bless him' and 'Absent Friends and the other battalion'. Then to the Sgts' mess for more wine and mirth, but by then most of them had become alcoholic casualties for we didn't get there till ten. We came back in a three-tonner and sang 'Blaydon Races' outside in the street, and then went inside and had a really good mush-up of about an hour's dancing and singing.

25.4.45   With St. George's Day over and Berlin a battlefield, and a practically surrounded one at that, a definite stage of intensity seems to have been reached and passed. We still await the official announcement that the Russians and Americans have linked up, but the inevitability of even this has already taken some of the polish off the event. The news from Italy is excellent and both the Fifth and Eighth Armies are across the Po. The advance is still going extremely well and I must confess I should like to be there to feel the atmosphere of excitement that must prevail, as well as being in at the 'kill' of the Italian campaign which had been this battalion's *bête noir* for nearly fifteen months. However, a soldier has to learn to accept his luck.

But I received a piece of exciting news today when at the end of a long Administrative Conference at battalion H.Q. the C.O. finished up by saying that the exempted groups for the Far East were 1-26. He said it so casually I could hardly believe him, and when he confirmed that it was in writing I nearly jumped for joy. Since then I have *seen* it in writing.

27.4.45   Each day, although spent calmly and peacefully, passes quickly. The pulse of time seems to be beating to the tempo of world events, and many exciting, at one time incomprehensible, things are happening. Today, for instance, it was officially announced that the Russians and Americans had linked up at Torgau. The great event took place on 25th April. It means that Germany has been rent in twain by the invading armies of the Allies, and virtually all that remains is the extermination of the various pockets of resistance. Those pockets are dwindling almost daily, and now have no outside communication of any sort. It is reported that Mussolini had been captured by Partisans near Lake Como, and Dr. Dittmar, the German radio commentator, has been captured on the Elbe.

Berlin, which was completely surrounded by Zhukov's and Konev's armies some days ago, is being liquidated street by street, whilst Stettin has been captured and the lower Elbe crossed in force. In Italy Verona has been taken and the two Armies are nearing Venice, Milan and Genoa. The Italian Partisans have risen. With such tremendously stimulating events at home, one cannot help asking, 'How much longer?' One cannot help feeling an inward excitement which has to be suppressed, difficult though this is. Our pleasant surroundings and the spring sunshine are, in a way, a somewhat two-edged situation. It is pleasant to wake up in the early morning with the sun streaming through the French windows and to look out and see the hundreds of swifts cleaving the air, high up and screaming with the excitement of a new day; it is pleasant to go out on the balcony, even at this early hour and discard one's pyjama jacket to sunbathe whilst waiting for your tea and hot water. Below you, dotted willy-nilly, lying on the deep blue sea, are numerous fishing boats and small sailing boats. The sparkle of the sea is glorious. Beyond are the mountains. To sunbathe in just the same surroundings all the afternoon is no hardship, but – one's heart aches for the fuller enjoyment of such beauty that will come,only when we are re-united with our wives, sweethearts and families.

29.4.45   Today's best news, though, comes from the Partisans in Italy, who say that Mussolini has been tried and shot, together with his ministers and many one-time Fascist officials. Apparently, he was shot first and then hung up by a rope. The Eigth Army have smashed the Adigi Line and are not more than twenty miles from Venice.

2.5.45   There was a hum of excited talk as we sat down to dinner
           tonight, the table decorated with the most exquisite roses. We
had just heard that the Germans in Italy had surrendered unconditionally,
and so the Italian campaign has come to a glorious end. When I look back
over the hard months we had there since the Salerno landing, I cannot help
thinking what a costly business that campaign must have been, with its
numerous desperate battles over mountains, rivers and marshes. To fight
up a narrow peninsula which is as knobbly as a backbone is a feat of arms,
the end of which comes as a fitting tribute to all concerned. It is appropriate that this first unconditional surrender of the Germans should have been
made to an Army Group that includes the old Eighth Army; may the
greater campaign on the Western Front soon come to a similar close.
News from that quarter has been of exceeding interest. The Germans
broadcast that Hitler had been killed in action and that Admiral Donetz
had taken his place. A real Wagnerian 'Twilight of the Gods' setting has
been built up around Hitler's death, with funeral marches, etc. Donetz
broadcast to the German people, saying that Germany would fight on –
what with, he doesn't say! He has already appointed a new Foreign
Minister, who is said to have inclinations to the Right (whatever that
means, especially in Germany) and news of Von Ribbentrop is conspicu-
ous by its absence. A war correspondent in a talk with Dittmar was told
that unconditional surrender was more likely to be requested from Donetz
than from Himmler. However, Eisenhower has confirmed the first meeting
of Himmler and Count Bernadotte, and also the story about Hitler's
cerebral haemorrhage, which rather conflicts with his dying in action.
Bernadotte on his return to Stockholm the second time says that he did not
see Himmler in Denmark, or bring any message back from him. He didn't
say, however, if he saw someone else. Why have Himmler and Ribbentrop
been superseded? Is it because they think the Allies might deal with the
newly appointed? Bernadotte says that Himmler told him that Germany
was finished. Praise be to the Lord! Surely it cannot be long now before a
complete surrender of the Third Reich, that Reich that brought hell on
earth.

6.5.45   Today is Easter Sunday in Greece. They have a fast, three days
           I think, which ended last night. Pandemonium broke loose
towards midnight, when they let off fire crackers and other pyrotechnics,
rifles, machine guns, and many other evil instruments of noise. Occasionally above it all could be heard the ringing of church bells. Then there
was much shouting and singing, and at one time I thought the devil had
arrived. It reminded me of the battle for Forli. At midnight the fast ends

and a gargantuan feast starts, from which proceeded more singing and shouting. It was a remarkable performance, an odd, seemingly undignified exuberance to celebrate the Resurrection. However, it is a joyous religious festivity, and I suppose it is right that people should express joy, no matter how inarticulte the method. Eventually the banging died down, for I dozed off in a restless sleep.

News continued to be good, but a fly in the ointment has appeared over the Polish question. It is reported, but not yet confirmed, that the Germans in Norway are going to surrender, it is thought to the British Army.

7.5.45   A great and memorable day for the whole world. This afternoon the wireless programme was broken for the special announcement to be made – that Germany had surrendered all her forces in Europe unconditionally to the Allies, including Russia. The announcer went on to say that telephone conversations were going on between Moscow, London and Washington, about the time the official announcement should be broadcast to the respective Nations. It was expected that Mr. Churchill might speak tonight to say that the war was over, and during the afternoon and early evening we eagerly awaited to know one way or another. Then at eight o'clock the announcer again broke into the programme to say that Mr. Churchill would speak to the Nation at 1500 hours B.S.T. 8th May, announcing the end of the war. He also stated that Victory Day in Europe would be tomorrow – 8th May – and that H.M. the King would broadcast to the Nation at 2100 hours on that day.

What words can express our profound gratitude and thankfulness that this terrible war in Europe has come to a victorious end? It is almost too big to comprehend; humbly we give up our thanks to the Almighty. When one looks back on this time last year, when we were living in slit trenches around Mt. Trocchio preparing for the great battle of Cassino and and the breaking of the Gustav Line; when one thinks that at that time the Continent of Europe had yet to be invaded – the peace that is ours today seems like a heavensent miracle. And surely – is it not a miracle of courage, of iron determination to rid ourselves forever of a scourge that had well nigh destroyed the civilization and the dignity of man? It was not only flesh and blood, but also the spirit of man's will. May the suffering of this generation, all the sacrifices, all the tragedies and miseries, all the heroic efforts that shine like a torch in this dark epoch – may all these things echo throughout the generations to come, so that they, in a Christian desire for peace, may look back with gratitude and be given thereby the incentive never to allow such a terrible catastrophe to fall upon men again.

Tomorrow is a holiday and so is the following day. May 8th should be instituted as a national holiday for ever, or at least some such day, dependent perhaps on the defeat of Japan as well, so that people can meditate on these things.

8.5.45   *Victory Day in Europe.* We have seen this coming for some time now and our hearts quickened at the thought of it, and yet last night as we listened to the news, a lot of us felt strangely calm – the climax had already been reached – this was the natural outcome – to quote a platitude, it was only a matter of time. The full significance of the fact has yet to be appreciated. Some of us retired to bed early to prepare for today but towards midnight the noises and alarms grew in crescendo. Finally it burst into full symphony, A/A guns, rifles, ships' hooters, church bells, horns of vehicles, and what have you, and the whole town seemed to be singing. Soon we were down again in the mess, and we had an uproarious time. There was singing, dancing, drinking; we went quite crazy, and I remember one officer having his hair shampooed with a bottle of Guinness! It went on till about 3.00 a.m., before we groped our way to bed. It was rather trying getting up this morning. The ordinary reality of day seems hard to reconcile with its historic significance. However, eventually we did go down to breakfast, having taken some asprins beforehand. Then I went to the barracks to congratulate L./Sgt. Addinall of my company on his award of the M.M.

After tea we all went to a Greek church for a short thanksgiving service. The small British congregation had gathered and we had sung our first hymn when the Archbishop came in, followed by half of Volos. He asked the Padre to delay the service so that they could join in our thanksgiving. The church soon became packed, people standing in every bit of space and up on the balconies at the back. There was a lot of noise and shushing. Then we sang our first hymn again, and the Padre gave a short address which an interpreter passed on to the Greeks, sentence by sentence. It was a somewhat trying process, but nevertheless a very spontaneous gesture on the part of the Greeks. Lined up outside the church they clapped like fury when we left!

9.5.45   The Cease Fire came into effect at one minute past midnight last night, but to save lives orders to that effect had been sent out to units during the day. Some fighting was still going on in Czechoslovakia, where the Partisans in Prague were fighting the Germans, and Russians were also meeting resistnace in their advance from the east. If the Germans continue to fight after the Cease Fire, then they would be treated as *franc tireurs*. In fact, news tells of fighting and looting and murder continuing there, and of a raid on Prague. Calls for assistance have been sent out by the Partisans' radio.

Last night we sat and listened to the B.B.C. Victory Service, which was very good, and it warmed our hearts to hear the great crowds in London acclaiming the King and Queen and Mr. Churchill. What a day for London. And the evening was fine for them too. Yes, I would have liked to have been at home in England last night. I wondered what Dulcie was feeling and doing. Volos was quieter last night, but merriment there was plentiful. We saw the first day of peace in and then retired to bed, thankful.

11.5.45   And so the first anniversary of the first of the great battles of 1944 – the assault of the Gustav Line – sees the end of Nazi imperialism and despotism in Europe. Who then could have seen our deliverance? The nightingales around Trocchio no longer sing to the accompaniment of the guns. No longer do the khaki-clad figures steal along the hedges there, company for the magical fireflies. Time, inexorable and irrevocable, has turned all these things from the actual to the historical. Dim memory looks back incredulously; the real is now mythical. Mars is in the descendant.

Now that the first flush of victory is nearly over, our thoughts turn to other things. The blight of separation is still upon us, like a canker eating into our spirits. We await eagerly for Mr. Churchill's speech on Sunday night, hoping he will tell us something about the redeployment of the forces at present in the field. We know that we shall have to stay in foreign lands for some time to come, but if leave is stepped up and the release scheme put into operation then I think we shall become more inured to this testing and tantalising period.

13.5.45   It has been a happy and peaceful weekend. On Saturday afternoon I went up into the Pilion mountains again, this time turning right at Porsaria and taking the road, where earlier on snowdrifts had prevented us going as far as we had wanted. Now these drifts, on the southern slopes anyway, were nearly all gone, although there were still many streams running. The shrubs and trees at this altitude are most attractive, especially the beech trees, which it was a joy to see again. I saw wheatears, stonechats, yellow hammers, and, my first in Greece, the cuckoo. I also saw many unknown and interesting-looking birds, and wished I had been able to recognise them.

We gave a lift to a cheerful old man who wanted to get to his village on his way to Zagora. This language difficulty is such a pity. He could have told me so much about the birds and flowers and people of this area. There was an abundance of a shrub with very similar leaves to holly, but smaller. Thinking of its connection with Christmas, I said 'Christos' and he crossed himself and patted me on the shoulder, laughing. I stopped the jeep at a part of the road that overlooks the sombre village of Dhiakia, and by various signs and odd phrases we tried to talk about the German reprisals there, when nearly all the young male population had been lined up on the edge of a cliff and machine gunned in cold blood. This was a reprisal for partisan activity. Standing there under the shelter of the mountains, this village looked very remote, and yet the full weight of Nazi terror had reached its peaceful seclusion.

Our next stop was a little plateau where a shepherd was minding his flock. He came up to us with a smile, saying 'Klaramiatos'. He had a most lovely crook and I asked him if he would give it to me, but it was his only one and he needed it for his sheep. Later I learned he spoke Italian so we got on a little better in our talking. He was a long-jowled, lean and weather-beaten old man, in rough clothes and shoes, with a good growth of beard. His eyes were pleasant, blue, humorous, and honest. I gave him some chewing gum as I hadn't any cigarettes. He was evidently sorry he couldn't afford to give me his crook, and kept mentioning the Sanatorium. It occurred to me that they might have a lot of walking sticks there for the invalids, but this proved to be a very hopeful deduction. So we left him with his sheep. Continuing our journey we got to the highest 'road' strata and from here had a wonderful view of Or Dhirfir, standing up above the clouds. Here the beech trees were in abundance, and especially round the Sanatorium, where we had to get out of the jeep and climb over paths running with water under the aqueous green of the beech leaves. There were some magnificent apple trees in blossom.

17.5.45   A scheme has been initiated in the battalion by which all the villages in the province of Magnesia are to be visited by patrols. The objects of the scheme, to quote operation orders, are as follows:-

(a) Show the flag.
(b) Cement the bonds of Anglo-Greek friendship.
(c) Ascertain the progress which is being made towards normal conditions.
(d) Ascertain the most urgent needs of the villages.
(e) Attempt to assess the political leanings of the populace,

In the sector for which I have been made responsible there are some twenty villages, seven only approachable by road, the others by mule or on foot. It is the high mountainous area to the north of the Lamia plain, and some of the peaks rise to 5,000 feet. It will take two days to get to some of the villages, so far are they tucked into the mountains.

We started two days ago, and I sent Tommy down with a platoon twenty-three strong to work the villages in the Pelasyia area, which overlooks Dhiavolos and Eubboea. Because of other duties, they could only stay out two days.

The scheme has been well received as it gets the chaps out of Volos and the barracks, surroundings which are apt to get very depressing. Yesterday, with my batman, Benny, and my driver, Cooper, and well supplied with sandwiches, tea, sugar and milk, and the inevitable water and billy cans, we set off from Volos at 0700 hours when the air was cool and the market streets relatively empty, although a few pedestrians seemed as stupid as ever, behaving as though vehicles were not meant to go on roads.

It was good, therefore, to get on to the open road, and to feel the cool morning air coming down the valley over the salt pans, where a small flock of waders had congregated. Their flight was like that of dunlin. There were a lot of villagers on the road in carts and on foot, farmers mostly I should say, who had beeng doing a bit of harvesting before the sun got up, or who were bringing oddments into Volos. An odd cart or so was loaded with newly cut barley. With their rough weather-beaten faces, their coarse and colourful clothing, their donkeys and dogs and children, they make a picturesque scene.

One could not help admiring the cultivation on the coastal stretches around the Bay of Alumios. There were great stretches of barley waving gently in the breeze, and field upon field of vines, their new green leaves showing up in the sun as only vine leaves can. Intermingled, of course, were the inevitable olive trees. In places, the fields had been harvested, leaving a brown, withering stubble that was as dry as cinders. Big mauve thistles, daisies, mallow and poppies bedecked the roadsides, showing up against the dead stalks of earlier flowers, now succumbed to the heat. The women in the fields, wearing their white hoods, stopped to wave and 'thumb' us. Some put up their clenched fists, which is, I believe, the communist sign.

We sped along the white dusty road to Alumios, which has a colony of storks nesting in it. I have never seen so many storks and nests before, or seen them at such close quarters.

In fact, bird life was abundant on this trip. We had a splendid view of an eagle quartering the ground, flying or sailing low with his magnificent broad wings with their great primaries. He had an enormous span, and a buzzard flying near him looked puny.

And so we reached Pelasyia and began our search for Tommy and his chaps. We went through it, first going on some way looking at harbouring areas, but found no sign of him. So we returned and took a rough track that leads to the sea and another village – Vathíkoila. Not far down this track we spotted the fifteen hundred weights under some olive trees. Tommy and party had left earlier for Vathíkoila, which, as it turned out, was a long walk. So we took the opportunity to brew up, chatting in the meantime to some of the men about their visit yesterday to Miloi. They said the people were most sociable and hospitable. They were completely destitute; still had no soap or medical supplies; food was practically non-existent, and that a large family never knew where the next day's meals were coming from. Such things as flour and fats were not to be had, and last year's harvest was nearly finished, and a month or so would elapse before the new one was brought in. There was ninety per cent scabies and malaria in most villages, and a lot of consumption. Malaria suppressives they hadn't had for five years and, of course, they had no lice powder, Some villages took a whole day to reach, and no doctors would come to them. The sick had to be transported to the doctor. The situation is chronic and it is not surprising that the communist regime is upheld. They have complete contempt for the present government, and I'm not sure I don't agree with them. Not the slightest effort is being made by the Greek authorities to alleviate the sufferings of their own people. The Red Cross in Greece have a terrific task of distribution, which lack of transport and civic co-operation make doubly so.

This policy of wet-nursing the Greeks has gone too far, and I think someone should tell them so. With the British here, we needn't do a thing, seems to be their attitude, and the peasants are suffering for it. To help *them*, I should say that medical supplies and their distribution should be handed over to the Army, for that would produce some results. Whenever the Greeks touch supplies, a racket starts! The clothing position is terrible and all are in rags. They have had no footwear for years. Tommy found an old man of nearly sixty who could speak English. He asked him to guide his party to a village, but the old man pointed to his tattered and worn-out woollen sandals and said – 'I am unable to walk far in these' – whereupon Tommy lent him his P.T. shoes. The old man was so excited, he tried to get them on before undoing the laces. When eventually he had got them on, he leapt into the air like a spring lamb and said, 'Come on!'

This old man told Tommy that R.A.F. Beaufighters had sunk two German transports in the Dhiavlo Oreon, drowning about 500 soldiers. Natural inquisitiveness brought the people of Pelasyia and other villages to the shore to see what they could see. An armed vessel was brought and fired on the people, killing about 120. That night the Germans shelled Pelasyia as a reprisal.

In an hour or so Tommy arrived with the old interpreter who was feeling his age a bit, and went off to lie dow in the shade. Tommy had great difficulty in getting him to return the P.T. shoes! They had had a great reception and each had to eat three or four eggs. The supply position was as in other villages, and they were crying out for medicines.

Then we left for home, arriving in for a nice cup of tea and two letters from Dulcie. Later we heard that age groups 1-11 would be out by the end of August, so I think I shall be very lucky to be home by Christmas, although Mr. Bevin did say a quarter of a million would be out by then, mostly from the Army.

19.5.45   I have spent two afternoons watching birds on Mt. Pílion. It has been good to escape the claustrophobia of Volos, where the heat makes one feel very inert. Up there it is a different world; the air is different, the vegetation is different, the mood is different. Yesterday afternoon I spent mostly on a whin-covered slope where bracken and grass and other shrubs intertwined themselves, making the steep guilles rich and verdant. Here Dartford warblers and whitethroats were much in evidence, while just below a nightingale was singing his heart out. Red-backed shrikes were as common as sparrows. To be among such dear company again, to be able to 'stand and stare', brought me a great sense of calm and happiness. I felt that for a short time I had flung off the shackled rigidity of army life. It was with gratitude that I found I could still enjoy these goodly things the country provide for us. Down below the ugly red-roofed Volos shimmered in the heat.

Today I took Tony, who wanted to walk down slopes to Porzaria. I saw a bunting that sang like a yellow hammer but didn't look like one, and a pipit too that suddenly dived out of the sky, making a peculiar noise. My shepherd kept his promise and I am now the proud possessor of a crook. The white clouds over the distant mountains were reflected, like a diaphanous aurora borealis, in the placid Gulf of Pagasitikos. It was splendid.

21.5.45   The heat is becoming oppressive, fiercely oriental. Already the land is looking withered and brown except on the hillsides. It is not possible to sit out in the sun in the afternoon, not if one wants to be comfortable. The season of the siesta has started, and it is the only sensible counter to this hostile manifestation of nature.

I thank God we are not in tents, and I pray that we don't go into them during the hot season. You need a thick wall to keep the heat out, and a white wall at that, and a storey or two above you. But French windows let the air in and shutters keep the sun out. The Greeks know enough about their climate to include such items in their architecture. Their houses are like sieves that drain off the sun, and in winter their adaptability allows a flood of light and sun. It is too early though to say that we've finished with tent life. It is too early by about nine months! For I have now been given a forecast, which is in writing, of when our release group may be expected to be demobilised. It is anticipated that it will be between February and April next year. Now nine months is not a long time in the history of the world; it's not even a long time in the history of a normal individual; but for a man to suddenly leave his young wife and his home, and all that it means to him, to be absent on and off for the best part of six years, during which time he has been doing things alien to his nature, but to which he has adapted himself, during which time he has experienced a spiritual and phsyical craving to return whence he came, during which time, though surrounded by a mass of humanity and friendly humanity his soul has been utterly lonely – then at the end of that long dusty trail I think it would be difficult to call such a person normal. He can't possibly have a normal attitude towards life; he can't have a normal attitude towards time. And he stares at those nine months with hard eyes and a grim heart. He becomes a battleground of the body and spirit. But there comes to him, as if by magic, a great ally – human nature. And it is human nature to forget, it is human nature to hope, and in the daily task, the trivial round, comes his salvation. It is as if he were a small boat on a wide sea – he has to attend to his sail, to the steering wheel, for otherwise his doom would be sealed; and his will is the wind that fills the sail.

24.5.45   At home party politics have come into the limelight, and party interests are now the gossip in a world shattered by war, and where self interest is the last thing required. All the important things are well tucked away in some dark corner of the stage, including the Japanese war. It is quite disgusting how separately that war has been taken, and as it's far from home, how unimportant it has seemed to the politicians. Churchill offered Labour a continuation of the Coalition Government till Japan was defeated. Labour refused, adding a suggestion that a General Election should take place in October. Churchill, of course, refused this, resigned and was reinstated by the King as Prime Minister of what has been called 'The Caretaker Government', and the General Election will now be held on 5th July. Labour deserve to lose.

27.5.45   The highlights of the past three days have been a visit by the General, a scheme for local leave, and the fact that I have actually had a bathe and enjoyed it! The General's visit, as far as I was concerned, was a complete waste of time, but as they usually are, that is nothing new. Tony tried to work out how much of his time in the Army has been spent waiting for Generals!

The announcement about local leave to such places as Cairo, Alexandria, Rome, by ship or possibly by air, coming as it did shortly after a long dissertation about the difficulties of increasing leave to the U.K., rather disgusted me. I may not be in full possession of the facts, but that is not my fault. It seems to me, however, that if they can arrange these seven day 'sop' leaves, using shipping, etc., there must be space somewhere – why not centralise it and send chaps home? One of the most ghastly results of lack of home leave is a high incidence of V.D., and just look where they propose men should go in lieu! When I say 'men', I use a misleading term, for at the moment the scheme only covers officers, which, of course, makes it worse; nevertheless, from the point of view of a single man, there's possibly something in it. He at least sees more of the world gratis.

29.5.45　　There was an agonising moment yesterday, when a draw from the hat for one officer to go on U.K. leave was carried out. There were twenty-eight names, and the C.O. put them all into a tin, shook them up, and asked the R.S.M. to take one out. It was a sickening moment – you could almost hear everyone saying, 'If only it is me.' Peter Gorst was the lucky individual. For the rest of the day I was most depressed – all the hopes that might have come to fulfilment were frustrated and repressed. However, to have had even a *chance* of going home was something. This is the second officer in *eight* months! I wonder when I shall get another chance.

31.5.45　　We are now distributing some of the UNRRA supplies to some of the villages we have patrolled. This is an excellent thing for two reasons. Firstly, the men are very happy to be able to help the villagers in a practical way; it is the natural sequence of their visits. Secondly, and perhaps more importantly, we actually distribute the supplies; medical supplies are all free but rich people are expected to pay up to seventy per cent for clothing. It is common knowledge that racketeering by Presidents of villages and others had meant no supplies for people who couldn't pay. So, instead of handing the stuff over to the President, we take it to the village, call all the people together, explain that it is a free issue, and distribute on the spot all we can. The villagers are overjoyed and shower eggs and retsina on the men, and offer to roast chicken. Fred came back today with an enormous basket of eggs for the mess.

Tony said that at a conference at division the G.I. said he saw no hope of us leaving this country before next December. Roll on that home leave!

2.6.45   A new month seems only to emphasise the utter loneliness and incompleteness of this separate life. Our eyes are for ever focused on an horizon, whose distance makes us feel it is an illusion. But even if it is a mirage, it is the only thing that sustains us. The iron bars of uncontrollable circumstances make a cage that is merciless and unrelenting. Within the shackled body hope and faith fight on. The struggle seems endless.

5.6.45   I wrote to the British Overseas Airways Corporation today to enquire about the possibilities of jobs after the war. A letter I've had from the Bank about salaries makes my return there a most depressing thought. I have contemplated writing to the Forestry Commission to see if they have anything to offer; now is the time, I feel.

10.6.45   It's inevitable that changes in personnel should occur nowadays, but when they come, they always do so very suddenly. The latest is that Coutts leaves us tomorrow for a 'displaced persons assembly area', but where or in what capacity is not yet known. Coutts has been my second-in-command since we reorganised last June. John Worthington, I am glad to say, is taking over his job, and will be here on the 12th, his rear 2 N.F. job being given to Peter Gorst. Bob Kershaw is off to command B company, and Hobby looks as though he will be away for six months with the R.A.S.C. So we are generally thinning out, and the mess has lost a number of cheerful inmates.

During my last two trips to the beach I have slipped off with a pair of binoculars to investigate more thoroughly the marsh-like hinterland. Amongst the salt pans, whose low rectangular walls are covered with low shrub, I have found many of the waders I mentioned seeing on the 7th June. I suddenly remembered the name 'stilt', and I've a shrewd idea these birds are black-winged stilts. At one time the view through my binoculars was of a deep blue choppy sea, with a small sailing boat crossing my vision, whilst in the foreground were the salt plans bedecked with sea shrubs and wading there were the stilts. It was indeed a colourful and uncommon view.

12.6.45   At about six o'clock, the dark clouds became even more menacing and after dinner there was much lightning to the south; very light rain began to fall at intervals, but it was so light that my balcony dried up completely between each fall. As I write the clouds are becoming blacker, and everything is oddly still. It seems as though nature is waiting for some magical touch before she renews the earth with her blessed rains.

Two more changes have occurred in the battalion following in rapid succession one upon the other. It is all very unsettling, I find. First, Dicky Richards is off to Austria as a Camp Commandant and has been given seven days' leave in Blighty before he takes up his new job. Then Philip came in tonight to ask me to dine at battalion H.Q. tomorrow night as Tony was going the day after under the Release scheme. He is age group 6. This makes me second senior major in the battalion, and I hope it doesn't mean that I might be asked to take over as second-in-command of the battalion.

Sir James Grigg has stated that a short leave scheme to the U.K. is to be started in C.M.F.* Reading his speech, I was amazed at the disparity between B.L.A. and C.M.F. figures. He said that in the B.L.A. over 7,000 were going home a day, whereas in C.M.F. the figures were about 2,000 a *month*. It astounded me, and if a considerable improvement or even parity is not reached under this scheme, when some of the B.L.A. fellows were only fighting at the most for eleven months, whilst chaps out here have been at it for two or three years, then it is a scandalous situation. What short leave amounts to I do now know, but seven days after two years absence would seem pitiful, unless, of course, it could be every three months. Better than a slap in the belly with a wet fish, as they say! – I suppose would be the official answer. All my mental energy is taken up with the thought and hope of an early reunion with Dulcie. Sometimes it almost reaches the stage of distraction.

15.6.45   This day two years ago was the last time I spoke to Dulcie, and that was a six-minute phone call. I shudder to think of that short, grim goodbye – it seemed to draw all life out of me. And now – 730 days have passed, during which our only means of communication has been the written word, and we have written about 650 letters to each other in that time. I know that life would have been unbearable without Dulcie's letters with all the news about Nicolas, 'Benallan', Kingston, and many local topics and personalities. In each one was a warmth and love that was most precious to me.

Peace has come again to Europe. This is a trying time, for now we all look forward to the peace of our final homecoming. Yes, indeed, a trying time that is best explained by Jaques in *As You Like It*:-

'Good morrow fool (quoth I). No sir (quoth me) call me not fool,
till heaven hath sent me fortune;' And then he drew a dial from

---

*Central Mediterranean Forces.

his poke, and looking on it with lack lustre eye says, very wisely – 'It is ten o'clock. Thus we may (quoth he) see how the world wags; 'tis but an hour ago, since it was nine, and after one hour, 'twill be eleven, and so from hour to hour, we ripe and ripe, and from hour to hour, we rot and rot, and thereby hangs a tale'.'

Thereby hangs a tale! Five years and more of our ripening have been stunted and frustrated. Five years and more we have been waiting 'to ripe and ripe', waiting with all urgency, for life is short, and soon it will be past 'ten o'clock' and we shall begin 'to rot and rot'. For, indeed, does not Jaques tell me later on that I, as a soldier, am playing my fourth act, and there are only seven! I am indeed at 'ten o'clock' and every day, every month, every year, means that I shall henceforth be on the downward road to 'second childishness and mere oblivion'!

16.6.45   From the great watershed of civilian life came all the streams and tributaries into that great river called the Army. Each chap, each individual, each small stream a unit, each tributary a regiment, that poured into the main turbulent force, becoming one with it and of it. Irresistibly that river force has pursued its purpose. Its task has been fulfilled. The world cleansed; and having run its course, it has reached its delta. The river divides and spreads into many small streams that 'meander with a mazy motion' of their own sweet will. And finally, each one returns to the turbulence and complexity of the great sea of life.

Yes, the affinity so necessary in war is being broken up, and most of us long for the sea. Tony leaves tomorrow. Paddy and Bert are off to a vehicle company in Rome. Hurry up, little stream, and find your way to the open sea!

20.6.45   More officers have been posted. This time it is Fred Dibble and John Scott. That is six we have lost in the last fortnight, and with detached officers we are becoming a very small mess. It has dropped from eighteen to eight and it seems quite odd. Fred Dibble, who was a regular soldier in the Middlesex, was wounded in his first ten minutes of action with us on the Ronco.

It is, indeed, a pity that this gradual breaking up has to be. How good it would have been if we could have all departed on one day – but, no – in the Army one is rather like an autumn leaf in a gale, and when the wind blows then the leaf must dance! And so this ten little nigger boys story goes on.

22.6.45   The evening is the loveliest part of the day. After dinner, for
           then, except perhaps when we are duty company, everyone
goes out; life in Volos begins then; the streets become crowded, the cafes
are astir, and those on the promenade have chairs and tables set out half
way across the road. Bizarre Greek music is to be heard everywhere. All
the shops remain open till well into the night, for the Greek does his
shopping at night in the summer months. There are dances almost every
night, and so it is natural, especially for a single chap, to go out and enjoy
himself with a Nursing Sister or a Greek girl. Wine flows fast and furious.

Tommy, who is a stay-at-home like myself, has gone on a course in
Athens, and I have not even got chess to fall back on. But I cannot
grumble, for my bed is of my own making, and at heart I am happier like
this than trying hard to lead a superficial life where, even in company, I
feel desperately lonely. On the other hand, I am not an ascetic, nor have I
the patience of Job!

24.6.45   Last night we had a storm, when towards evening dark creep-
           ing clouds came over the hills from the northwest. Soon the
lightning stabbed the sky, great blue flashes that lit up the gradually
darkening atmosphere. Then the sky went black, and with the rumbling of
the thunder, a wind got up, a strong wind too. Looking across the bay
from my bedroom window, I saw what at first I thought was a rain cloud
passing over the water; then I could see it was dust. But, thankfully, this
storm did not bring dust alone. After this came heavy rain. It was the
loveliest thing that's happened in months. To see the roads and roofs
sparkling in the wet, to see the rain drops bouncing on my balcony, and
best of all, to breathe the divine smell of rain on a burnt-up world – that
was wonderful. It was so cleansing, so long needed. But the first shower
soon dried up, although there were puddles in the road. Then after dinner
the storm came back again – from two sides. The sky could not have been
a blacker hue, deep blue black. And then came the heaviest fall of rain. It
was good to hear it splashing and beating on the window, the air becoming
sweeter every minute. After that the storm began to lessen and finally
departed – and sleep came easily last night.

This morning I went up towards Portaria, as I knew the air would still
be fresh up there. On the way up I saw great blue thistles and yellow-
flowered ones, which are very common here. A heathery-looking pink
flower was plentiful too; it had a strong sage-like smell. The gardens
looked lovely with lots of fruits and flowers. I got out and walked. The
atmosphere was moist and autumnal. The brown hillsides – the quiet – the
fresh smells – the sultry call of a turtle dove – the withering hollyhocks,

and a breeze and clouds over Pilion – yes, for a moment I got that feeling that comes so often to me in July and August in England, the feeling that the year had turned.

26.6.45   A speed limit has at last been laid down on the road to the barracks – fifteen m.p.h. Every day I do this nightmare ride, and each time I gasp with relief when we are through! Horses, carts, donkeys, men, women, children, all in the road, never looking where they are going, never dreaming they are on the road. At night it is literally a solid mass of people. It's a question of ploughing through them, not avoiding them. How could the Germans have thought they would conquer Greece! I can't imagine.

28.6.45   Bob Hutton has been out with some of the company surveying the villages of Plátanos and Kokotí in the hills south of Almiros. I went down there yesterday to find their harbour area and see how things were going. It was a hot day but thankfully there was a breeze. What a pity the roads are so shocking for the continual jolting and banging, the twisting and weaving to avoid holes, is apt to fray one's nerves, and detract from what would otherwise be a most enjoyable scenic run.

I stopped for a short rest at one of the beautiful bays on the road that hugs the coast before Lea Ankhialos. Taking a short stroll I suddenly realised someone was calling me. Someone who could speak good American. He asked me to come and have a chat with him, and I joined him in the shade of his olive tree and had a pleasant interlude. He was Greek, one of many who have lived a great part of their lives in America. He went out there in 1922, only to come back again to fight the Bulgarians. Off he went again in 1924 and this time stayed till 1936, when (again like so many Greeks) he returned once more to his native land. He seemed very happy, and his pleasant western type of face always wore a smile. He liked America better than Greece, not only because of the better living, but the people were not so class-conscious. You could say 'good morning' to anyone in America! He was pathetically short of clothing, shoes, etc., and bewailed the fact that when he came back from America he had complete suits and underclothes, topcoat, but – 'The Goddamned Germans took everything and I'm damn near naked.'

Then we talked about his land – 'I gotta a little bit of land up here, and I've come up for the day to have a look around.' His cart was standing under the deeper shade of a pear tree opposite, and this, he informed me, would be his bed for the night. His watchman, a Rumanian, who looked like Popeye, then joined us, a delightful old man, with a nut-brown, twinkling face and eyes, and a Russian hat. I was given a note by the

American Greek saying that anytime I was passing I could take what pears I wanted. It was addressed to the watchman. He signed himself James Angelis. Before I left we had discussed politics, hunting, the weather, and he had told me about a skirmish that took place nearby between Germans and Partisan forces. 'They were sure shooting to beat the band, yes sir!'

That little interlude added colour to a tedious journey. He lived at Ankhialos, the next village we passed through – a village in which hardly a house is intact, a reprisal effort. The tragedy is that they cannot get materials to do any building.

4.7.45   The new month has brought forth nothing new in our lives. The General Election – it is polling day tomorrow – has left us rather cold, and we shall all be glad when the papers cease to be full of the screeching of various politicians. Each Party, I believe, has said that our future depends on our vote at this Election, but none of them give us anything to have faith in.

The most interesting thing of late in the Army papers was a report that the LIAP* allotment for this theatre was to be increased, as much as by five times. It has been 3,000 a month; now they hope it will be 15,000, but whether this is a combination of the long and the new short leave, it didn't say. If the battalion's allotment was to be increased pro rata, it would mean that an officer ought to go each fortnight, supposing the same ratio was kept. Anyway, it's nice piece of wishful thinking and no doubt will carry us through this month when we can think up something else!

A rumour has it that our winter quarters are going to be at Khalkis. Might be worse!

I had an enjoyable day yesterday when, in the morning, I went for a bathe with the company. The water was as smooth as glass and it was glorious for swimming. There was hardly any movement of ebb and flow as it met the shore. In the afternoon I took John up Mt. Pilion for his first visit.

It was a particularly hot afternoon, and so it was most pleasant to get amongst the beech, chestnut and oak trees, where the air had the warm smell of bracken. We relieved our thirst in a lovely stream by a wood, where, looking down, one has a bird's eye view of Dhakia. John wanted to see the Sanatorium and eventually we fetched up there. The stream, the beeches, the luscious nettles, the fruit trees and roses, and the snapdragons of the now neglected garden, made Volos seem very far away. 'Le Docteur' was away but his niece was there, and on the porch we were given wicker chairs and chatted in our best French. This delightful

*Home leave.

Asylum, the result of thirty years' work, was destroyed in a few hours by the Germans, who dive-bombed it with Stukas. 'Pourquoi, Monsieur – pourquoi? Les Allemands sont très mauvais; ils y n'avons de coeur'. In the corner of the porch were the remnants of some of the bombs, ugly souvenirs of a horrible deed. All around the area were the German machine gun posts still with odd bits of ammunition and ammunition boxes. From these places they used to fire at random on to Dhakia, a helpless target in the valley below. the people of the Sanatorium, just an odd family, were not allowed out, and for three months they were without supplies. The Germans would not let them into Volos or even to a nearby village. Sitting there by the rambler roses with the house martin flying to and from its nest on the eaves above, the cool shadows of the beech spreading across the garden, it seemed inconceivable that this remote mountain retreat for the sufferers of tuberculosis should have been the scene of unwarranted reprisals by the hated Hun. Attila's bloody sword has stained many a green and remote corner of Europe and Asia, and the minds of men have been stamped indelibly by the horrid brutalities and loutishness of the German race.

6.7.45   Yesterday afternoon John and I visited Makrinitsa. It was a cool day with rain about; in fact, it seemed to be raining over the hills across the bay. Just beyond Portaria we stopped on a bridge that crosses a shady ravine, a cool, pleasant place with a delightful mountain stream. It was like a bit of Northumberland. The bridge was recently built – in 1929 – and the old bridge still stood there, a very ancient affair. In the corner stood a large barn-like building that was once an electricity station, and we went behind this to clamber up the green slope, down which the water had been diverted by means of a trough. It was all so cool and green, and butterflies flew hither and thither. The poetic movement of nature was much in evidence here after the dry barren monotony of most of the countryside. This idyllic spot had a very strange and restful effect on the mind – here one could feel at peace.

Here in one small dell seemed to be the very essence of all these things that, since childhood, had been to me the very embodiment of the living country. Under the great overhanging crags, above which the eagle flies, we passed on our way to Makrinitsa. We were greeted by many small boys in anticipation of which I had brought up some chocolate. When this was distributed we were well and truly 'Zeeto Englishi!'. John has been looking for a stick like mine so we sent them off in search of one.

John was as intrigued as I was when I first came on to the 'Square' with four great planes, one of which has a bell strung on it, and in its base has been built a door. A picture of the King of the Hellenes was pasted on another tree. We looked in at the tiny Church nearby, with its little balcony for women and the usual ornate ikons of Christ, St. John the Baptist, etc. An intelligent lad seemed to be in charge of the key, and it was he who later let us in to the Church of San Praria, to which we had climbed by the steep, narrow, cobbled path. Again the usual ornaments, more if anything, but the pleasant thing about this Church (built in 1767) was its cleanliness and its beautiful and peaceful cloistered courtyard, very unusual for a Greek Church.

7.7.45   Today is the last day for two men of the company, Fusilier Cox
           and Pte. Cairns, who are the first to go under the Release Scheme. They are in age groups 11 and 9, and both are over forty. Cairns, a cook, was always with one of the platoons in action and would never consider being sent further back. At last we are really seeing the scheme in action – men being sent home – what great hopes it gives us that soon we shall be doing likewise – going back home; no more of those terrible partings.

Another good thing happened today; the company was given four vacancies for LIAP out of about ten for the battalion, double our usual figures – and a covering note stated that further increases were likely. Age groups 1-21 are not eligible, which is understandable, but which nevertheless increases the chance for those in the higher groups. It is one of the greatest pleasures I've had in the Army – to get those selected into the office and tell them they are going home for twenty-eight days. At first they are thunderstruck; then their faces broaden out into great jubilant grins. But how many millions of little human happiness and tragedies will for ever go unrecorded in the Army? How difficult it is, particularly for an officer, to get behind the military facade. How difficult to know the private life, a man's thoughts, hopes, feelings, likes and dislikes, perhaps even his *'affaire d'amours'* – for all these things are hidden in each individual, whose surface military life discloses nothing.

10.7.45   Today is Nicolas' third birthday, and as I write this at ten
           minutes to five, I expect he is enjoying the little children's party that Dulcie has arranged for him. I can shut my eyes and so easily picture the scene and hear the happy chatter of both children and parents. I can hear the clicking of spoons against china, and see the cakes that Dulcie has no doubt provided, despite the food restrictions. I expect Nicolas will proudly show any presents he has to his young friends. I can remember so well the tea parties of my own young life, and it is difficult to imagine that one day (next year, I trust) I shall be watching my own boy

doing likewise. I think perhaps it will be one of my greatest regrets in life that I have missed these early years in the life of Dulcie's first baby. For I think there must be something quite unique and ephemeral about the emotions that are evoked by the various subtle changes in a child at this stage. However, this enforced denial has been lessened considerably by Dulcie's many lucid and descriptive letters, and thus in a way I have been able to share many of the delights which she has experienced concerning Nicolas.

15.7.45   John Worthington once said all you need to make a comfort-
able living is a 'bottle of ink, a pen and paper'. A capital, in fact, that is perhaps the smallest of any vocation! Harraps, the publishers, are, I see, offering good prizes for best novels written by men or women in the armed forces. Well, I have pen, paper and ink, why can't I do something about it? I have often tried to think up suitable settings for a novel. I have even sketched out on paper one or two of them – but whence comes the spark that will set the ball rolling? I don't think I'm without imagination, but perhaps I am confusing sensitiveness with imagination. I don't think the physical effort of writing frightens me. No, I think it's lack of knowledge plus mental laziness and indiscipline. The ability to concentrate and control one's thoughts about any given theme is perhaps the first step, the ability to transcribe those mental conceptions to the written word is perhaps the second, the ability to do it so well that the reader understands what was happening in the author's mind is perhaps the third; all that is the arduous task that is the author's lot. Yes, John, pen, paper and ink in the hands of such an individual might mean entry into the land of milk and honey! But I think, nevertheless, that writing is more an acquired art than anything else. One may have a 'bent' for it, but by God, it's the training of that bent that is difficult. I've got a feeling that not many authors are carefree happy chaps!

18.7.45   Sometimes I send the company bathing all the morning, and
have some tea sent down to the beach at 1030 hours. If I am lucky I manage occasionally to join them and have my swim in the morning. Then in the afternoon I read or sleep or write. I am now reading John Buchan's autobiography *Memory Hold the Door*. I find it extremely interesting, especially his early scholastic life – a life that must have been the background of my own father – cultured, leisurely, spent in the unreal medieval and almost monastic surroundings of lovely old colleges in the 1890s.

A great friend of John Buchan's was Lord Lucas (A. T. Herbert) who was killed somewhere on the Somme in the Great War. Maurice Baring, a friend of them both, wrote a lovely elegy on Lord Lucas, which I thought was worth reproducing here. Lord Lucas, incidentally, was a great lover of the countryside, and had a good knowledge of its wild life. He also had a great passion for music:-

'So when the Spring of the World shall shrive our stain
After the Winter of war,
When the poor World awakes to peace once more,
After such a night of ravage and of rain,
You shall not come again.
You shall not come to taste the old Spring weather,
To gallop through the soft untrampled heather,
To bathe and bake your body on the grass.
We shall be there. Alas! –
But not with you, when Spring shall wake the earth,
And quicken the scarred fields to the new birth
Our grief shall grow. For what can Spring renew
More fiercely for us than the need of you?'

Such a fine elegy might well be a fitting tribute to all those who loved their youth, and whose youth has become eternal.

20.7.45   The rhythm of our life in Greece has been completely upset just recently. The mail, instead of arriving in the morning, and being distributed by lunch-time, now arrives any time in the afternoon. This outrageous alteration in the structure of our daily lives has thrown us completely off balance. Before, having got through the drudgery of a morning at the barracks, there was always consolation in the fact that, at the end of the bumpy dusty jeep ride to the mess for lunch, there might be waiting for you your mail from home. If there was nothing – well, perhaps you were lucky enough to get the paper. That moment of anticipation acted like a booster and tided you over the rest of the day. But now it is quite different – almost a gritting of dentures! The atmosphere at lunch is quite tense – there is a stoical air of endurance about the table.

And so I sit at my desk in my shuttered room, writing these odd notes to help pass the time away. It is a terrible thing to want the time to pass away, and even under wartime circumstances it is very stupid of me, no doubt, to allow myself to get into such a state of mind. For, after all – this *is* real, I can ignore its reality, or treat it as a dream, but I cannot dispute it. I should accept the fact, and absorb intelligently what goes on around me. Time, after all, is a state of mind. Occupy the mind and time looks after itself, make it a vacuum and time becomes a prison. The wind howls through my shutters, sparrows chirp on the buildings outside; I hear an anvil being struck, and voices; all this is real – now – as the ink which makes these words is drying – now. In twenty years' time, perhaps, I shall look back on these words with eyes that see differently, and a mind that thinks differently. But of one thing I am certain, I shall be sorry that this ink has been dry for twenty years.

23.7.45   The mail has upset me a little – it has come all right but there's a gap, Dulcie's FOUR HUNDREDTH LETTER has gone astray! I suppose I must have a relatively tidy mind for I just hated getting No. 401 before No. 400. However, doubtless it will turn up.

25.7.45   I feel myself getting very short tempered these days. Trying to analyse my physiological condition I am forced to admit that no vast changes have occurred to upset my morale, nor has it been assaulted by any particular calamity. No, I think it is the insidious accumulation of a series of minor mental buffetings in addition to an aggravated sense of frustration. The mail is all topsy-turvy; the Greeks seem even more stupid than ever in their lack of road discipline; the filth of the roads seems worse than ever; the fact that Dulcie has to use all her ingenuity to get her shopping done, as compared with the masses of food one sees here; our slender chances of getting home on leave; the possibility of going under canvas at Stilis and not Khalkis; hearing that 46 Division* have gone to Graz in Austria; and, of course, the continual bodily perspiration by day and night – all these things *do* tend to fray the nerves.

The sort of thing that infuriates me are the precautions we occasionally have to take against demonstrations by the populace. The latest and perhaps the '*pièce de résistance*' is that tomorrow we have to have men standing by in case the local population make demonstrations as a result of the outcome of the British General Election, which will be made known then. Imagine the process reversed – Greek troops standing by in England for fear of an English demonstration on the result of a Greek Election! That is what is sickening us here, the continued mollycoddling of a nation that seems to be making little effort to stand on its own feet. What will we be required to do when the Greeks have their elections here?! Another thing that irks me is the thousands of pounds that are weekly pouring into the pockets of greasy Greek business people almost direct from the British taxpayer, and there is nothing to show for it. No, I begin to weary of Balkan indiscipline.

---

*Brother's Division.

26.7.45   The main topic of the day has been the frequent reports of the
           Election results. So far I have heard nothing official on the
wireless myself, but by midday reports showed a definite swing to the left,
and by teatime the Labour Party had been returned! And by a big majority
apparently. I look forward to tonight's nine o'clock news, when the final
position ought to be announced. Generally speaking, the tone of the mess
is despondent, which bespeaks of a sense of insecurity. I think the cause
of it is the fact that Mr. Churchill has been dropped, and that without his
leadership and worldliness we shall lose face internationally. Internally it
remains to be seen what the new Government does to fulfil its pledges. If
they go ahead at the task of reconstruction with the same vigour as they
went into the Election campaign – then we should have nothing to grumble about. The result of the Election again reflects the trend of world
political thought.

I must say I feel a deep personal regret for Mr. Churchill – the man who,
in the most catastrophic hour that has perhaps ever beset the civilised
world, came forward, and at first by his inspired speeches and obvious
confidence so raised the morale of the British Nation, at that time standing
alone in the fight against the Axis, that later by their spirited efforts, the
people were rewarded by the fulfilment of a victorious strategy, which had
largely been planned by the Premier. We owe much to Mr. Churchill –
perhaps more than much – the whole world owes much to this man, and in
distant countries he is somehow symbolic for all that the British have ever
stood for. So it is somewhat natural that we should all feel that something
has gone out of our lives. But such are the whims of democracy that 'those
who hold us together in the hours of darkness are forgotten at the dawn'.

27.7.45   The final results of the General Election must surely have
           surprised even the most confident Labour man! It finished with
something like 386 seats for Labour against 194 for the Conservatives,
giving, I believe, one of the biggest majorities in a British General Election for many years. It means that the opposition is practically negligible,
and if Labour want to push anything through the House, it seems *prima
facie* that they will take a lot of stopping. Twenty-six members of the present Caretaker Government lost their seats, but fortunately Mr. Churchill
and Mr. Eden have retained theirs. It is certainly an incredible and unexpected result, unexpected at least as regards the enormous majority, but I
think it means that those persons who voted took great care about their
decision – for surely Mr. Churchill must have been a very popular wartime
Prime Minister, but his glamour and personality have not swayed the
people – they voted for a policy which they thought would give them a

better chance in life, regretting probably, a lot of them, that it meant the end of Mr. Churchill's leadership. In the circumstances, I feel a big majority is a good thing; it makes for a strong government, and if the Labour Party don't behave like a child with a new toy, I don't see why it shouldn't work. They want to make a programme not too complicated or too vast in scope, and keep to it. If they try to do too much on the Home Front, it will be to the neglect of foreign policy, but that *must* take up much of their attention. We have to remain trusted friends with America and Russia, the three knitted together into an inseparable team. If this fails then perhaps much of the sacrifice of the past grim years will have been wasted – if not completely so. It will be like a game of chess in some respects, for it will be no good if we concentrate only on our own pieces – your opponent in the meantime is making subtle moves that will later perhaps prove disastrous to you. It applies not only to the political but very much to the economic field – this essential need for absolute co-operation.

Mr. Churchill, therefore, offered his resignation to the King, and one does not need a lot of imagination to appreciate what must have been the emotions and thoughts of these two men, who, during the war, must have built up a great admiration and friendship for each other. It must have been hard indeed for the King to see this great Prime Minister cast away overnight.

Mr. Attlee was also at the Palace and the King summoned him to form a new Government. Now these two men return to the Potsdam Conference, whence they had just come. How incredible and ironical it seems that their positions should be reversed? It will be interesting to hear the reactions of Russia and America to this massive swing to the left. The majority of the Greeks are, I understand, despairing at the fact that Mr. Churchill has not been returned. Some, in fact, have asked how long it will be before we get rid of the King! But so far they have not been demonstrative. May the Labour Government see to it that we are not much longer in this 'Goddamned' country.

30.7.45   With many signs in the form of advance parties of 12 Brigade that the long impending moves are at last to take place – the mixed bag of rumours that it has all produced has at last crystallised itself into a move to a tented camp near Stilis, which, thankfully, is near the sea. We learnt this today at a battalion conference, and apparently the original intention of going to Khalkis has been frustrated by the Greek National Guard not being in a position to move out of the barracks. So the stupid British, who, after all, are only here to intervene in the event of further trouble, have to go into tents. But, as the Britisher is wont to say, I suppose we mustn't grumble, for have we not for the past four months, and for most of the hot weather, been in good solid stone billets, which have kept the oriental sun off our backs?! The move to Stilis is timed for the middle of August, so we should only have a month or so of really hot weather under canvas.

The most important item on the conference agenda was the question of LIAP. Division want to know (and in haste!) how many men of the battalion could be got off in LIAP before 30th November, i.e. how many the battalion could afford to send that would still allow us to work operationally, supposing the 'Greek disease' was to break out again. So company commanders went back to ruminate on this pleasant subject, and I came to the conclusion that I could get the whole company away in that time, spread out as four parties of fifty, or eight of twenty-five, and this, strange to relate, included *all* officers.

What all this means I am not quite certain, except that I know they want us to be fairly up to strength by November because of the Greek Elections. If it means that at least leave is a real possibility, then a move to a tented camp will not, I think, have much effect on morale.

The result of the British General Election has, I think, at last sunk in and the first exultant flush of victory, or the weeping and gnashing of teeth, whichever the case may be, has died down somewhat. Australia, New Zealand and South Africa seem to be pretty pleased about the result, although one South African paper said 'the experiment would be watched with sympathy, but also with some anxiety by the world.' Canada and America seem most concerned about the loss of Churchill as an international figure, rather implying that perhaps a change of Government is not at all a bad thing. A statement by Professor Laski, the man on whom so much wrath was spent during the Election is, I think, worth reproducing here; what it means quite, I am at a loss to say:-

> 'At long last we have made possible full friendship with the Soviet Union. At long last we are going to be in a position to do full justice to our Spanish comrades and we shall give no help, as a Labour Government, to decayed monarchs or obsolete social systems.'

3.8.45   The first communiqué of the Potsdam Conference was issued today. Hitherto all we have been told about this momentous Conference was the sumptuous menu of the delegates – in a Black Market world a rather ironical piece of information.

However, it was all taken in good part, and after the Churchill-Attlee reshuffle the thing seems to have come to reasonable conclusions. The main points of the report are:-

1. Germany to be completely disarmed and de-militarised.
2. Regular armed forces and Nazi Organisations to be abolished.
3. The making of arms, aircraft, and ships forbidden.
4. No central Government for the present, but local government to be restored on democratic principles.
5. Poland to get a big slice of Germany, all Silesia, most of Pomerania, and a large part of Brandenburg, Danzig, and the southern half of East Prussia.
6. The northern half of East Prussia, including Konigsburg, goes to Russia.

That's a promising start, to be sure, and with any luck *Germany* should not be making war in Europe again in twenty years' time.

6.8.45   As a change, on Sunday afternoon I went up to the higher slopes of Mt. Pilion; continual scratching on the earth does not give you a very good view of life, and therefore to go to the high places has its spiritual, as well as physical, rewards. The smell of pines and bracken, the bright little houses, the deep shade of the trees, the blackberries, sloeberries, peaches and pomegranates; the sweet chestnuts, the brightly coloured, green-bellied, long-beaked exotic birds that gather on the wires, the goats and goatherd, the savage dogs; the tall thistles, the rock and shrubs, the very massiveness of the mountain, gives one a newness of life. The hot August sun beat down out of a sky edged with white cloudlets, but as we climbed the air grew cool and scents of bramble and briar brought back nostalgic memories of England. It seemed a lonely pilgrimage.

Yes, loneliness and insignificance were my reactions on that Sunday afternoon. Sitting on a grey rock I could see the lower slopes of Mt. Olympus and Lake Limin, whilst immediately before me, as though in some giant saucer, I could see, on the one side, the brown and puckered landscape between Lamios and Volos stretching far inland; two heath fires, together with the general heat haze that enveloped this vast area, added so much to its unreality and its lifelessness that I might have been observing the moon at close quarters. On the other side, dazzling in contrast, was the deep blue sea set out in bays of varying size. I could see right across the Gulf of Pagasitikos, the sand on the shore as white as salt;

again, the haze blurred the distant contours. How many summers has the sun beaten down on this scene, earth and sun pitiless in their indifference to each other? Man's creation, his strivings and struggles, the passage of time, the meaning of life and death itself; such fleeting thoughts resolved themselves into the question – 'What am I and whence cometh my fathers and whither do we return?' For, indeed, I could see great beauty, my eyes hovering over the elements of land, sea and sky, the intermingling of which words fail to describe, but I saw not as a kestrel sees, and I was sad and could not fully comprehend my feelings. Looking at Volos, Keats' poem came to mind:-

> 'O Solitude, if I must with thee dwell,
> Let it not be among the jumbled heap
> of murky buildings; climb with me the
> Steep, –
> Nature's observatory . . .'

A pensive mood, and dreamer of home; have not these last few days coincided with a visit by Dulcie and Nicolas to Mrs. Harvey's at Lymington, which has brought back vivid memories of a happy time when Nicolas was, to quote Dulcie – 'No more than a bout of indigestion!' There was about that time, something special, a term Dulcie and I always used to apply to any set of circumstances that by their very nature brought such happiness and understanding, the quality of which was ephemeral. It was one of the dewy gossamers of the cobwebs of our life together. It has passed forever and the nature of such ecstasy may never be ours again.

8.8.45   Our move to Stilis has been somewhat clarified of late. An annoying aspect of it is that we have to leave our mess on the 12th, so that the Black Watch can come in. And yet we do not leave Volos till the 15th, which means finding another mess for that short period, and also officer's billets. Until we receive more tentage we are still to have company messing at Stilis, and as far as officers are concerned I know that this meets with approval.

I shall indeed miss the comfort of four strong walls, with its cleanliness and buglessness, its protection against the strong sun, and perhaps, most of all, its privacy. We have indeed been fortunate to have spent these last five months in such comfortable billets, but that does not console us much.

9.8.45   Just recently the world has been apprehensively startled at the announcement by President Truman of what is described as the 'fission of the atom'. When we were schoolboys, I well remember the talk that used to go on about the splitting of the atom, and if I remember rightly, in our peculiar way we all thought that when this unthinkable event came about – well, it would mean at least the end of the world! What the exact scientific significance of this discovery is, I do not know, or understand, but as I see it, it means that we are able to harness tremendous energy which was once latent. It seems that if this discovery can be applied commercially, then such things as internal combustion engines, petrol, electricity, jet propelled aircraft, will be quite antiquated. This new conquest of the powers of nature by man will in this event so revolutionise industry, and presumably, therefore, the life of man, that all other discoveries of the past will pale into insignificance.

10.8.45   As from yesterday, Russia has been at war with Japan. This seems a natural corollary of the closest co-operation of the Big Three. It has been hoped for and expected, especially in America, for some time. But this declaration of war is a well-timed one. Great Britain, America and China have recently issued an ultimatum to Japan to surrender unconditionally, or take the consequences. Japan refused. Then came the atomic bomb; the first well nigh destroyed Hiroshima. Now comes Russia's declaration – following naturally after the refusal of the ultimatum with which Russia associated herself.

For some time since the capture of Okinawa, the main activity has been a large-scale softening up by bombing. Behind the scenes has been a colossal build-up, presumably for a direct assault on Japan. There have been changes in command, and huge transfers from the Western Front. The stage is undoubtedly set for a great offensive, and if Japan does not capitulate now, then the reward she will reap will indeed be a just one.

I wrote the last pages before I went down to dinner; when I got downstairs into the mess, I was greeted with the question, 'What's all this about the end of the war?' So staggered was I that I said, 'You mean the Japanese war, I suppose?' And, indeed, it transpired that someone had heard on the wireless that Japan had accepted the terms of the Potsdam ultimatum. After dinner I listened avidly to the news and, sure enough, it was so. Japan had accepted the terms, with the one exception that the Emperor be allowed to remain the Sovereign.

The Tokyo radio had broadcast this acceptance to the Japanese people, and the request was being made to American, British, Chinese and Soviet Governments through the Swedish and Swiss Governments. It remains to be seen if the Allies agree to the one condition asked for by Japan, but if they do then the Cease fire, that final Cease Fire, that we have so long waited for, will shortly be sounded.

A year ago today we were coming out of the line from the Florence battle; no-one could have convinced me then that in one year hence Europe would be at peace, and the end of the Asiatic war at hand.

14.8.45   What a heavenly thing it will be to get a long night's sleep again. Night after night I have tossed and turned in a restless sweat. I might get off for an hour or so, only to wake dripping with perspiration. Besides that, of course, one has the catcalls of Volos' night-life. It was pretty bad in my old billet that was a serene paradise compared with this one. Just opposite my room is an open air cinema, which blares forth in every tongue known to man, and an open air theatre, which is an all-Greek affair. These places are surrounded by high boarded railings, but, despite this, crowds gather in the street outside to try to catch a glimpse of the film, whilst thousands of small boys clamber up the railings. There is much shouting and screaming, and vendors selling their wares, etc. This goes on well past midnight. To one who longs for sleep, it is nothing less than a sort of maddening human inferno. How hateful man is in the mass, pressing and pushing and yelling, with a lack of dignity that gives all his activities the atmosphere of the 'hill of apes'. It is quite terrifying at times, and I recoil in disgust and want to run away.

In many ways, therefore, I was hoping that this move tomorrow to our tented camp near Stilis would enable me to recover a little mental serenity. A pity then that the reports of our new abode hold out no hope at all for an even frame of mind. John has called the place, 'The Dust Bowl Hell', a barren, treeless site where a hot wind whips the dust into great clouds. Drivers who have been there come back with grim stories of sunstroke and scorpion bites, and never have I known the men so depressed. I think it is ironical that we should be dumped in such a wilderness after the gutty time the men have had here. The doctor is going to be a very busy man! For it is not natural for Englishmen to live under flimsy canvas with a kamsheen blowing at something like a temperature of 110 degrees.

16.8.45   Just as cold numbs the mind, so I think does heat. The journey down from Volos yesterday was so hot as to make most of us go into a sort of stupor. It was terrific, and many vehicles had to stop because of over-heating. In some cases the petrol was vaporising before it reached the carburettor. So we pushed along the white dusty road through a brown sullen land. Even the olives seemed to droop in the heat. Great heath and forest fires covered whole mountains and smoke billowed into the air in the manner of a volcano. One thing I did notice were the familiar larks, who normally plop up in front of your vehicle and plop down again nearby. But today they were hunched under the shade of olive trees on the roadside, their wings spread, utterly exhausted.

I had two longish halts to cool down vehicles after mountain roads, and to quench our thirst. For the first time this year I wore sun glasses, and glad I was of them, too. Stevenson's adage that 'to travel is better than to arrive' was very true in the case of our new camp. It is on the coast just past Stilis, set amongst a grove of thin olive trees which provide little shade. Its worst feature, at least at this time of the year, is the hot kamsheen wind that whips the dust into a frenzy. We arrived at its zenith, and after that long journey it was not a very welcoming scene.

18.8.45   The bustle and anger of settling into a new camp has died down somewhat, and matters were considerably eased by the kindness of the weather, which ordained that the wind should change and blow off the sea. This both cooled tempers and bodies, and it was really wonderful not to perspire in the way we did at Volos. The monumental fact that final peace had come to the world again was completely overlooked because of the vicissitudes of our new environment. It is proposed we have our own private V-J days next week sometime. But such is the momentum of life today that we cannot stop to ruminate over the meaning of things and try to understand their implications. We are simply swept along by a relentless pressure of new events and ideas. Then came news of a speed-up in release, and that simple, practical but vital thing seemed to clear the air, because I think it is army life that to a large extent clogs and frustrates the mind of all clear thinking. Yesterday, too, I had a letter from Dulcie which contained some most delightful photos of herself and Nicolas on the beach. They spoke of joys to come.

20.8.45   Yesterday saw the end, and I think for ever, of D company mess. For now that we are concentrated it was inevitable that we should have a battalion mess, and peace being upon us once again, presumably it will stay thus for many years to come, years during which I hope the shape and form of any messes will never trouble my mind. After a late dinner, for the battalion held a mess meeting beforehand, we set to in a most natural and unselfconsciousness way to a round of popular songs. It was a pity we had not all the mess as it used to be to finish up, but, nevertheless, it was a goodly representative gathering. The hot, sticky atmosphere did not deter our full throatedness in any way and that, despite the lack of drink. We sang until after eleven, and, as usual, all the old favourites came out in due turn.

23.8.45   It is becoming more and more difficult to reconcile our present mode of existence with the fact that war is no more. I do not mean to say that directly the Cease Fire had gone I expected to be transported magically back to civilian life, but I do expect our life today to be organised in the light of present conditions. Surely now, the less organised things are the better; any form of community has to have a good administration, but its working should be so smooth, so intelligently applied that each individual feels he is an entity and not just one of a mass. The bulk of the army is composed of civilians – and surely now is the time to start that mental reorientation towards civilian life, for we do not want to arrive there too inexorably steeped in gregarious and sheep-like ways. We want to build up now the ability to run our own lives, and not have them run for us. We fought for freedom, we have gained a victory, but there seems to be no air of victory about the place – no feeling of – 'Now we can live.' Our attitude is almost apathetic, negative. This emptiness is not, I am convinced, a question of environment. Natural enough, then, that I have felt somewhat miserable, not to say bitter, and this at a time which should surely be characterised by a sense of relief and joy. I should have thought it reasonable to suppose that life now would be made as pleasant as possible. But no, we still have stupid impositions put upon us – the 'carry the baby' mentality still permeates our daily life, and the sense of claustrophobia is appalling. I feel now a complete revulsion for everything that is army, and under present circumstances I find that communal life is just too much, I would be quite happy never to see a uniform again. I should love to dump all the paraphernalia of war into the sea – and forget forever the bizarre existence that is built up round it all. But the fact remains that until age group 25 is released I must owe allegiance to His Majesty's Army, however much I despair and tug at the chains. It is the last lap, the hardest of all, when to give up would be so easy. But, oh, the artificiality, the futility of it all.

24.8.45   The world awaits the signing of the unconditional surrender by Japan, and the entry of Allied forces of occupation into the Land of the Rising Sun! Japanese delegates met with members of General MacArthur's staff at Manila to receive instructions and to report back to the Emperor. Now allied warships are moving into Tokyo Bay, and it will be on the *Missouri* that the first surrender will be signed. Allied paratroopers are standing by to occupy Tokyo. It has been a somewhat long-winded business, due no doubt to the lengthy communications, causing delays in receipt of orders by local Japanese Commanders, some of whom even when they did receive them found such an act so contrary to their creed as to cause them to ignore it. What the position is now on the various fronts is difficult to say, but I imagine there is not yet that complete feeling that all is over, and that the need for vigilance no longer exists. It will be interesting to note the reaction of the Japanese populace to the Allied occupation forces. Has the militarist Cult of Bushido reached many levels of society, or is it mainly a creed for military and political leaders?

The main problems of transportation of displaced populations, of the concentrations of Japanese forces, of the care of prisoners, of the vast economic relief of a war ravaged China, will need herculean attention and action. They are seemingly so complex that the layman can have little idea of what all this will involve. The economic reconstruction of the Far East will be the task of a generation, and until order is established there, the standard of living of the whole world must surely suffer. The world today stands at the crisis of a grim shortage of food, clothing, shelter and heat, the bare necessities of life, in fact. Man's immediate task is to avoid worldwide famine and pestilence. And so it irks us more than somewhat to be clicking our heels in army camps wasting precious time. Today and tomorrow are our ersatz V-J days, but they mean nothing to us, each day is alike. We are more than disgusted about an announcement concerning release to the effect that it was hoped that 23 group would be out by the end of the year. A week or so ago it was hoped that the 28 group would be out by the end of the year. Life is bloody!

25.8.45   The V-J celebration took the form of two days off duty, and as it is never possible to get away from the Army, the holidays as such were barely noticed. Entertainment for the troops is just non-existent, except what we produce ourselves in the way of a dance band and concert party. Free beer and retsina, I suppose, was something – no doubt used in an effort to fight their immediate environment rather than to celebrate the coming of peace! The lack of mobile cinemas is particularly noticeable, for that is a medium of entertainment which gives a lot of contentment.

Mr. Ismay's announcement about release came at an unfortunate time, of course, i.e. that he hopes to *begin* the release of 23 group by the end of the year. Then he goes on to say that release is being actively reviewed – so even now we are not on a firm base. At present I am entertaining the hope of being released at the end of January 1946 – but I keep a very open mind about it now.

So the mental stress of the body's captivity must continue yet awhile. It's like watching the kettle boil – the more you watch it the less it seems to boil. The more you long for time to pass, the more slowly it will go. Yet it is mighty difficult to train the mind not to brood on these things, but to

seek employment elsewhere so that the time will pass quickly. It is curious, this trick the mind plays with time. A leave goes like lightning, and
yet so does going to the dentist when you don't want to! In the former, I
suppose, the joy of living is re-captured and to live joyously is to live
timelessly. In the latter, you fear going to the dentist and in your mind the
approach of the inevitable goes all too quickly. Yet in some ways is it not
strange that the mind does not rationalise these 'time' hallucinations for
the benefit of the individual? One would have thought if a certain event
was most desirable, then the psychological processes would have tended
to ease the gap in some suggestive way. But I am getting out of my depth!

The fact is that my body is here undeniably on this patch of ground in
the Bay of Maliakos. The tent, the red dust, the three sheepdog puppies,
the ugly wire and camouflage nets that screen my view of the sea – all
these physical things are irrefutable. I can see them – I can touch them –
and yet I cannot escape them. I can see the full harvest moon rise majes-
tically over the mountain tops, its soft light spreading peacefully and
beautifully over the bay, and yet I enjoy it not to the full. I hear a wader
call down on the beach, I see olive trees silhouetted against the diffused
light, and yet I enjoy it not to the full.

29.8.45   The last few days have passed quickly and touchily! Rather
           like an enraged dog asleep and better left asleep! A
somniferous atmosphere of suppressed hope, anger, and disgust hangs
over the camp. The men are unhappy and bitter about home leave, and
leave to Athens, about release announcements, about welfare, and about
their present environment. It is brought home to them, especially when
they get letters from relatives in Germany and Austria, where by comparison every facility exists. They feel that none of the promises have been
fulfilled and although I try my hardest to raise their hopes about LIAP,
they always look at me with a particularly 'lack-lustre' eye. It is bloody
for them. It's bloody for the people who can do nothing for them. If only
we could tell them *definitely* that they would be going on LIAP, and *when*,
morale would shoot up like a rocket. And yet, despite their moroseness,
there has been little trouble – touch wood – but we have had a host of
applications for transfers to parent and other units, which is natural. And
yet the C.O. is very hopeful and confident about LIAP whenever I talk to
him, and personally I have felt happier these last few days despite the War
Office's announcement of Release date for groups 19-23. 23 group is to be
released between 24th December and 20th January, nearly a month, which
looks as though I shall be lucky if I am out by March; in other words, I am
back to where I started.

The weather has been much more pleasant of late, with a nice breeze, and a lot of cloud about. The sunrises and sunsets are particularly beautiful – the Gulf placid and steel blue – the mountains with hazy-touched contours reaching into a pastel sky. How characteristic is this Greek scene, with its perfect contiguity of sea, sky and mountain – a poetic and magical blending of the elements, the like of which must be seldom seen in other countries.

At night the moon has taken up the tale of this perfection by spreading its ghostly light over the hilltops, by diffusing a magical gleam over the sea, and silhouetting in a delicate tracery the olives and gum trees at the water's edge.

The heights of Thermoplylae look magnificent and remote, and I have promised myself a day out to explore them. As yet, I have not been out of the camp since we arrived, and with the General coming next weekend it looks as though I shall be kept in for a while yet. Parnassus stands out like a vast Epsteinian monolith, a crude yet lovely monster.

31.8.45   And so ends August in the usual blaze of sunshine. Today it has been perfect, pleasantly hot, but with a nice breeze. The sunrise was again very lovely, and I stood and watched the rosy light shed itself over the great shoulders of Mt. Parnassus, which was silhouetted against an aqueous sky. It made a lovely scene. The sea looked more attractive and enticing than for a long time and I thoroughly enjoyed my bathe, from whence I could still see Parnassus set in a misty frame of giant mountains.

We had a mobile cinema here last night (*mirabile dictu*) and I must say it is rather pleasant, this open air cinema business, for to be able to look up and see the Milky Way or to watch a shooting star and the Plough, relieves one of that sense of claustrophobia which is the effect of many cinemas – and, of course, the air is fresh.

I talked to the company for an hour this morning on morale and life generally. They have been very low of late and my theme was 'Sweet are the uses of adversity'!

2.9.45   The weekend was somewhat disorganised by the Divisional Commander visiting us. In fact, he stayed the night and, of course, we had the usual formal dinner. Worst of all though, he made me miss a film with Margaret Lockwood in it – I like her – and we don't exactly get an orgy of films here.

Today makes history in the Parkhurst family – I wrote my first letter to Nicolas, at his own request.

3.9.45   And so the last six years have turned full circle. Today the world is once again at peace. Today we occupy Berlin and

Tokyo. The war is over. But peace is not just the negation of war. The peace between 1918 and 1939 was perhaps negative; its negativeness led inevitably to the second war. No – peace must be vitally positive and constructive, never again must man again take the blessings of peace for granted, for if peace is to be enjoyed and lived to the full, then the minds of men must be free of the fear of war. We have fought twice for peace – now we must learn to maintain it, and maintain it in a world that is fit for men to live in, and one which gives him complete freedom of spirit. To maintain peace, we must understand it and try and analyse the reasons why it has so often been disrupted. An organisation, backed by force, is being instituted to maintain world peace. It is a kind of global police force controlled by a world Security Council. If this Council works in harmony and with tolerance and vision, and above all with integrity of purpose of each of its members – then this powerful 'Guardian Angel' of peace should be a good deterrent to those who seek to settle political differences by war. And unless mankind reaches a much higher state of morality, I am afraid this organisation will always be necessary, just as national police forces are. Nations will still have to keep armies, equipped with all the dreadful modern impedimenta – and so *if* nations fall out – the instruments of war are at hand, and how well the instigators know it. Someone said, 'In peace, prepare for war!' Surely that is not still to be our watchword for generations to come. Our ethics must run hard to catch up with the atomic bomb.

5.9.45   Our minds are still centred on LIAP and Release. The Minister of Labour has announced that it is not the difficulty of allocating manpower or the inability of demobilisation centres to cope with large numbers. Industry, in fact, can absorb and needs men in vast numbers for the changeover to peacetime production. The limiting factor is still transport, a factor which has been aggravated in the sense of release by the surrender of Japan. There are over 150,000 prisoners of war alone, to be transported home, and they have, rightly enough, a very high priority. Then we have an area of responsibility in the S.E. Pacific which includes many islands and uses vital shipping. So, quite rightly, the Prime Minister in a recent broadcast told us to be patient, that a constant review of the situation was to be ensured, and that the Government would release men as quickly as possible. We did not, he said, want to make the same mistakes as after the last war, for as a member of the United Nations we had to remember our commitments. So I am afraid we must put up with the inevitable. If local leave and LIAP is stepped up, as they have promised, then things shouldn't be too bad. A piece of news about LIAP came in this morning to the effect that persons in age service 23 and under were no longer eligible for LIAP. So that puts me very high in the battalion roster for officers and once the big allotments start I feel I have every chance of getting home. Dudley cannot go till the C.O. returns from LIAP. Hugh is next, but rumour has it that he has got himself engaged to a nurse at 53 General Hospital, so maybe he won't be so awfully interested! Then comes myself and Roy, unless Philip (age group 23) has signed on for a regular commission. So, with baited breath, we wait and see.

8.9.45   I had a very interesting day yesterday when I had to go to the village of Makiakomi to visit the scene of an accident in which two Greek civilians were killed. I have been made President of the Court which is to investigate the case. And so Gill and Bob came with me as members. Makiakomi is about twenty-five miles west of Lamia, and so we took sandwiches and made a day of it. The road up to Lamia was, of course, familiar, and I took note of the eerie staging camp where we stayed on the way to Volos, with its lonely church and the single pencil-line cyprus trees, and the marsh opposite with the grim walled-in farm. Beyond Lamia was new. It was a brown landscape at first, and the destroyed and desolate railway on our left, with occasional batches of rusting engines listing at all angles on the broken line, added to the dreary picture. A dead railway system is a horrible thing to see, and it will take many years before the Greek railways are in working order again, very many years.

Further south the great mountain mass of Oiti reared itself with a relentless majesty into the sky. These heights are forbidding indeed. We then came to a more fertile part of the country, with trees and crops. Sweetcorn was plentiful, and so, too, was the cotton, lovely to see; some of the plants were still in flower but most had reached the cotton stage. The flower is not unlike a musk rose. Many bridges were being built – in the slow Greek fashion, and we had several diversions. We passed through some very grim and forlorn villages, the depressing and dilapidated houses made of a local mud brick. How poorly the people and children looked, wretched, dressed in rags and most without footwear.

Makiakomi is, I think, the most destroyed village I've seen in Greece. It is, in fact, utterly destroyed. This wanton act was the result of the killing of about seventeen Germans by the Andartes. As a reprisal, every house in the village (a largish one) was burnt to a shell. The President said they used to do about six to ten houses a day until the whole village had been completely burnt. It was done with the mad methodic way of the Teutonic mind. The President hoped that each family would have one room by this winter! But when these people will be properly housed again is hard to say. It was a tragic sight, and there was tragedy and dejection in those villagers' eyes – but not defeat. It was a terrible sight to see these people sitting outside their burnt-out houses, all of them in the most shocking clothing and no footwear. A crowd gathered round us as we studied the scene of the accident – a woman nearby was sitting on the pavement feeding her baby from the breast. She was weeping, and did she not have something to weep about?!

Soon, a lot of jabbering ensued and my interpreter told me they wanted to show me the head of the child who had been killed. This I declined. Several of them had seen the accident but I only took one man to be a witness at the Court. I would have liked a representative gathering of English people to have been with me on this visit, and to look into the faces of a suffering people.

We then went to the police station, which was a small inconspicuous building recently made habitable. There it was we met the President, who told us many interesting things about the village. For food UNRRA had done them well, and for medical supplies they were lucky to have a hospital nearby. Clothing, there wasn't any, and children who had been born within the last five years had never seen footwear! Building material was very short, but some timber was coming now, and tiles, etc. We saw signs of this outside the village ourselves, small dumps, etc. Transport, of course, is non-existent except by the dear old moke. The President spoke a little English (I expect he had been to America) and bore himself as a President should. They always stand out, these men, and usually have very honest faces.

Having arranged with the police for the witnesses to be collected on Monday, we took our leave. This visit to Makiakomi made a sombre impression. It is useless in Greece to judge the standard of living by the towns – one has to go to these wayside and remote villages to get a true reflection of the state of affairs. Most of these people Leonard thought would want the King back – Leonard was our interpreter, a Greek boy of eighteen years, who was a very intelligent chap. He said, even if the elections were held, they would never be run properly – even dead people were known to have a vote in Greek elections!

9.9.45   Two years ago today – Salerno – now a grim dream; one year ago today, in our concentration area near Gradona, just before the hellish Coriano battle. I see I finish up my entry for 9 September 1944 with 'May 9th September next year see us out of this business and may providence be kind tonight and give us a night's sleep'. Well, here we are then, one year hence and my wish has been fulfilled. We are out of it. The fighting and all the physical and mental weariness it entailed are over. We are at peace again. But the war has left its mark. World economy is strained as never before. For a year or so civilization will still hang by a thread. The days of abundance are a long way off.

Most of us still have our own struggles to contend with – mostly concerned with the continued separation from our homes, many concerned with homes broken up by unfaithful wives, many with the fact that they have no home or job to go to, many with bereavement. Yes, indeed, the war has left some terrible scars on humanity, scars, many of which will take a long time to heal. But it is infinitely better than defeat. Only by our own efforts will we reap the fruits of victory.

13.9.45   The Court of Enquiry concerning the accident in Makiakomi seems to have kept me fully occupied for the last three days. We sat all Monday, and anyone who has had to deal with Greek witnesses will know what a trial of patience and endurance that was! And we finished on Tuesday morning, but couldn't conclude with our opinion until we had visited the scene once more. So yesterday off we went again and there again deliberated on the 'whys and wherefores' of this incredible accident, the evidence of which is very conflicting. Again it rained, and again on getting back to camp, it thundered. In fact, last night the storm was fierce and Gill had a narrow escape from lightning which struck nearby, stunning him and making flashes come out of his boots! Small red patches came up on his left shoulder, but he was quite O.K. The signal lines were hit and the wire snapped in your hands like dead twigs. We had a wonderful display of rainbows and cloud effects and colours. After dark a rare sight was given us in the form of a rainbow caused by the moon.

The cloudier skies and cooler temperatures are getting the birds on the move again, and many times have I heard the sad and piquant note of a willow warbler in the olives. Today, too, I have seen fly-catchers and shrikes; hoodie crows seem to be the commonest resident birds in the area at the moment. The next few weeks should see the movement increase – I was hoping to see the storks migrating but so far I have seen no signs of it.

15.9.45   Today has been gloriously sunny – Greece as I shall always remember it – with the white fleecy clouds skirting the hilltops. It was good to get all my clothing out of my tent and dry it, and during the day I had some shale put down and now it looks altogether much more cheerful with that wet, sticky mud all covered. It was somewhat sacrilegious, therefore, to have to go and shoot our own pieces as a rehearsal for tomorrow's demonstration. But how these Greeks love it – they have a definite streak in them that makes them relish these instruments of war. The more's the pity that we don't hide such things from such people!

16.9.45   A beautiful crisp and blue dawn over the Bay of Maliakos – the mountains clearer than I've seen them for a long time and Parnassus looked magnificent in its rocky drapery. I usually wake before the dawn to see a bright and lovely star shining just over the olive tree opposite – I think it may be Venus. It was a glorious shimmering day, the sea an incredible sheen of dazzling colours, making strange illusions of the islets and rocks the far side of the bay. A pity that such a sabbath morn should be shattered by the explosions of bombs and firing of M.G.s that we had to do for the Greek Army. Before it started, from near a lovely walnut tree, I watched flycatchers, shrikes, grey wagtails, hoodies, and an old raven flew over grunting like a pig. Such a morning as this should be set aside for such a pastoral and soothing pastime.

The afternoon was a happy one to compensate. A letter from Dulcie saying John* was going on LIAP; a luxurious sunbathe, which did my old bones a power of good after all the wet, and then a bathe in the sea, which was exhilarating. This evening I feel fitter and more ready to meet life than for a very long time.

18.9.45   A year ago today it was that I moved my H.Q. to the slope beyond Coriano, which was to be home for a fortnight. And what a wet time it was, and noisy. Now it is all like a distant dream – or perhaps a nightmare – but whatever it was, it was irrevocably part of my life's experience, and doubtless will have its effects. At the moment my memory of the place is very vivid – I can see the gaunt outline of Coriano ridge, the knocked-out tanks, the flashes and din of the 5.5s just below us, the very look of the dusty and ill-kempt and battle-scarred grapes, the German dug-out near my tent, our cookhouses, the search-lights, and the stars – and so I could go on – putting every piece in this memory jigsaw.

21.9.45   I think I shall remember this day for the rest of my life. I wonder? I think I will. It is difficult to express just why, to express the culmination of events, of hopes and fears, of longings, that seemed to make life a prisoned hell. But the difficulty does emphasise the many changing scenes, the numerous experiences, the mental impressions, the broken reactions of hope, fear, joy, cold and heat, hunger and plenty, the emptiness of time, that have all manifested themselves since I left Dulcie on that 31st May 1943. Yes, the emptiness of time, for time

*Brother.

and nature are inter-related and man's life is conditioned thereby. He lives it out in the framework set by time and nature, and the cycle of his life takes on a definite shape. The roots begin to grow deep, and for two generations those roots have been cruelly clawed out by man's inhumanity to man. Dulcie and I are two such people of the second generation. We have been married nearly seven years, and altogether since then we have spent barely eighteen months in each other's company. And today I have been told I am going on twenty-eight days *HOME LEAVE*!!

Yes, and it is as definite as I suppose anything in the Army can be. The word 'exigences' must always be kept well to the fore in such circumstances. I am told we leave here on the 25th September, that is Tuesday – FOUR DAYS' TIME – it seems quite incredible. It is better than any dream. I had a letter from Dulcie yesterday, and she said her patience was wearing thinner and thinner – for hopefully waiting is a trying business. My reply to her will surely seem like a work of some fairy godmother. How happy it makes me to be able to write such happy news to her after all the brave and anxious waiting, all that responsibility she has had. Dear God, we have much to be thankful for, when you think of the poor fellows who have been killed, and vice versa – of the wives who have died in the air war. We have a home, a lovely son, beautiful surroundings, and, above all, our faith is still strong in the goodness of life. Our faith in each other, our love of home and all it entails, of the country, of the simplest joys, is as abundant as ever.

22.9.45   I seem to be living in a whirl of activity, and excitement, both bodily and mentally. Such things as planning what I should take with me, my letter home to Dulcie telling her the great news, the feverish activity in the office brought about by the large party going on this LIAP, handing over to John, all seem merged in a kind of hazy, rather hectic, dream. To sit quietly and read I find well nigh impossible. Last night sleep would just not come, for on these occasions, visions and pictures float before me of a happy meeting, of a joyous reunion, of seeing Nicolas, and 'Benallan' again, in fact, all those wonderful things that have of necessity been submerged and held far back in the mind, all have suddenly come rushing to the fore. I feel like a caged lion, but a happy one! It is all so unbelievable, so difficult to grasp. I can still quite clearly see all the men in the dining tent, with me taking a Quiz, and when it was nearly finished Dudley coming in and going up to John grinning all over his face, and then hearing the words, 'Does he know he's going on the 25th?' I knew instinctively he was referring to me, and I knew it was about LIAP. At first it just washed over me, then it began to penetrate, then its full significance began to gather momentum – and yet I still am not fully orientated or even convinced. Philip and Roy are going with me, and over 130 other ranks, which is a far larger number than I ever hoped for even in my most hopeful moments. The effect showed itself last night when much singing and other signs of jubilation were to be heard over the camp. Men kept going to the cookhouse to get tea because they couldn't get to sleep. Nothing better could have happened to raise the morale of everybody. Bob said I looked ten years younger last night, but all the excitement is most exhausting, I find!

23.9.45   And the happiest Sunday I've had in months. In all the rush I have forgotten, I believe, to mention that the sulphonimide tablets the doctor gave me had a very unpleasant delayed effect. For six days I had terrible headaches and eyeaches, and I got very worried until I happened to mention it to the doctor, who explained what it was. I had my last ache yesterday afternoon, a terrific neuralgia pain on the right side of my head – but today, nothing. That was a joy in itself, and to top it all the weather has been really beautiful. There has been a gentle breeze and quiet-sounding sea; patches of white cloud have been thrown haphazardly over a glorious sky, a true Grecian day, in fact, without that horrid electrical atmosphere we have had of late. This morning I was busy with further preparations, but I wrote to Dulcie.

A note arrived today to say we were to be at the Reception Camp by 1200 hours if possible, so we are leaving at about 0445 hours. What this means, if anything, I don't know, but it seems quite on the cards that we may go to Italy by air. The time of leaving caused a bit of a stir with Roy and Philip at first – for myself I know I shall be only too ready to get up at 0345 hours to go home – I shall probably be awake anyway. I would prefer that to travelling through the night.

It was beautifully peaceful sitting in the warm sun, especially with headaches gone, and ruminating on the joys of leave. As I sat there I could see the grey-red rocky hillside above the camp covered by a green shrub, a typical Greek hill – hard but beautiful. In the distance I could hear the croak of some hoodies, but otherwise, except for the sea and the gentle movement of the now very laden olive trees, all was quiet – the quiet of the afternoon – that special atmosphere which surely must be universal. It is as though the world is brooding quietly.

24.9.45   And so finally I am ready to go – everything is packed, even the twenty-eight mepacrine tablets! I have said my goodbyes to those who will be released before I am back. I have written my last letter from this camp to Dulcie, and now comes the speculation as to what kind of journey it will be. Everyone in the mess looks at you in a strangest sort of way, a way which says –'lucky fellow' – but I know just what it feels like, and I sincerely hope they will soon be following my lucky footsteps. It has been another glorious day and I sunbathed again, in such a happy frame of mind, reading, and revelling in the knowledge that soon I would be home with Dulcie and Nicolas. My mind hasn't been in such a peaceful state for months. For the first time since May 1943, all the 'weariness, the fever and the fret' of soldiering abroad is beginning to pass away. It is my own private PEACE. Today, in fact, sees the end of a chapter in my life.

Now it is late evening, after dinner in fact. The mail arrived late but there was nothing for me. So my next communication with Dulcie will be in person. What a heavenly thought after all this time, during which our separate lives and thoughts have been expressed in the written word. The moon is just up – it is on the wane and an odd shape, but thankfully still very bright, which will help considerably early tomorrow morning. Just risen, it casts a lovely narrow golden beam across the bay and with the hill silhouetted beyond the scene is altogether delightful. Cicadas are singing everywhere, and their sound forms the familiar unchanging symphony of the Greek night. The Greek fishermen are already out in the bay, and sometimes you see a boat blackly silhouetted in the path of the moon. The scene in the early morning, in the first hour of dawn, looks like a beautiful painting – the very essence of quiet and peace. The fishermen have a habit of banging on the sides of their boats, I think to attract fish, but I am not certain. The dull thudding goes on throughout the night.

So, in this atmosphere which surrounds my wanly lit tent, I sit and write these final notes before going to bed. My LIAP kit lies about me, a valise with a couple of blankets, a mac, grey bags, etc., and a big pack with all my notebooks and the 431 letters Dulcie has written me since I left her just over two years ago. That is quite a heavy package and to me a valuable one which is going on my back. These diaries have always constituted a minor worry for they were illegal in wartime and I daren't ever send them through the post because of the censor, and, of course, the risk of loss was great anyway. But I hope they have not been a waste of time. They haven't for me, personally, for although at times they have seemed a burden in that I seemed never to have the courage to stop writing them, they have given me a great outlet and diversion in the difficult days, and looking through occasionally I find much to interest me still, and, who knows, they may take a certain vintage as time goes by! Perhaps Dulcie will be the only person ever to read them, or parts of them, and it will be interesting to hear what she thinks of them.

I am wearing battledress tomorrow and it seems most likely that today will be the last time that I shall wear the shorts and stockings dress in the military sense anyway.

And to quote Samuel Pepys' famous words, 'So to bed'. And in that bed what dreams may come?! Everything comes to pass, and I thank God that I have been privileged to enjoy this exquisite anticipation, and, please God, realisation.

26.9.45   We arrived at this camp (Rouf Barracks) at about 1330 hours, and how thankful I was, but somewhat dazed, needless to say. Then came the business of sorting the men out, etc., finding our own quarters, which we were pleased to find very comfortable – a spring bed and good washing facilities being provided – quite magnificent to rest here for a night. My back (small of) had come up in a big lump and I ached and was very heady. It was not known when we would be leaving, but it seems it will probably be by ship. There was one chap of LIAP 24 who was still here, but I think he goes today. After a few meals and a quiet sit down in a comfortable deckchair in the cool of the evening, I felt fit enough to write to Dulcie to give her my latest position.

29.9.45   A notice in the mess requested officers not to leave the camp before 1400 hours owing to 'sudden movements'. After a few days, of course, this was thought to be the work of some humorist as 'sudden movement' seemed the least likely thing to happen. But, hopefully, we stayed in duly till 1400 hours, reading, writing, and what have you. Yesterday morning Roy and I started on a game of darts about midday and we were just about to start a 'round the clock' when someone came in shouting our names. We were going by air today, Roy on flight 127, myself on flight 126. I was to be at Kalamaki at 1300 hours. It was then 1215. Never have darts been dropped so quickly! I rushed upstairs, packed, wrote a short note to Dulcie, and then had lunch. It was to be my first air trip and they all said, don't eat a lot of fat, so I had a lot of bread and tea. The dinners here, anyway, were always particularly greasy. Then came a lorry with eighteen chaps to pick me up. I was setting off on a new experience and how glad I was to be getting out of Greece.

After arrival at the aerodrome, we were shown our plane – 'H' for Harry, an American four-engined Liberator, had the roll called, the kit put in the bomb bays, a short talk about the trip from the pilot, and some do's and don'ts, and then we were fitted in. The pilot said I could travel on the flight deck, for which I was grateful as I could see more, and being the centre of the pressure of the plane, it was smoother and also warmer.

I sat behind the pilot and flight engineer, and beside the wireless operator. Another officer was given the seat above in the gun turret, which I didn't relish as it was not made for tall chaps. Then various noises occurred, and things started to happen; soon we were moving down the runway getting ready for take-off. The pilot got the O.K. from Control, the engines roared, and the ground was shooting away from under us. Almost immediately I was looking down on Athens. It really was quite incredible to be looking out of a little window through which I could see one engine and propeller and, beyond, sea and islands. It was a curious sensation, this looking down, and in the air you have no telegraph poles to give you an idea of speed. Time seems to stand still! The pilot was kind to us and flew right down the Corinth Canal to avoid bumps. The plane, as it happened, was as steady as a rock the whole way, like being on a Southdown bus on a very good road!

The scene mostly was of the wrinkled and patterned sea, of dark blots of islands, of coastline and seashore, or distant hills and clouds. When we reached the Ionian Sea there was more cloud and then shadows moved across the sea in a ghostly migration. It was a lovely sight altogether. And so to the Adriatic, where we flew up the coast past Brindisi and Bari. The weather was glorious now, clear blue sky and visibility of twenty miles. We were flying at about 2,000 feet. Then we turned inland to Foggia, a perfect landing – I didn't even know when the wheels touched down – efficient reception, good meal and fine sleep; and move to Milan tonight, leaving at 2330 hours. We should be there on Monday and off on Tuesday for Calais by Wednesday, and then, by the grace of God, off on Thursday for dear old Blighty.

2.10.45   My thirty-first birthday and my third spent in Italy. I had an interesting and happy day exploring Milan and buying presents for Dulcie. This morning I took a train down to the city centre, first making a call on the Field Cashier. The train service is really first-class, and the trains themselves are very clean and smooth running. Most of the populace seem to have season tickets and they are always crowded. The conductor takes tickets sitting down at a desk. He does not clamber about as in English trains. The doors open and close like those in the London tubes. Milan shops are stocked with every conceivable luxury, and I wished I had been a millionaire, for there were many things I saw that Dulcie would have loved, especially clothes. This morning I contented myself with the purchase of some cosmetics, which I understand are still short in England. This afternoon, with Philip, I was tempted to a lovely silk scarf, which was a luxury, but which I think Dulcie will love. It will also serve as a headdress. Then as a toy for Nicolas I bought a collapsible giraffe. It's an amazing thing which stands on a block of wood, and by pressing in on the table, the giraffe collapses into a floppy heap. Release the pressure and he stands erect. I hope he likes it. We visited the bombed-out Scala Opera House which is on the highest priority for reconstruction. Work was going on at a very energetic pace, and I should think the end of the year will see it completed. It holds 4,000 people and is a magnificent place. The stage is the largest I've ever seen. I like Milan, it seems a lovely city and very clean.

Today our names went up on the board. We leave tomorrow at 1630 hours, which means, unfortunately, that we go through Switzerland in the dark. We ought to arrive about 0500 hours on the 5th, but how soon we leave Calais I don't know. We should arrive in England on the 6th. This evening we called in at the R.T.O. and reserved our seats on the train. It is indeed difficult to suppress the intense excitement of these happy days.

8.10.45   The last three days travelling through France have been one long spell of unreality. It is difficult to grasp the fact that the dreams and longings of the last two unpleasant years and more have been fulfilled at last. To assimilate one's new, yet old and familiar surroundings, to renew old acquaintances calmly and steadily, is, under the circumstances, well nigh impossible.

At first I tried to grasp all these impressions in one gasp – rather like a man lost in a desert, at the first opportunity of relieving his thirst, has to use all his will power not to drink too great a quantity. The mind can only absorb so much at a time. For the first time I think I am in the frame of mind to be able briefly to recapitulate the events of these last memorable and happy days.

First then Calais. There we were concerned chiefly with the final documentation, change of money, issue of Naafi, which was done with factory efficiency. My cold was aggravating and I visited the M.I. Room to see what they could do. They gave me a nose bath over a bowl of hot water in which methyl crystals had been placed, and also gave me a bronchial mixture. It was a great relief. The weather was glorious, sunny and warm, and very comforting after the chilly night and the cold nissen huts of the camp. So the time passed quickly until we were taken to the docks. Soon we found ourselves getting on to a single-funnelled steamer. I remember vaguely some instructions being given out over the tannoy, and particularly I remember, 'You should be in London four and a half hours from now!' Then we were told we could send telegrams home and I realised we were moving.

The sea, over which hung a distant autumnal haze, was calm and still, incredibly calm, for which I was most truly thankful. True to style and all the story books, loomed the white cliffs of Dover, and on this particular afternoon they glowed rosily in the setting sun, which in the mist gave a beautiful curtain effect. But it was England – after all this time, and after this long journey. We crowded to the decks to watch the dear old homeland draw nearer. This was my first glimpse of Dover and Folkestone; Dover Castle, in which the 2nd battalion were stationed at the outbreak of war, showed up clearly.

We got into Folkestone harbour at about 1700 hours and how good it was to see an old English pier, with the green slime and seaweed, showing the big tides of the Channel. Ropes were thrown and gulls hovered and called. A rotund policeman, hands behind back, calm and dignified, walked up and down the quay with a stately gait. Solid and comfortable stood the boat train that waited to take us to London. The gangways were thrown down and before long a mass of men struggling with kit – yet orderly – went past various officials to have documents stamped, and then through the customs. The customs officer let me through and I was met by a happy and officious movement control officer who waved me into a first-class carriage. My kit went in the van next door; now the excitement was intense. The train was so comfortable – and it was a step nearer home. It all took place so quickly, this transfer from boat to train, and we had not long to wait before the train pulled out. How cosy and friendly the green wooded countryside looked. A Naafi car on the train provided us with tea and cakes, which were most acceptable. We didn't arrive till about 2050 hours, which meant that I'd missed the train to Lewes. So I phoned Dulcie, intending to catch the 9.28 to Brighton. How amazing and lovely it was to hear her voice again. I had pictured it all happening so often and yet when it was real it was difficult to know what to say!

We arranged for a taxi to meet me at Brighton, and I arrived there at eleven o'clock. To my joy, Dulcie was there waiting for me – she had arranged for a friend to look after Nicolas for a while. Silently and swiftly we sped through the dark night, the road smooth and gleaming in the headlights. It felt strange to be on the left-hand side.

Finally we turned the corner up the Kingston lane; it seemed not to have changed in the least; then down the hill, and in a few moments we were in 'Benallan'. I was home at last. Thermopylae to Kingston – the journey had come to an end. I was lost in a glorious sense of relief and comfort.

11.10.45 I find little inclination to write notes about these happy days.

My notes of the past two years have perhaps been a form of

mental diversion, at once an outlet, and a screen behind which I could live a little life of my own. This present happiness has seemingly drowned all incentive. And yet, what a shame! For, indeed, I am passing through and enjoying a rich experience, one that I hope has been the happy lot of many servicemen who have spent years in the spiritual loneliness of foreign lands. It is a common story today, and these reunions, some temporary, some at least permanent, are the central theme in the lives of millions. They are a major part of the resettlement and readjustment that has to follow the chaos of the last six years. Unfortunately, it cannot always be a case of the happy ending. What grim disillusionment, and lack of faith, must ensue in these tragic instances. Indeed, there is not an atmosphere of certainty for many as yet. The war itself, following as it did years of threat and uncertainty, has come to a close, not in an atmosphere of concrete security, resting as we had hoped on a sense of complete world co-operation, but rather on one where the dominant feeling is – 'Well, at least the firing has stopped.'

But this is a digression from the joys of a temporary reunion. And yet it is difficult to describe the emotions that have emanated from this glorious, but oh too transient sense of comfort and serenity.

The task of assimilating the '*fait accompli*' of a three-year-old son, who has (perhaps only to the biased mind of an incredulous and long absent father) a very positive and endearing personality, has been absorbing and stimulating to a degree. The process of finding my feet, of orientating and accommodating myself to this new factor in my life, has brought an awareness that having children is no light-hearted hobby! I am afraid I haven't the pencraft to be able to depict all the subtle shades of a child's personality. It is a mixture of mundanity and ethereal intangibility. I could say he says 'so and so' but it would not describe the wistfulness or the intriguing inflection or intonation of voice in which it is said. The platitude that there is no child like one's own needs no substantiation and bears considerably on any attempts at an impartial and impersonal description.

To me, however, after this long absence, it seems that Nicolas expresses himself very lucidly. You are able to talk to him in a normal way, and generally he understands completely what you say or a line of thought you may be trying to impart. He already possesses good thought processes, and in the matter of alternatives you can almost see the 'act of consideration' before a choice is made! Like any healthy child, he is full of zest and fun, and will mimic and imitate to his heart's content. It is amazing to hear such well-known phrases as 'crack of dawn' or 'I do indeed' come out at the most odd and unexpected times, and often with great relish, and a glint of wickedness in his eye. 'Hey presto' often comes out as 'Hell's presto', which has its derivative in 'Hell's bells', a form of oath used at times by Dulcie.

17.10.45   One day melts imperceptibly into another, and the precious happy time slips by, regardless of all that it means to us. The new environment and atmosphere, from which emanates this serene state, hasn't a daily measuring stick. All time is one, and only when one enjoys an especial highlight does the dark thought of another separation occur. It has been a time of being rather than doing, and being in the background of 'Benallan', of dear old Kingston village, and the soft contoured evergreen downs, with their white chalk paths and steep, yet fairy-like combes, that are so characteristic of all downland; a background of large, friendly elms, of that national character the rook, of dear mellow houses and cottages and their gardens, of misty yet summery October days. When the sun goes down in an atmosphere of cold bluish haze, that is the mark of all that is autumn.

21.10.45   Rain for the first time since I've been home – a fine misty drenching rain from the south. As I write I can hear the water dripping into the water butt, a pleasant sound when one is safely and cosily esconced at home on a Sunday morning. Up until now this October weather has been halcyon, and Dulcie, Nicolas and I have spent much of it in the open. Twice we have been to the seaside at Seaford; the first time we both bathed but it was too cold for me after the warm waters of the Aegean, and the second time Dulcie bathed alone, and even she said it was colder – that was the 18th October.

Last Friday we had a glorious walk through Buckhurst Park. This lovely forest scenery contrasts strongly with our local and relatively open downland. And in an October sun that must have reached a temperature of over sixty degrees, with all the lovely variegated colours of autumn exposed to their great advantage, one couldn't help but be deeply conscious of the landscape which was doubly enhanced. How rich and lush were these lovely English scenes compared with the bare and barren Greek countryside? I wonder what those hardy Greek shepherds and goatherds would say on seeing such a wealth of grass? How intimately friendly is this land with its hazel hedges, its small fields and woods, its warm red-bricked and secluded farmhouses, with those quaint oast houses cowled like nuns, its grass-edged and oh-so-smooth roads, its rambling five-barred gates and enticing stiles, and perhaps, best of all, the glory of the trees, stately beeches, now turning to a warm amber, the chestnuts that seem to have a certain air of dampness, which perhaps emanates from the moist leaf-strewn ground about them; the ancient oaks whose leaves seem to resist so strongly the turning of the year; the dark towering firs, the less solemn pines, and the ladies of the woods – the silver birches. And pride of the hedges are the dark glistening hollies showing off a glorious crop of deep red clustered berries, vying in this respect with the drab and perhaps less poetic hawthorn. The grey and ancient village churches push their towers up above the yews whose curious lantern-like berries are already beginning to fall.

And in this panoply of the woods live those birds – the winter residents – that must have been part and parcel of this land for hundreds of years – the tits, finches, yellow buntings, thrushes, woodpeckers, jays, and, of course, the ubiquitous robin, whose winter 'creekings' can be heard in almost every hedge and garden. So, whether you hold your head high or low, there is always some fair view, be it only a murky leaf-strewn pond, from whose bordering sedge swims an unexpected and comic coot.

This, then, was the background of our walk which started at Eridge station along the lane to Motts Mill, through Buckhurst Park, where we collected sweet chestnuts, and horse chestnuts for Nicolas, and in a grassy ride we lunched in the warm sun. Then on to Withyham and back through Five Hundred Acre Wood to Friar's Gate, Maiden's Hill, St. John's Common (which has been desecrated by an army barracks), and finally Crowborough in time for tea and the four o'clock bus home.

28.10.45   The lovely Indian summer ended in the great storm of the last five days which has at last abated somewhat, although there have been further gale warnings. For the present the wind no longer shrieks around the house, Much damage has been done along the coast and many mines washed ashore. So great has been this storm that all cross-channel sailings had to be stopped, and this has brought me some good luck. My leave has, as a result, been extended for four days, and I now return on 7th November. I have, therefore, a particular liking for storms at the moment. John has, likewise, had four days extension.

One piece of news that has depressed us somewhat and I have not so far mentioned in these notes, is the postponement of release of all officers of groups 21-24, for at least three months. This is the first breach of faith by the Government over the release scheme, the principles of which they have so often affirmed would not be broken. Now a person who happens to have been commissioned is to be held back, more than a person who happens not to have been commissioned. It has been viewed with utter disgust, more so as in the last official announcement it was naively stated that the Government was always aware of the shortage of officers. This is their way of filling the gap! It means, of course, further hardship in longer separation, delay in returning to civil life and civil occupation, delay in studying for the professions, delay in marriages, not to mention the further sense of uncertainty, and loss of faith in one's own countrymen. The official statement went on glibly to say that it was hoped the release dates of later groups, i.e. 25 onwards, would be delayed 'little, if at all'! Group 25 (officers) should have begun to be released at the latest by the end of January or beginning of February. And yet group 21 (officers) is not be completed now till 12th February. How long will it take to release groups 22, 23 and 24 officers? I shall indeed be very surprised if my release is not delayed more than a little. I await with the keenest interest for the dates of release of group 25. It is most upsetting to have to contend with such bad planning at this stage, and it is only to be hoped that Mr. Lawson is doing everything in his power to alleviate the effects of this monstrous decision.

4.11.45   And so this glorious, this serene interlude, is coming to its inevitable close. The inroads of time, innocuous enough to the blissfully unwary, are at last beginning to assert themselves. But to be wary is of no help, and indeed only serves to emphasise one's helplessness. Time, the insatiable locust, gathers everything in its path, and its movement is irresistible. But though time can devour, it cannot destroy. Therefore, my mood is not to contend but to be thankful. These days have been everything that I could have wished them. Not for many years have I enjoyed such peace of mind; indeed, not since we were first married in 1939. However, this joyous reunion has not deluded us about the malevolent gods that still stare sometimes through our windows. Shadows cast up by an unsettled and unhappy world sometimes cast their shapes over the happiest of people. And who but fools would ignore them? Who, after a war that really started in 1914 and ended this year, can afford to ignore them? 'The peace that passeth understanding' is far, very far, from the hearts of countless millions. The world is still a grand hunting ground for the devil. It is amazing how many people still get endless pleasure from goading the devil on his works. Incredible it is then to say, even for a brief spell, that I have been content – against this dark background, but such is the case. For my own little background has been 'Benallan' with its embodiment and sense of home as inspired by Dulcie and Nicolas. To be home, to have a home, that is without doubt the prayer of the times. To have such a home, endowed with the sense and happy spirit that marks my own, is an ideal not easily surpassed in days such as these. Some people have told me I look younger of late. Perhaps it is not surprising – even I can feel the effect of the mental and physical relaxation that this home leave has brought me. Such, however, have been the vicissitudes of our generation that it seems almost wicked to say one is happy!

11.11.45   Thus a week sees me back on Italian soil and many things that I would like to have noted have been left unwritten. However, perhaps in the future I may be able to recapture some of it. Many impressions have been received and emotions felt in this last brief span of happiness, which culminated in the inevitable and sad parting. Dulcie and I have had many partings since 1940, but I think perhaps this last one was almost the hardest to bear. It was as though a way of living had been shown to us, in which the practical and beautiful had been pleasantly combined – and then suddenly it was rudely snatched away from us. For it was long enough to make the end seem dim, and we lived as though it would never be. The greater then the shock. And because the fighting was over, the necessity for my return, so we rationalised, seemed no longer to exist, but whatever we thought, it had to be, and I think we were both glad when the last day was over.

'Pop'* took Nicolas for a walk in the afternoon and when they returned I was, as Nicolas says, in my 'soldier's clothes'. Finally then came tea (Dulcie had saved a poached egg – even I remember how upset Nicolas was that he didn't have one, eggs being his great weakness), then our last goodbye, and at last valise and pack on the pushchair, out of the warm lit cosiness into the dark night. The lane was particularly dark that night and long will I remember Nicolas' shadow in the circle of light made by Dulcie's torch. He danced with delight at the sight of his huge head and feet, and made many attempts to catch his shadow. This, at any rate, served to distract our sad thoughts, as did his undiminished joy on finding a cat at the bus stop. Then round the corner came the well-lit double decker bus, and soon even Dulcie's waving hand faded into the darkness. The emptiness and helplessness that follows these cruel partings must be familiar to millions of people. Time and events surreptitiously soothe the troubled mind.

14.11.45   We reached the Transit Camp at Novara, a city some thirty miles from Milan, on 10.11.45 and were housed in the barracks of the ex-17 Italian Regiment, whose battle honours (some I noticed in the last war) were displayed in the main entrance. Like all barracks, it was austere and ugly to a degree, just a mass of concrete rooms and staircases.

---

*Father-in-law.

However, we were made very comfortable by the German prisoners of war and Italian women who worked there, and the food was excellent.

On the 11th, we left for Taranto but detrained instead at San Spirito near Bari. It soon transpired that we are likely to be here for a week or more, and when possible we would be taken to our boat at Taranto. But nothing is certain at the moment and we all well pleased for this further delay in rejoining our units.

Scanning through the news of the past few days, I found a further announcement about officer releases has been made. It was to the effect that groups 22, 23 and 24 would probably be out about the end of March, and 25 *et seq.* would come out with their respective groups. It follows, therefore, that group 24 is being released over a period of about three months, group 25 starting release presumably about the beginning of April. The question immediately springs to mind – how long will it take to demobilise group 25 which has 80,000 more men than group 24? If group 31 is still the target for the end of June, it will have to be completed by the end of April at the latest. I think April is a fair bet to see me out of the Army. May the next five months speed by as they have never sped before. But I still cannot understand why group 24 is taking so long, but maybe my assumptions are all awry.

After a wet night, the weather cleared and this morning I sat out in the warm sunshine on a small balcony overlooking the Adriatic. The smooth sea was broken only near the shore upon which a lovely surf was breaking, the regular waves rolling forward leisurely and rhythmically in long foáming lines. On the grassy shore I heard a meadow pipit, whilst away in the olives, chaffinches and great tits called; occasionally a charm of goldfinches would fly in happy concert. Beyond, rather stark and ugly, rose the buildings and chimneys of Bari.

16.11.45   Transit life in a Camp in the flat olive grove country of south east Italy is pretty lifeless and negative, and the proximity of the more lively seashore is only tantalising in that prisoner of war hutments, damned wire, and so forth, prevent free and undisturbed access.

The cloud scenery over the Adriatic has been fascinating to watch. For whilst over the land the sky is usually clear, over the sea those high, amorphous and faintly translucent cumuli – the 'battalion' of Rupert Brooke's 'Pacific' poem – seem strangely stilled. There, in those high, ethereal places, light and shadow harmonise in beautiful pastel.

Then one has to return to the frightening vulgarity of a transit mess, with its bar and high stools, its painted pin-ups, its billiards and darts, its impersonal masculinity, its whole blatant gaudiness. Could anything be colder or more unhomelike? And sometimes at night its hard toneless walls reverberate with the hideous shattering din of a dance band.

These are the things that men provide for men's comfort and enjoyment. When the welfare of men has to be considered, these are the things that naturally spring to mind. For most, perhaps, they fulfil a necessity, for a few, I know, they make a great void, so lacking of all the warmth and gentleness is it of the life I have just left behind me. Here I am lonely and cold, so I fill the gap with what books I can get (and what a dearth of them) and with memories and longings. But these last are often two-edged in their action. Oh, but what a waste it all is – what a dreadful imprisonment.

The German bar attendant will turn on the wireless; sometimes it will be a lovely symphony – I strain my ears to catch the theme – but the clatter of drunken voices, the sound of billiard balls, feet, and voices and voices and voices. But it is useless – be it Beethoven, Brahms, Sibelius, Mozart, Dvorak – it is quite useless; here music falls on the stoniest of stony ground.

29.11.45   Much, and yet nothing, has happened in the last nine days. It has been a story of moving from one place to another in various forms of comfort and discomfort, and then of our final arrival at Khalkis, when, strangely enough, we were hurled into a whirlpool of bureaucratic military activity.

First, a move to Taranto, then boarding H.M.T. *Matoroa*. Again, waiting, lines of men jostling, kit, waiting – so endless, so purposeless. Such a damned waste. I was glad to get to my cabin, and even more glad to go down to dinner, for by that time I was ravenous, and I was on the second sitting. The lounge was really too crowded to be enjoyable, but it wasn't unpleasant by any means. This was the afternoon of the 21st, and we were due to sail then, but this was postponed till the afternoon of the 22nd. The weather had not been very promising and I was indeed relieved to find the sea so calm. It was most pleasant to saunter round the decks in the evening, all very well lit, and occasionally good music coming over the tannoy system. I could not help remembering the strict blackout of my previous trips. There is a great atmosphere of spaciousness and adventure about the boat decks at night.

1.12.45   The mad Greek who drove us to the 30 Reception Camp gave us all a horrible feeling in the bottom of our stomachs. He would approach a busy traffic centre, push in the clutch, change into some sort of gear, and then press on a very doubtful footbrake, and just hope for the best. As for blowing his horn – it was incredible, a continuous effort in whatever the circumstances –   most often when vehicles in front were quite unable to move away. 30 Reception Camp was cold and messy; perhaps my cold gave me a wrong impression, but I shall never like that place now, having been off colour on both occasions there. We waited there nearly all day for our kit, and once it arrived we were despatched in a 3-tonner to the 4 Division Transit Camp at Kifissia. We arrived there after dark and found the officers' quarters without lights which was cheerful to say the least of it. I was feeling so seedy that once I had procured more blankets and made my bed I retired forthwith and let the cold moaning wind make its ghostly noises to its heart's content.

The next day was pleasantly sunny and I felt a little better. I got up late, and was not sorry to be leaving the badly kept billet which houses unfortunate officers in transit. It was dirty, it was bare, and even with the sun it presented a cold appearance.

This first week has been busily spent settling to a life that we left over two months ago. Peter Gorst had to go after the first day to take over 4 Division Transit Camp, and there was much to do, but once we knew the latest position regarding routine, personnel, LIAP, Release, etc., most outstanding items were soon dealt with. The new C.O. seems a typical regular and doesn't bother us much.

We live in the Hotel Pallaria and mess in the old battalion H.Q. – mess rather well, in fact, – but, oh, those long-winded dinners! So our life is stretched along the Khalkis seafront, the barracks and the mess being the extremes, the Pallaria the happy medium, where a room each with a bed, table and a wardrobe, gives us sufficient comfort, and that desperately needed privacy.

8.12.45   Recent information has brought the shock that our stay in Khalkis may come to an abrupt end. Accordingly, the gloom which is the natural outcome of the uncertainty of our release and the negativeness of army life has now been deepened by the fact that we may be rooted out of the deep emplacement of our winter quarters, into which we are well and truly settled.

The new threat has arisen because India is demanding that all Indian troops be returned immediately, and if the demand is met, 4 Indian Division, who are stationed in the Salonika area, will be relieved by 4 British Division. A move by road to Salonika in winter, some 300 miles over the most bloody road and passes, is not exactly an enticing thought. The shortage of drivers, due to LIAP and releases, has meant that the bulk of our transport has been put into cold storage, and a move now would mean that every 'odd sod' would have to drive. It is to be hoped that carriers would go by sea, or, better still, not go at all.

Happily, the Indian request is being fought tooth and nail at a very high
level, and our proposal is that 4 Indian Division stays until after the
elections in March. If that is not accepted then the Divisional Commander
has made a special plea that we stay in our present area till after Christmas, which would be something. It doesn't look as though we would get
any extra transport, so how we would move in one go, I just don't know.
The journey, I understand, will take about six days. I have no wish
whatsoever to see Salonika, and I sincerely hope that the move doesn't
come off, or at least is delayed till the elections, by which time I hope to
have been released! Just now we are preparing for the worst, but praying
like hell for a favourable decision. This business of playing the 'shadowy
nurse' to the Greeks is becoming intolerable. Why not leave Salonika to
the Greeks? They'll have to be left alone one day.

12.12.45   The last four days have been marked by the return of John
              Worthington from LIAP, looking in a very rude health, and
bouncing about like an enigma on a bit of elastic; also, as ever, by lengthy
screeds to write regarding army organisations – a seemingly never-ending
occupation, and I suppose rightly so, at least if they took any notice of
what one said; some release news, and last but first – some letters from
Dulcie. Salonika is still unpleasantly in the balance, and if we do go the
carriers and heavy kit will go by sea, and consequently the driver situation
is not so drastic, although it's bad enough to have to prepare a plan to stop
drivers' LIAP until after the move, if it comes off.

If the Division does move, we have been given an extra commitment of
providing a staging camp at Levádhia. This would be the first staging
camp *en route* for units from the Athens area, etc. There is nothing really
that we can do until there is a decision by the gods – those military and
political men. In the meantime, it looks as though the Greek winter is
about to kick off. There was a cold nip in the air this morning, with a lot of
cloud about. Then a breeze sprang up which pressed the cloud down over
the island in an impenetrable blanket. By afternoon the breeze had become a stiff breeze, and tonight it's a howling north wind which makes
noises in the streets and around the houses reminiscent of *Wuthering
Heights*. The sea soon showed its teeth and caught the Khalkis fishermen
unawares in the channel, and their boats tied up at the delivery points
on the promenade quickly began a bucking stampede. There was much
shouting, pushing and pulling of ropes, and other aquatic devices, a spot
of fighting, and I should imagine a great deal of Greek blaspheming, as
the excited men got their boats under some sort of control. The mimosa
trees, which relish the calm heat of summer, sighed and swayed in this

demoniacal wind, which sends all Greeks scurrying along the bare street for shelter and warmth. As I sit in my room I can hear the sea swishing to and fro over the promenade. Tonight the bleak hills are astir with the weird moanings of the northern gods.

14.12.45 And as so often happens in Greece, the howling wind ceased suddenly, the clouds passed by, and a clear cold starlit night which brought frost was followed by a most glorious sunrise. The slanting rays of the sun striking the red rocky earth, and the red tiles of the humble dwelling houses, bring forth a warmth of colour and tone which is most beautiful. The cloudless azure sky vies with the sea for a blue that will shame the other; but each is unique and glorious, the deep blue giving a moving solidity to the sea, the turquoise an ethereal remoteness to the sky above. The shapely mountains, some with their first touch of snow, leave colour contours in the sharp frosty air. Dappling sunlight glistens on the mimosas that line the pavements. The smooth sea is alive again with caiques and other boats, for these seamen have a lively trade to pursue. And very picturesque it is to see one of these boats come into the promenade loaded with fruit and vegetables and fish, etc., and, of course, they take useful things back to the remote parts of the islands. Today, for instance, I saw tiles being loaded on.

Thus it is today, Greece in winter, and for me Greece at her most beautiful. The air is clean, the elements are sane, and the colours subtropical. Typifying Greece are the predominant blues of all shades, and merging into the blue a curious whiteness. The whiteness of sun, of the sky where it goes to meet the horizon, of house fronts, of seagulls, of reflected sunlight, of a train of clouds hugging the mountain tops.

This then was the scene that confronted me this morning as I walked to the barracks, and on my way I could not resist taking a look at heaven on earth from Khalkis bridge. The woodwork of the bridge was still covered in rime from last night's frost, and that somehow amazed me in that, looking down on the twisted and worn wood, I could not help thinking of the arid and violent heat that must fall on those same boards in summer. It was a fleeting thought, however, for I was soon gazing with a wondering admiration at the snow-clad beauty of Olympus, and all the lower snow-touched ranges of the island. The beauty of mountains is greatly enhanced when seen from the sea, which was what I was virtually doing. Blue, blue, dark blue, white, perhaps the dark necklace of pines, the warmth of red stone, sharp points of white, but mostly blue; what words are there to describe this lovely scene? For words are much too clumsy a medium for the interpretation of colour. It was a symphony in blue and white; many a

time in the barracks did I look up at the clear sky and the dark line of
the hills, feeling a hapless imprisonment. Inside the dark heavy walled
building the rooms struck chill and bare, and whenever I looked out of
my windows my eye met the blue sky over the roofscape of an eastern
town.

Back at the mess, I found three letters from Dulcie and decided to read
them in the little walled-in garden behind the mess, where there would be
no distraction, and where the warmth of the sun was glorious to feel. It
was in this garden, where the chicken called with a sleepy resonance,
where the tangerine and lemon trees showed off to advantage their lovely
fruit against dark sunlit leaves, where looking up over the four encircling
walls I could see the dome of a mosque-like church silhouetted against the
pure blue sky, it was here that I read the news I had been waiting for –
Dulcie was to have another baby. Curious that this unknown child should
be somehow connected with this little garden, which with its newly-dug
beds, the chicken, and the black pig, its oriental trees, I shall now never
forget, and he or she may never see it.

17.12.45   The latest announcement regarding release indicates that of-
           ficers of my group are to be subjected to a deferment of nearly
two months. The other ranks of this group are being released between
10th January and 5th February, which means that they will be leaving
Greece in a week or so. 25 group officers are not even mentioned, but the
announcement states that the release of 24 group officers will commence
on 20th February. No completion date was given. There has never been
any official pronouncement that 25 group officers would be deferred. The
groups specifically mentioned were 22-24, and further statements have
tried to make it clear that subsequent groups would be delayed 'little, if at
all'!! What, I wonder, is the official interpretation of the word 'little' in
this context? To Mr. Lawson, or the Service Chiefs, six weeks may seem
'very little', but the officer who is abroad, and has had some years' service
abroad, a further six weeks of enforced separation from his home, and
return to his civilian occupation, represents an iniquitous, and in the
circumstances, a thoroughly surreptitious deferment, for which, courtesy
if nothing else, would deem some kind of explanation to be necessary.
Officers have had plenty of uncertainty about their release but to add to
their lot this kind of underhand deferment is adding insult to injury –
hardly the treatment they deserve. In effect, this latest bleak statement
seems that instead of leaving Greece towards the end of December we
shall be lucky to leave till after February is out. It's an unhappy way to
finish one's war service.

24.12.45   The latest information about our move to Salonika is that it is
            unlikely that the battalion will leave Khalkis before the middle
of February at the earliest. Other units of the Division are moving before
that, and it is hoped mainly by sea. In the meantime, D compay has been
given the job of the Levádhia transit camp, as I had wished, and I have to
make a recce there on the 27th, to study the layout. There is no exact
information as yet as to the date of our being able to function, or as to
 the nature of our responsibilities but there will be much to do, and I
expect to leave Khalkis by early in the New Year at the latest. I have
grumbled about transit camps many times, and it seems only right that it
should befall to me to run one of my own! – whatever the difficulties. It
will, indeed, be nice to have the company detached from the battalion
again.
25.12.45   *Christmas Day*. And, pray God, the last Christmas Day in the
            Army. But I have no feeling of Christmas today, except per-
haps that I have a rather unhappy feeling in my stomach, which, I think,
must be the result of last night's orgy at the Sgts.' mess! In fact, it's a
moot point as to what is the real cause of my tummy trouble, for I am not
the only sufferer. In the early hours of the morning there was a constant
flow of traffic to the 'seat of custom', and on one occasion I'm afraid I
very nearly fainted. Dripping with sweat, I staggered back to my room,
dried myself and was amazed to see a white ghostly face staring at me in
the mirror. It was horrible. I thought I had detected bad beer in our own
mess last night, and when at breakfast this morning there was a general
comparing of notes, the doctor brought out the version of bad beer. The
grim humour of it all is that we are meant to be playing the Sgts. at
football this afternoon in a Comic Game. The way the Army spend Christmas is enough to drive some men out of it. To me it seems a toilsome day.
    But whether it was bad beer or just the odd mixture plied to us by the
Sgts. I do not know. Sgts. usually have peculiar ideas about a sociable
evening. To the initiated all may seem well at the start – a glass of beer, a
game of darts, a quiet chat; now this is all right, you say, but you say it too
soon, for just then some very old Sgt. comes up who knew you in so and
so, and remembers Salerno, and before you know where you are, there is a
double neat whisky at your hand, and finally the stage is set. All your
good resolutions about making *this* evening at least a reasonably sober
one are at once at stake. To refuse is courting trouble, to drink all they
offer is knocking at hell's door; it resolves itself into a game of getting
the other chap drunk first so that he won't notice you are only sipping
the whisky! Sherry, beer, port and solid whisky or gin, what a heathen

concoction indeed, but it's nothing to a Sgt., at least to some. For suddenly there will be a gathering round and a tottering body will be carried out of the room in a horizontal position. But one takes no notice of that. It's a good thing these parties only come once in a while!

During the party there was a horrendous thunderstorm with hail, the culmination perhaps of what has been a spell of very sultry weather. When I got back to my room there was a great puddle of water on the floor – my French windows had been left open and the hail and rain had driven in. All my Christmas cards were flat on their backs. Today the wind has veered and it is again in the north and much fresher.

And so, weather beaten and somewhat torn, we stand this day and look back over the last six grey years. Six grey years of war. And today, amid the perplexity of current affairs – the fighting in Java, the different policies, ensuing friction in the zones of the powers occupying Germany, the threat of Allied disunity, the grim reality of the vast American loan with its hard terms, demobilisation, votes of censure against nationalisation, crime waves, war criminal trials, conditions in Europe, the continued shortage of housing, clothes, coal and food – amid all this we sink rather tired into the armchair of this Christmas and thank God for small mercies, hardly hoping or daring to expect more.

My thoughts turn naturally to home, to Dulcie and Nicolas. Nicolas, now fully aware of the Christmas atmosphere, will, I expect, be thoroughly happy with all his new toys and presents. He will have entered into the spirit of the day with an energetic excitement. Would I were there to see it all. And you, Dulcie my love, with your new child, what I wonder are you thinking? You, at least, who have had the responsibility of bringing up Nicolas during these hard years, will know that the next years ahead will not be easy, but then you are confident, and for that I am eternally grateful; for how can a woman who has no confidence be happy about the child she is soon to bring into the world? You, darling, have not only the confidence of motherhood, it is greater than that, it is the confidence in life itself. And so, darling, with my release and homecoming, then the advent of Toni (and who can deny our wish for a girl; my wish in particular is for a 'second you'), our eyes and thoughts turn naturally from the present to the not-too-distant future.

> And so his sojourn came to an end
> And looking up, he saw a bright light
> And he made ready to go.

I pray God that with the passing of the years, the sense of wonder that Christmas engenders will not diminish. This thought came to me in a

Church Service we had on Sunday. It was a carol service, and I love to sing carols. For the familiar tunes of the favourite carols are, to me, an embodiment of the Christmas spirit. The very music provides a nostalgic atmosphere. And yet on Sunday morning something was wrong. There was a feeling of emptiness, a feeling of doing something because it had to be done. And I don't think it was because it was an Army Service, or anything like that. It was just that the spirit of Christmas wasn't there. The piano was tinny, I grant, but where there's a will there's a way, especially with carols. Perhaps it was the fact that it was so disconnected with home. Perhaps it was the noisy Greeks who had come to watch the Service; it may even have been the unfamiliar smell of a Greek Cathedral. Anyway, the Service seemed like so much clockwork; we stood, rising rather half-heartedly and on the wrong note; we sat to listen to a lesson; we stood again and so on. It was frigid, automatic, unfriendly and unfelt.

29.12.45   Subsequent events had almost put out of mind what was, in any case, a feeble Christmas. Even the joy of the sun was denied us, and that was sufficient to make the day a very ordinary one. Boxing Day was dull, wet, and generally unpleasant, and nothing special happened to break its monotony.

The following day I had to make my recce for a transit camp at Levádhia. This was the last day I had to do it, as the C.O. was in a Conference at Division on the 29th, and had to have my report on the 28th. During the night 26/27 a strong wind got up, bringing great gusts of rain, which at times were torrential. It was that macabre northerly wind that has a heaviness about it, and moans madly and incessantly about the windows. When Pickering, my batman, came to wake me, he could hardly push the door open against the draught that came through the French windows, and when he did succeed the windows burst open in a crashing frenzy. It was 6.00 a.m. and very dark. I could hear the rain spluttering on the streets, and the mimosas sighing furiously. How loath I was to leave my warm blankets. The long journey ahead seemed, amidst such comfort and cosiness, a frightful effort. But up I had to get and soon I was struggling, head down, to the mess, where I had breakfast with Peter Gorst who was to accompany me.

We left soon after 7.00 a.m. I had three Sgts. and C/S Candler in the relative comfort of a Ford fifteen-hundred weight and Peter in a jeep. I had had good reports of the road worthiness of a Ford, and I was very glad to have listened to their advice for, despite all, I think it was about the most comfortable vehicle I have ever travelled in on the so-called roads of Greece. In the half light of dawn, the water-filled ruts and holes had the glint of armour. The gleam of the lights we used till over the pass, which takes you out of Khalkis, touched the armour with gold. The olive trees, dancing madly in the wind and rain, were to be seen in the same yellow light for a few brief moments. Frantically they shook, bowed, sighed, and were gone. The wheels of the car frequently dashed spray against the windscreen from the many lurking puddles. The mountains were covered in a great swirling woolly mist. The light of day brought with it only better visibility, and little colour.

The brown water-logged fields were brightened occasionally by the fresh green of winter wheat, or a patch of thin grass brought up by the recent rain. Near some pines we came across a large gathering of hoodie crows, and in the hawthorn-strewn fields magpies made a great fuss as we approached. The road shone with the colour almost of blood, for the water had been infected with the red soil. Red streams born in the fields and on the hillsides rushed across the road at many points, taking away what little surface there was. Thus might we have been moving along some strange sea, for mile after mile we bobbed and dipped and splashed and churned along the pitted, grim and watery road. Save for the odd birds, a shepherd and his sheep, or a hardy peasant on his mule, it was a bare empty road we travelled that morning.

Once through Thebes we began the most treacherous and never-ending stretch to Levádhia, a route now familiar for its scenery of sombre mountains, derelict villages, as well as a quite unbelievably bad surface.

After being on the road for nearly four hours, we finally reached our destination, and I went forthwith to the place called 'Peter's Corner', which was, in fact, used as a Transit Camp. Then came the business of finding the O.C., looking for accommodation, and getting all the information we could. It transpired that the only real accommodation that could be used to extend the present facilities was a school that stood next door. I saw the Authorities, who seemed ready enough to let chaps sleep there if necessary, even in term time. This would have to be ratified but, failing the school, tents would have to be erected if you were to accommodate 400, and this was the last thing I wanted to do.

The whole business was rather confused for Capt. Frost (the O.C.) had been told by the General that he would be there till March, and Capt. Frost said he could run it even for the larger numbers with about a further ten men, bringing his total up to about thirty! The idea of taking a company there was absurd as this would reduce considerably the accommodation for those in transit. He had, of course, heard nothing about our coming to take over, and the end of our visit saw us pretty mystified as to exactly what was happening about this Transit Camp. But later information was to throw considerable light on the matter.

We stayed to lunch and soon after began the long journey back. It had now stopped raining, but that didn't make the journey any shorter! I met the C.O. in Thebes, on his way to Athens, and put him in the picture, and he said he would try and get out of doing the job, but Division had been definite about it being our responsibility.

During the day a letter about the Levádhia Camp said that 2 N.F. would absorb the present staff and that a Major or senior Captain would be appointed as staging post commander. The Camp was to be functioning by the 14th January and we were to increase the staff as we thought fit. So now it remains to be seen what the C.O. decides. If he sends me, it means virtually that I lose command of D company which would, under the new circumstances, stay practically intact. At this stage I should be unhappy to do this for the sake of running a camp which is already being capably run by an officer who has been there six weeks. And information has now reached me that we will not leave Khalkis till March, by which time I hope to be released. The C.O. is back tomorrow and we have a conference on Monday, but I hope to know one way or another by tomorrow.

And so, in rather a hectic aftermath, Christmas has been forgotten and our thoughts are centred about our activities in the early New Year. But with the first party of 25 group departing on Monday, it is just as well that I am given no time to brood on the circumstances of the release scheme. *Tempus fugit* indeed, and well it might! For how glad will I be to cast off this khaki life for ever. Life today is like a fever that never lets you rest. Will it always be like this?

30.12.45 My fate has been decided, and I leave for Levádhia tomorrow to take over the Transit Camp. The C.O. said he wanted me to get the thing started and then he hoped to get me back in a fortnight or so! Knowing the Army, I can see myself staying there for a goodly time. The rather complicated administrative instructions brought forth many problems which can only be solved on the spot, and some of them will be pretty good headaches as far as I can see. The C.O. wanted D company to be dissolved and the personnel posted to other companies. Later I got him to change his mind, for this would have meant chaos. Much better to treat my party as a detachment and leave the pre-framework of the company in working order to keep continuity. It was rather a rush order to move tomorrow, but I want to get there as soon as possible and I am only taking a small working party, sending back for specialists after consultation with

Frost. I shall miss my room overlooking the harbour and the fishing fleet, but such it has to be. Rather ironical that today I should be saying goodbye to men of my own group. It is indeed an unexpected parting of the ways.

3.1.46   The fact that the New Year has begun has been lost in the seething activity of taking over Peter's Corner Camp, and getting it looking to my liking. And there was much about the place and its existing staff that I didn't like, and I'm afraid I lost my temper occasionally and made myself generally unpleasant. But the place was filthy, the staff casual and ill-dressed, and there just was no air of purpose about the place whatsoever. So I immediately became a kind of 'atomic broom' and started sweeping at hurricane force. The building itself is an old asylum, and at times during these last three days I'm sure it must have been saying to itself – 'Just like old times!'

I had a quick inspection of the whole camp and found it quite filthy, dangerously so, in fact, and I thanked heaven it wasn't summer. There were old uncovered latrines, which had reached cesspool saturation, and finding an impermeable bottom had formed disgusting pools that would never have gone away. It was not just a matter of filling in, for as you heaped the earth, so an equal quantity of most undelectable liquid went overboard, making things a most horrible mess. We had to use a lot of ingenuity to complete that unpleasant task, and I was never so happy as when I saw the 'Foul Ground' signs standing like crosses marking the evil place! It turned out that the whole sanitary system was vastly overburdened, and I couldn't rest until things had been put right, and a method of daily disposal enforced. The whole place had an aroma of swill, and I can remember now that first night when the stink even bothered me as it invaded my room through the open window. How I longed for some creosote to arrive! And so, besides getting some sort of office routine established, the last two days have been an orgy of cleaning up, both inside and outside the buildings.

So by yesterday evening much had been attended to and I feel very much happier about things, and to cap the day most gloriously came four letters from Dulcie, and two Christmas cards. It really was a joy to receive that mail and learn all about the Christmas festivities at home, for it was the first time that Nicolas was truly aware of Christmas as such, and what a haul of presents he had. I lost myself completely in those happy homely scenes, and admin. orders about the move to Salonika, the camp, and all its petty problems went to the winds for a brief glorious spell.

We get all sorts of curious people through here. A day or so ago we had a Graves Registration Officer whose job it is to go out and collect bodies dead or alive. He said he often had some interesting cases! Often his only means of transport was mules, by which he would make his way to some lonely spot where a crashed airman had been buried, or to some remote mountain village in search of information.

Then at lunch today we had Charles Dickens' grandson, a Capt. Richard Shuckborough, M.C., a divisional staff officer well known in the Division. Tall and large-framed, his big head and the set of his hair were faintly reminiscent of Regency times. He told us a story (amusingly) of a certain officer in the Division who had to fly from Salonika to Athens, who after certain frightening incidents at last realised that his pilot was quite drunk. So drunk, in fact, that he passed out. A Sgt., unqualified in the art of flying, took over and the pilot was brought round to make an odd landing at Athens!

Our biggest trouble here is lack of accommodation for those in transit. We have two large nissen huts, and when they are filled, we sleep men in the corridors of the building, and in the dining hall. And so we are surrounded with men going on release or LIAP, new reinforcements, drivers, and other casuals, all making a nook for themselves to sleep the night. If we fill up here, we then resort to the billet in the town, and if even that overflows, our last reserve will be the school or tents, when they are erected. Accordingly, we get all manner of men in many moods; a truck load of 'group happy 25s' set off their high spirits against the unfortunate young men who have just come out as reinforcements, and have tasted for the first time the joys of travelling the Greek roads in the back of a three-tonner. There is, then, almost every night a great murmuration of voices outside my door.

The Communists have been troublesome again in Levádhia and in Lamia, and shootings and grenade throwing have taken place. Prices are quite exorbitant for all the ordinary and necessary foodstuffs, and the average Greek has so little faith in his currency that he will just not sell anything.

The Government is so inept that the Black Market thrives whilst all the poor people go hungry. Great disturbances have arisen at the distribution of Red Cross parcels for the needy, for knowing of old how the well-to-do and favoured ones usually come off best, they attempt as it were a stampede to ensure they get something. Presidents and Greek clergy are not to be relied upon for the distribution of food and clothing. It is indeed a terrible land.

5.1.46   Sam, the interpreter, who helped us out over the school, has some interesting stories to tell, mostly about his own life. He often gets the odd job to do for us and the other day when he was in I had a chat with him. He fought with the Americans in the last war, thereby I understand entitling himself to become a U.S. citizen, and served in the occupation of Germany for eleven months. He also served with U.S. army in Mexico, looking for revolutionaries and such like, but it was no good, he said, 'in those dam' mountains'! Then, like most Greeks, he came back to his land of origin to settle down on his earnings and live a relative life of ease, as one could in peacetime out here. He married and had children, and everything in the garden was lovely, especially, according to him, under Venezuelos, but not so hot under Metaxas, whose *dictati* methods caused much bloodshed. Then, of course, came the war, and the campaign against the Italians, who for all their superior equipment were outmatched and outfought in this hard land by the ferocious ill-equipped Greek army. But the Germans wanted Greece as a jumping ground for the Middle East. They intervened and like a tidal wave swamped the whole country. Instead of the daily sight of train loads of happy singing Italian prisoners, who at the sight of a Greek woman forgot all about their army life – instead of them came the grim unfriendly Germans, and not in trains.

It was Easter when they first poured into Levádhia, and Easter is a time of great joy in Greece. The people dress in their best clothes, they sing, they go to church, they hold colourful festivities. The church bells were ringing and most of the people were inside the churches when the Germans came. Suddenly they heard the din of hundreds of aircraft and the sound of guns. The churches were machine-gunned from the air. Many people were killed at their prayers, but mostly they stayed in the churches. Then down the road came the thunder of tanks and vehicles, and marching troops who were full of the 'Heil Hitler' stuff. Hundreds of swastikas flew on the tanks and vehicles. Immediately all the public buildings were taken over and guarded by German troops.

Sam got to the hospital before they came to take a note from a dying New Zealander, who Sam said was 'nearly going crazy with some pain in his head'! Sam was asked to get the note to the New Zealanders some way or other. The next day the man was dead, and the Germans had taken over the hospital. Later the other patients were evacuated as prisoners.

One incident Sam remembers very clearly. Some German troops were marching in one of the streets when a German aircraft came over and machine gunned them – a German soldier fell dead. The pilot had thought they were Andartes, but over the air he heard what had happened and landed in a nearby field. When he got to the town he found he had killed his own brother. The man was buried and the pilot went back to his aircraft, but he did not show what he must have been thinking.

Then after the first flush of another Wehrmacht victory came the long grim occupation, with its starvation, its shootings, its looting. Methodically the Hun set about bleeding the country white, both materially and morally. They took what they wanted and paid for nothing. It was the custom of Greek girls to store up a supply of dresses to last them a lifetime; the Germans took the lot. Trainloads, said Sam, of dresses and valuables went back to Germany. But the Greeks are a hard people and were never completely broken. They have been used to strife all their life, and it wasn't long before the Germans began to be afraid of their underground activities, for fear breeds such things as mass shootings, and the burning down of whole villages. The cold unfriendly German soon learnt what a hostile country he was in, but very often the Greek Communists carried out acts which were contrary to the general wishes of the people. They would lie in the corn and shoot up a car. Fifty young men would be seized and shot out of hand. Once, he said, after a bomb had been thrown in a window where some Germans were having a party, a great mass of people were surrounded in Levádhia and threatened with shooting. The men were grim, silent, but the women, weeping and wailing, implored that they be spared. A German officer said they would be reprieved if they all made the Hitler salute, which they did, of course, looking, said Sam, like a lot of 'silly flowers'! One version I heard about the starvation in Athens was that the villagers put their prices at an impossible level on purpose because of the treatment they had received from the Athenians in the past.

Sam, of course, had to touch on politics, and he thought the forthcoming elections would be all right and that the Liberals would be returned. He said King George would never come back because he backed many of the unpopular things Metaxas did as dictator. What these things were exactly I don't know; political opponents were disposed of in curious ways, but I thought that happened so often in the Balkans that it would be taken for granted!

But they beat the Italians under Metaxas, and they haven't been united since. Sam voiced the often repeated request that Greece should become part of the British Empire – 'You boys want to stay here for fifteen to twenty years, and then the country will get settled down.' I think a very large percentage of Greeks would be happy to see their country married to Britain, but unfortunately for our imperialists, it is not 'form' nowadays. He had nothing to say for the Communists, the trouble-makers out here, and I feel that his request for us to stay here largely originates from the fear of what the Communists will do when we leave. And there is no doubt that we leave a very potent evil force, which is hooliganism and not communism, lying doggo at the moment. Occasionally it erupts to let off a little steam, serving as an evil portent of things to come to the peace-loving Greeks. Sam thinks that a large number of the best Greeks will emigrate if given the chance, which will, of course, make the country even weaker. Yes, this short rotund and benevolent little man has had a curious life, and now he wants to take his children back to America to educate them and give them a chance to lead happy lives. But his wife, he said, doesn't want to leave Levádhia, and so he is going without them, that is, if he gets the chance. When asked if Levádhia was his home town Sam said, 'No sir, my home town is Kansas City.' Service in the U.S. forces brought Sam a certain wealth in the form of bonds which are still in America.

Writing about Sam has brought to mind a certain joke about the U.S. Army after the last war. An American was explaining to an Englishman about a certain very large BELL in America which, when rung, could be heard for miles and miles around. 'That's funny,' said the Englishman, 'in 1914 we blew a very large TRUMPET which the whole world would have heard but the sound didn't reach you till 1917!'

Sam finished up by telling me briefly of the last horrible sixty days of the German occupation when, whilst retreating northwards, they stripped the country bare, taking everything they could lay their hands on. Bridges were blown, and the German sappers completely wrecked the railway system. Years of toil and strain were all brought to nought in that dreadful finale. What a setting indeed it would have been for the bloody and terrible revolution that nearly came about.

Things have been very lively at the Transit Camp. The D.A.Q.M.G.'s forecast that the staging post business might fall through altogether was confirmed the following day, at least tentatively. The order states that if sea lifts from Piraeus to Salonika continue as scheduled, then staging camps would not be required. We were ordered to complete plans so that the place could be established as a staging camp again at short notice.

I reckoned to be here for three or four days to complete all outstanding work, but I didn't reckon with the weather or with the General. Since then it has been raining without a stop, which has held up most of the work, and in the hills it has been snow all the time. Passes between Lamia and here, and between Thebes and Athens, have become very treacherous, and this in turn caused the General to spend a night here last night. The poor man's saloon car just couldn't stay on the road, and he had himself towed into Levádhia by his jeep. After a pretty nerve-racking journey in the

dark, he arrived here about 2330 hours, somewhat chilled and bleary-
eyed. However, a good meal (God bless the cook!) and a large quantity of
rum soon put him in good fettle, but he didn't sleep, and this morning at
breakfast he was a bit quiet and more like a General! He had been up to
Volos on a duck shoot, and came away early to avoid the bad weather
before going off to Salonika. This morning he started talking about commitments and said he thought 2 N.F. might have to take over the Camp
altogether, so that the old staff could go north to help their already 'Up-to-
the-eyes-in-it' Brigade! He said he would have to investigate it when he
got back, so, irrespective of the new move circumstances, it's quite possible that we remain after all. The fun came this morning when the jeep
wouldn't start. Before long, and after a certain amount of pushing and
heaving, he was sweating profusely, and was even heard to deride these
'bloody shooting parties'! But eventually all was well and he disappeared
in a cloud of rain, duffle coats, gascape, and kit.

9.1.46   Yesterday the weather turned clear and sunny with a crispness
           about it, and I could not resist going for a walk in the afternoon
to taste the freshness of the valleys, and to gaze wonderingly at the snow
draperies of the mountains. I went along the road to Delphi, passing the
German cemetery that is just on the outskirts of Levádhia. I visited this
place one day before, and a forlorn scene it presents, with most of the
crosses missing, some tilted at all angles, some broken and many without
names. I studied the names and dates of some of the crosses, and saw that
many had died in the autumn of '43. I could not help noticing that one
fellow had been born the same day as I, and I tried to picture that day and
the fates that had placed my birth in England and his in Germany. I
wondered whether his mother was still alive, or whether, like mine, she
had been spared the grim knowledge of this second world catastrophe. It
would have, indeed, been an interesting study to be able to observe the
course of the two families since 2nd October 1914. When I visited the
cemetery for the first time I had noticed a rather dilapidated house on the
opposite side of the road. This afternoon there was a sorry scene there for
the heavy rains had made the whole of the front wall collapse. An old
woman and several little girls, presumably her children, were forlornly
gathering up the worthwhile bricks from the heap, but being mud they had
crumbled. The small rooms of the house, now exposed, had been emptied
completely, and it was obvious from the shaky condition of the rest of the
house that reconstruction wouldn't be worthwhile, even if materials were
at hand. So another homeless family is added to the millions in similar
straits all over the world.

Further on, past these morbid scenes, the view was idyllic; Parnassus at
the head of the valley dominated everything, lifting itself out of the lower
slopes in one graceful sweep, and then just beyond the summit, dashing
down in sharp descent to valley level again. It is an abject business trying
to put on paper the glory of a sunlit snow-covered mountain, for words
cannot depict all the loveliness, all the subtleties of light and shade, all the
fascination and majesty of hill solidity, and the amazing serenity that are
its special endowments. One can remember the mood of contemplation,
just as sometimes one can remember a dream. But as a dream is gone in a
flash and for ever, so too does the actual visual and sensual setting of a
particular scene pass into eternity. I can remember, for instance, as I stood
on that road to Delphi, the beautiful warmth of that January sun as it fell
on my khaki battledress; the delightful and happy notes of meadow pipits
and goldfinches; the somniferous sound of sheep bells from across the
valley mingling with the swish and gurgle of a sparkling stream: in my
mind's eye I can conjure up the harrier being chased by a hoodie crow; I
can see, down the road, the little donkeys and horses laden with brushwood, trotting laboriously ahead of their Greek masters, who, to keep
them in check, made peculiar and reverberating labial noises. I can see,
too, the new green of the valley and the lower ridges and beyond, towering into a turquoise sky, and touched by the merest fleck of clouds,
heavenly Parnassus. But this moment, this special setting has gone.

11.1.46   Yesterday I made a journey that I have been promising myself
            for some time. I visited the ruins at Delphi, and thereby en-
joyed an experience which I suppose will be unique in my life. It was just
such a heavenly day as had been granted me on the 9th; a day that makes
you feel restless, that makes you lift your eyes to the far horizons, and
wish yourself away from all the petty turmoil that daily besets you.

So I decided that it was the day for a visit to Delphi. I got Brown and
Candler to come with me, and after an early lunch we set off in the jeep,
with Fus. Speem driving. How infinite, I thought, as we sped along the
twisting road, must have been the causes and circumstances to bring the
four of us together, moving along the mountain road to Delphi at this
particular moment in time. It was quite inevitable that it should happen,
and yet if, as babes in arms, some seer had said to our mothers – 'Ah yes,
let me see, yes on the 10th January 1946 your boy will be visiting the
ruins of Delphi.' How unbelievable it would have seemed.

On my previous walks, Parnassus had seemed just over the brow of
the next ridge but this illusion was soon exposed to us. For mile after mile
we meandered through a scrub and rock-strewn countryside, where an

occasional mountain stream brought the only life and movement in these otherwise still and remote surroundings. On our left ran a high ridge on which the snow line was clearly defined. Dark blotches indicated clusters of fir trees, and when the road ran close to the ridge, a dark sombre shadow was cast over us, and the air was cold. Fortunately we were mostly in sunshine. On our right it was for some time more open, with patches of cultivation, but mostly grim rocky hills were the dominant feature. The whole area was strewn with rocks and boulders and the soil must have had a meagre depth. In the far distance we had a lovely view of hazy snow-capped ridges and mountain tops. There never surely was such a still cloudless day. There was about it the indefinable hush of a June evening. If it had not been for the peasants cutting the brushwood, or loading it onto their donkeys and horses, or for the hardy goatherd tending his flock, we might well have been travelling through an uninhabited land. Strangely enough, the road was uncommonly good, unexpectedly so, in fact, in such a barren and menacing landscape.

And then after passing through a fairly wide valley, in which I found crocuses blooming in the stony fields, we came to a fork, where by the side of the road stood the grave of some Greek who had died I know not how. Here, from an old man who happened to be there with his donkey, we understood that we had to take the road to the right. This led into a narrower valley, almost a defile, and then climbing, twisted through a very rocky and precipitous landscape. Many of the culverts and bridges on this stretch had been blown at some time or other, and such places, now in course of repair, needed careful driving. Soon we were under the fearsome northern precipices of Parnassus, a great grey towering rockface now caught in the afternoon sun. Down in the rock-covered valley below we could see a small party of Greeks with their donkeys, and how minute they seemed, moving slowly and laboriously along a mule track. We reached a col between two valleys and here the road crossed to the Parnassus side.

We were high up now, with a great valley dropping away on our left. Far away to the west was a magnificent view of the distant mountains, and all this part of the road gave me the sensation of being amongst the mountain tops, for we were on a level with the hill crests on the opposite side of the valley. Deep down below was a dark mass of olive trees, whilst the slopes, some at least sixty degrees steep, were often terraced and planted with small vine trees. The walled-in cultivation here was quite amazing, and must surely have bred a very hardy and patient type of Greek. In and around the many re-entrants and spurs of this complex corrugated mountain fastness we went, and quiet and subdued it made us all feel. It was strange to us that people had known and lived in these valleys for thousands of years. So remote did they seem from the pastoral scenes of our own country. Here was the embodiment of the endless struggle between nature and man. It was in a mood of awe and fascination that we completed the last miles of our journey. We had been about an hour and a half on the road.

For the last half hour the road had wended its way along the slopes of Parnassus, which towered above us, serene, aloof, and very still. Soon we came in sight of the quaint village of Arakova, built up like a heap of playing card houses on a prominent spur. It gave much the appearance of some of the Italian medieval hill villages, perched up in defence and defiance to all comers. Passing through the narrow street I noticed that many houses had been destroyed, mostly by fire. This was presumably the grim work of Germans or Italians. Old women sat outside their houses in the sunshine spinning the yarn from the wool with those sticks they have for the purpose. We had one pleasing glimpse of the Corinth Canal, which far below us struck an unexpected blue tongue of water into the dark landscape.

Suddenly we saw the ruins, outlines of lovely temples, where still endured some of the massive columns. The rectangular serenity of these ancient buildings, especially the Temple of Apollo, offered a magical contrast against the saturnine and frowning precipices under which they had been built. The amphitheatre built into a hollow on the hillside above the temples looked very beautiful and complete in the afternoon sunlight. Here, and amongst the Temples of Marathon and Salamis we wandered, bewildered by our lack of knowledge, and the austerity and massiveness of the architecture that surrounded us. It was indeed difficult to reconcile it all with the hand of man.

We walked the sacred path of Apollo, where, stopping to wonder at the scene and bemused by the beautiful warmth of the sun which fell full on the hillside, we saw high above us several eagles, sailing with great outspread wings outlined in the clear blue sky. How fitting they seemed, like ancient guardians of the place. Some other birds, flitting about the hillside kept uttering a song, not unlike a wood warbler's, and I wondered if they were wall creepers. Such birds as chaffinches, chiffchaffs and tits, which were also there, were quite out of place in such revered and majestic surroundings. Do the ghosts of such birds, as the ghosts of men must, wander still among these places, where people of an ancient era had their homes?

13.1.46 Continuing with our visit to Delphi, I ought to mention that we went into the museum there, chaperoned by a delightful old Greek with a great moustache, who, in his uniform and peak camp, could easily have been taken for one of the keepers at the Zoo. Unfortunately, he had no English, as they say, and as we had no Greek things were a trifle difficult. Then he said – '*Parlez-vous français, monsieur?*' And I said, '*Un très peu, monsieur.*' Whereupon he immediately called up a friend to the rescue, who said he spoke French '*Un peu*', and proceeded to gabble it off like nobody's business. However, we all got on fine, and it was almost with reverence that the old boy showed us the visitors' book. He took obvious pleasure in pointing out that Ronald and Joan Scobie had signed the book just recently and he showed us the names. He requested us to sign, which we did as ceremoniously as possible!

The museum was rather bare, for many of its priceless contents had been taken away and buried when the German invasion started. However, there were still items of great beauty and interest there – for example, the statue of the Dancing Girls, and the Phoenix, and a peculiar font-like piece of stone work, on which the sacrifices to Minerva were apparently made. There were all kinds of delightful bronze works there; such things as the women used to manicure their hands in those days, tiny jars, swords, and other relics. The Curator produced a book in which was an excellent reproduction of Delphi, based on the ruins, and he was able to show us where some of these original statues were, both in the book and on the ground. He helped one to get a better mental picture altogether. There was, too, in the building an excellent reproduction of the entrance to one of the temples, and that again helped to complete in your mind what you saw in the present day.

Time was against us, however, and where we would have liked to dawdle we had to rush. Before we set off home though I had to go to Delphi itself and enquire of an hotel there whether they had rooms for Frost, who might be spending part of his honeymoon there.

The weather since our visit has been as perfect as ever. Most afternoons I have taken a stroll along the Delphi road, there to be met by a regular cavalcade of Greeks with their donkeys and ponies heavily laden with firewood. The load consists of two bundles, very evenly balanced and securely tied with rope, which are suspended on each side on projections of the wooden saddle put there for this purpose. Hence, one often sees the comic picture of some poor little donkey coming down the road with its head seeming to protrude from a mass of greenery. The daily trek, which is a long one, must run into hundreds of donkey loads a day, and at this rate each succeeding generation is going to have a longer walk for its firewood. But as Sam said – 'We'll have to get some of this atom stuff!'

This afternoon it was so warm I took my jerkin and a book and clambered up among the olive groves, there to read in pleasant sunshine and pastoral peace. Eventually I found a suitable rock for a back rest, and, placing my jerkin on the ground, proceeded to settle myself. In this delightful setting I started to read about William Cobbett. The only sounds that assailed me were the mellow notes of sheep bells, an occasional shout from the shepherd at an erring sheep, the curious grunting noises of some nearby ravens, a chiffchaff or two, and perhaps the brief piping notes of finches flying overhead. I wonder what old Cobbett would have thought of it all? He would probably have been happier on his horse so that he could get a better view of the agriculture of the country. Perhaps, studying the rocky hillside, he would not have been surprised at the poverty of the villagers. It would be interesting to know how these workers of the land fit into his definition of freedom. 'Freedom', he wrote, 'means – and it means nothing else – the full and quiet enjoyment of your own property. If you have not this, if this be not secured to you, you may call yourselves what you will, but you are slaves.' But the sun and drowsy sounds about me caused the book to slip out of my hands and, Cobbett or no Cobbett, I stretched out under that rock and went fast asleep.

21.1.46   The last four days have passed very rapidly. On the 17th I had a message from Peter to say that Denis would not arrive till the 18th after all, and this made me quite furious, and I told him just what I thought of 2 N.F., and the way they had haggled over everything we had asked for. My view is that just now we are the only outside commitment the battalion has, and as such should get priority. However, it wasn't Peter's fault, and I knew it! Whether my fury secreted some curious glandular mixtures into my blood, I don't know, but I felt rotten for several hours afterwards and couldn't eat any lunch. Anyhow, Denis duly arrived at midday on Friday, and for two days we were very much occupied in the hand-over of Peter's Corner. On Sunday Mervyn Frost returned from Athens and handed over the Canteen Fund, etc., and today ought to see the thing complete. We have had heavy traffic both in high ranking officers and other ranks this weekend, which was most timely, for it gave Denis a good picture of the running of the place. On the 19th we had Gen. Callander, G.O.C. 4 Division, and last night Gen. O'Dair, D.S.O. & M.C. & bar, and the CRA 4 Division, also five other officers, and on top of that nearly 200 other ranks, mostly reinforcements, youths

of nineteen or so who had been in the Army just about six months. It was a
tremendous business fitting all this crowd in, and the General and C.R.A.
had to sleep in the mess after dinner. However, he was all smiles this
morning, shook hands and said he was very grateful for all we had done.
Many of the men had no blankets, and we had only enough to let them
have one each. I felt awfully sorry for these fellows coming out here like
this when the war is over, but I suppose it will do them no harm. It amazed
me to see them, after a long weary bumpy ride in the back of a three-
tonner, lying down on the matting in the corridor, trying to write a letter
home – 'Hey Bill, how do you spell the Acropolis?', and similar questions
kept being flung about the building, and the arguments and swearing that
ensued quite amazed me. They did go to sleep eventually.

So this morning, to the sound of the singing Greek girl employees, the
place is to have its much needed daily clean out, and now that all these
persons have departed on their way we feel we can breathe again, and
altogether our spirits are much more buoyant. But we have another large
party tonight. I might be returning to Khalkis tomorrow if the hand-over is
complete, but I think it's more likely to be Wednesday.

24.1.46   It was with no real regret that I came to leave Levádhia on
            Tuesday. The place has a certain dreary and morbid atmos-
phere, especially in bleak weather, and the asylum building, with its dark
and austere rooms, was never conducive to an exuberant spirit. I wonder
now if really I have travelled that grim and barren road from Levádhia to
Thebes for the last time? The bitter wind and the rain made it more
unfriendly than ever, a long rough trail by marsh and mountain, and
Thebes at the end of it has nothing very worthy or homely to offer. No, I
was glad to descend the mountain road that brings you to Khalkis by the
sea. How clean and fresh was its appearance compared with Levádhia. It
was with gratitude that I found my old room at the Palleria reserved for
me, and it wasn't long before I was installed, with the room laid out much
as it was before I left it. Unfortunately, there wasn't any mail waiting for
me as I had hoped.

The following morning was heralded by a conference concerning our
forthcoming move to Salonika. It dealt mainly with the advance party
which was to leave by 6th February. Major Cox-Walker, my first company
commander in the Regiment, who has recently joined the battalion, was
detailed in his capacity as acting second-in-command to accompany the
party. It was not mentioned whether officers of my group would go to
Salonika or not, but I imagine it is unlikely as we may be leaving the
country at the end of February.

To my great joy I found two letters from Dulcie awaiting me in my office, and these I covetously placed in my pocket until I should get a quiet moment to read them. But the ways of life are unfathomable, and when I did open them I was not prepared for the shock and sad disappointment they contained. For Dulcie had had a miscarriage, and had written these letters in bed at St. Michaels.* Toni, about whom I had heard the first joyous news in that little garden on that beautiful 14th December, was not to be born after all. The possibility of such a happening had never entered my mind, for it seemed so remote that Dulcie, so strong and energetic, so confident, should be assailed by such a sad thing. At first I could not grasp the truth of it, but when at last the full realisation came, the sad blow was softened greatly by the comforting knowledge that Dulcie herself had come through her unexpected and unhappy experience very well. It is only natural to try and put a cause for her great misfortune, for she had no shock or fall. Dulcie offers the theory that it is a combination of strain, anxiety, separation, and poor diet. Be it as it may, the sad business has occurred, and pray God that the cause is some special combination of circumstances and not something fundamental that might cause a similar occurrence if and when we try again to have Toni. The tension and strain of these war years after the birth of Nicolas, during which she had the sole responsibility of his upbringing, when bombs and rockets were falling, and the almost nightly symphony of sirens and anti-aircraft guns, must have taxed her nerves to a high pitch. This, coupled no doubt with my absence on the Italian front, and all the hardships, food scarcities and vicissitudes of Britain at war, made her of necessity a buffer between all the evil of that time and little Nicolas. She alone was there to deflect all these harmful and hateful things from him. Our long and unnatural separation was ended for a brief spell last October – but even that was followed by another, and inevitably grim parting. Is it really surprising that nature has refused us this blessing of a second child? For nature demands a natural balanced and wholesome life, and these last tragic years have been anything but that.

27.1.46   The dreary haunting wintry weather continues, and today there
            is snow on the near peaks. It is unusual to get such a spell with
no sun at all in Greece. With the battalion in a state of flux, a somewhat unstable and depressing atmosphere is setting in. Many officers are leaving on various postings, and the new faces that come in their stead only serve to increase one's restlessness. The sense of disintegration therefore

---

*Parents' home.

is acute, and I am daily more inclined to feel – 'Well, I shall soon be out of it too.' Luckily I have plenty to do or else I would go nuts. This is especially important after Dulcie's misfortune, which makes me want to get home more quickly than ever. This 'wishing away' of precious time is a dreadful reflection on the state of the world today, and I pray that the lot of future generations will never be such that men and women are not content to live in the present.

30.1.46   How good to wake up feeling happy, well, and full of energy.

The early morning noises from the fishermen, the street boys selling cigarettes, indicated before I was up that the weather had changed. That maniacal howling at my window had ceased at last. Tranquility reigned amongst the elements. I rose and, looking out of my window, saw that the woolly clouds were lifting and parting, to reveal once more that halcyon sky. The rays of the early morning sun were already lighting up the snow-covered mountains, and the dark sea was turning gradually into that miraculous blue. Nature had ceased overnight to be malign, her claws were drawn in and she was purring and all benevolent. How could my spirits feel anything but light and gay? I felt almost as though I had climbed out of a dark and gloomy valley, filled with ghostly trees that sighed and bent and beckoned warningly at me, and reached the summit of some high ridge where all was light, and my vision unimpeded by menacing mountains. here at last was the vista I wanted to see. Here was the promised land, and all's right with the world!

And in this mood I sauntered gaily to my breakfast of porridge, egg and bacon, toast and marmalade. it was indeed a land flowing with milk and honey. The 30th January. Another day nearer my release. My spirits welled up, and mentally I was almost home. Was this release fever? Even the barracks in the sunshine seemed pleasant, with the chiffchaffs in the trees, and wagtails dashing here and there. As I walked from one block to another I could feel the warmth of the sun being absorbed by my khaki, producing that delicate dreamlike smell of bracken and bluebells!

The feeling that I had come out of a dark valley increased hourly, and inwardly I prayed that it was so for mankind all over the world, who surely have been in the valley of despair for over six years. Perhaps it was the goodness of God, through the benevolence of nature that had made me sense a turning point.

4.2.46   The new month ushering in, as it does in these southern climes, the first gay promises of spring, brings me a new lease of life. And on this, my seventh wedding anniversary, and the sixth consecutive one spent apart from Dulcie, the gentle zephyr of promised release and reunion bring a warmth of mood that has not been mine for some time. God willing, the new month may see at least the beginning of the release of that mental stress occasioned by our enforced separation, as well as the long delayed start of my physical release from the Army.

Release and reunion – those two words have been the light that has lit up the haunted darkness of these past years. They have been the hope and strength of millions of men and women for six long years, the thought of their realization the very bedrock of their morale. Without them all would have been despair. To future generations – if peace be theirs, and God grant that it is – this grim separation, this long enforcement from home and country, this nightmare movement of populations, homeless, workless, foodless, will perhaps be hard to comprehend. Has ever the fundamental rootedness of human nature been so strained in history before? I doubt it. The whole fabric of civilization was, to all intents and purposes, in a hellish crucible. The moral disintegration that has resulted will affect, even though they may not be aware of it, those future generations of which I speak. And we are, at the time of writing, a long way from being out of that crucible, though, thank God, the hell heat is not quite so great. For nearly all of us, with our tender roots, have somehow or other to reconstruct and renew on this soil of the modern world, a life with a lasting stable morality.

Since I last wrote we have had another spell of that moaning grey wind from the north, and with it this time a lot of rain. But it soon cleared and once more we are enjoying these lovely spring days when sea and sky are so richly blue that they look like picture postcard presentations. I had an enjoyable walk yesterday with Peter Green, who is a keen botanist. I took him down the lane where I used to take the company for marches last year. Great tits were singing merrily in the olives, and chaffinches and chiffchaffs were numerous.

7.2.46   The last three days, whilst I have been acting, acting, acting
           C.O., in the absence of Hugh Wilkin, have nipped along nicely. On Tuesday afternoon I managed a short walk with Peter and Philip on the mainland, and in the hot sunshine we had a happy time looking at birds. Khalkis on a sunny day never fails to impress the mind scenically, and as we topped the brow of the hill and looked down on the harbour with its delightful caiques and fishing boats, and the promenade bedecked with those white and not unattractive houses, and beyond the mountains, we just had to stop and admire it all.

Last night, after dinner, we sat around the fire talking about U.N.O., the American loan, the new rationing in Britain, and, of course, Russia was a subject all by itself. They have recently declared that the presence of

British troops in Greece was a menace to world peace, and, of course, U.N.O. have been in a pretty turmoil, although Bevin stood his ground well. This morning it seems that the Russians have dropped their demand for the withdrawal of British troops from Greece, and the matter is now closed. I wonder? And I wonder what they will hatch next? It was something to know, anyway, that it was only Russia who thought we were imperilling the peace, and as long as the Greek Communists are unable to carry out Moscow instructions doubtless they will continue to think of us as a menace.

14.2.46   The last few days have gone so quickly that I am unable to remember the events of each day. The C.O.'s return from Italy, after a stay which produced a crop of rumours and a certain amount of gossip, coupled with the proposed visit of the G.O.C. 13 Division, has caused the usual military stir that is inevitable on such occasions. The window dressing, the scurrying, the cleaning, the menu in the mess, the sleeping arrangements, and all the other hullabaloo that goes on prior to a General Officer's visit has to be seen to be believed. A small crisis has arisen in the mess regarding the latest wish of the C.O. He wants the vegetables served by waiters, rather than having them more or less 'dog-fashion' all on the plate. Of course, there aren't enough dishes to go round, but the C.O. insists that the *top* table is served thus, even if the rest get a dog-dinner! Naturally, Philip and John hold up their hands in horror at such a suggestion, and haunting agonising memories of Pylewell came twisting through their minds. To differentiate in the Army is to separate, especially in the mess, and most of us see in this the beginning of another separation. Yes, shades of Pylewell are beginning to creep back again. I almost said unobtrusively but, no, it is almost blatant.

The General was to have arrived today but the weather decided otherwise. Last night a bitter wind sprang up from the north that howled and thundered at the windows all night long. In the early morning light I could see big blobs of snow tearing into the glass. It was amazingly sudden and I noticed that the little hillock opposite was sprinkled with snow. It was bitterly cold walking to breakfast and the pavements were slippery with watery snow. The hills were invisible. Later in the morning the clouds lifted somewhat to reveal the white slopes, but the wind and snow persisted. It wasn't surprising, therefore, to hear that the G.O.C. had postponed his visit for a week. You could almost hear the general sigh of relief and puckered brows became all smiling again in no time. The mess is particularly crowded at the moment, there being nearly forty officers present. In fact, hardly a day passes without some new face appearing.

Peter Gorst is coming back from C company to take over from me prior
to the move to Salonika, and today I handed over the P.R.I. to Hugh,
for which relief much thanks. We have had confirmation that 25 group
officers will not go to Salonika, and my heart is very warm at the thought
of release and reunion with my dear Dulcie and son Nicolas. Perhaps in
about a fortnight I shall be about to start that journey that will take me
back to their sweet company. But nothing is certain in this hard world,
with its troubled politics, its hungry peoples, and its homeless masses. The
word 'famine' is on everyone's lips these days – a reality to millions and a
threat to many more. It is in such times, when the mind is seared with
unrest, when children are a big responsibility, that husbands and wives
need each other's comfort. I pray God, then, for our speedy reunion.

17.2.46   Today has been indescribably beautiful. This morning was
            perhaps one of the loveliest I have experienced in Greece. The
wind died in the night and the sky cleared. The chugging of the fishing
boats in the early morning gave full measure of it. The whole earth was
glittering with the light of the sun on the snow and the sea. The glory of
the morning was enhanced by the fact that the snow was down to the sea.
George and I went to the bridge to view the scene from there. The blue
glittering sea, on which rested like a 'painted ship' a red fishing boat, took
the eye to the snow-clad mountains, and then inevitably your gaze rested
on the wonder of Dhirfir, the very incarnation of stillness, of immeasurable serenity. The sky seemed to hold the essence of both sea and snow,
the turquoise blue fading imperceptibly into a white light. No wonder the
Greeks thought the gods lived in the mountains. Today, rearing up out of
the sea, in shadowed drapery, their white sweeping outlines gave the
aspect of some natural yet magical cathedrals.

Happily then did I get up, singing my way through my shave, full of the
thoughts of release and reunion, and the joy of the day. Being Sunday
nothing was on at the barracks, and after signing a few things I made my
way with stick and binoculars along the coast of the island to a lighthouse
that stands on a rocky promontory. Birds were everywhere to be seen;
black redstarts, wagtails, siskins, larks, gulls, meadow pipits, linnets,
chaffinches, and many others. I had a superb view of the siskins feeding in
a flock, male and female, and the contrast was clear to see.

20.2.46   There has been great activity since I last wrote, and on my own
            account joyous activity at that. When George and I went to see
the C.O. about leaving the battalion on the 26th February, he said he had
just received information that the move of the battalion had been put
forward a week. They were now to leave on the 27th February, and

embark on the 28th, so he could do nothing but accede to our request. And so mercifully we leave the battalion just when it gets itself involved in a complicated move to a place that is even further away from home!

Since the C.O.'s conference on the 19th, all normal routine has ceased and packing is the order of the day, an occupation, the theme of which suits me well just now. I hope to have divested myself of D company by the end of the week, and Peter is well ahead with the take-over. It was a happy moment when my clerk handed me papers appertaining to my release, the first that I have seen. I have just come away from my final medical examination; the doc. had a thorough do and pronounced me quite fit, for which many thanks. My mind is now turned towards home and the future, and concentration on Army matters is diminishing daily. I have now five full days left with the battalion, and it's difficult to be too concerned about its future welfare!

Tommy Prior left today for Salonika to take over the officers' shop. Tom, as Bobby says, is the salt of the earth, and nothing better befits his solid, cheerful, genuine and friendly character. Tom has the independent spirit of a Wat Tyler, and he has a love of home and the land and its care that would warm the heart of old Cobbett. After being so long together, it was sad to say goodbye. But it was only goodbye from the point of view of our Army careers; already we have planned to keep up correspondence and arrange to meet in England later.

24.2.46   My last weekend in Khalkis, and with the battalion, has come and gone quickly and quietly. After a cold windy day yesterday, the weather made a somewhat surprising change, and today I could not have wished for better. Sunny, clear, fresh, and a blue shimmering sea, it was the kind of day that, to me, typifies Greece. After a practice pack in the morning, I went to the barracks to give in my library books and water bottle, and get my pass for Athens. Peter was deeply engrossed in the last minute details of the move, and as I talked to him about it I felt a glorious detachment from it all. I cannot say how thankful I am to be leaving the Army, with its forced community life, its petty regulations, its everlasting masculinity, and, above all, its unrootedness and lack of purpose. How many hundreds of years will it be before the world is rid of these parasitic organisations, which bleed the wealth of mankind because of his political undevelopment – in short, because of fear.

Thus ends my notes whilst with the 2nd battalion. It has been a long sojourn since the 8th February 1941 at Pylewell, when I first joined them. It has been a long chapter in my life but I cannot say that I have any regrets at its closing.

27.2.46   Everything comes to pass and hence accordingly here I am,
           seated at my desk in room 112 of the King George, Athens,
writing up my old notes. The passing of time has always been a difficult
thing to understand; events come and go, and you can't have them back
again – not that you always want to! But sometimes you like to recount
them in your mind so that you can either cherish the more, some particular
memory, or gloat over an incident which was particularly distasteful or
grim, which you know, gladly, can't return. Hence this diary – any diary?
Scenes, incidents, and men, come and go, and the impressions go on until
death. Some remain firmly rooted, always at hand when required, an
accumulation of the sub-conscious in cold storage, and on call for any
particular moment. Others, and some fleeting and beautiful, never take a
firm hold in the mind, and if we are not careful are lost for ever, like small
earth passing through a sieve. So these 'little things' pass through the
mind and, generally speaking, it is often the small earth that we want to
keep, for out of it springs the best nourishment. I wonder what is the
determining factor in this mental selection; I expect the psychologists
would say that you remember a thing because you want to, and vice versa.

To harp back to these last three days. Monday, my last day with the
battalion, saw me the proud possessor of my Release Book, and various
movement orders and certificates appertaining thereto. I felt as though I
was holding the handle of the door that leads back to civilian life. But I
still had to open it and pass through, with my neat bundle of new civilian
clothes! But to be holding the handle was something, and I shall keep hold
of it now until I've opened it and closed it on the other side.

In the barracks I had my last 'cup of char and a wad' in D company
office with Peter, and then I strolled round to the M.T. with George to fix
details for the Utility that was to take us to Athens the following day. This
done, I began a long series of goodbyes, wandering from one barrack to
another. I covered as many people as I could – people who knew me, that
is – for the new reinforcements make up a big proportion of the battalion
now. My own company came in for special attention, of course, but I
could not miss such people as R.Q.M.S. Cook, who had been my C.S.M.
at Salerno, where he did a magnificent job, and C.S.M. Watson, who had
been one of my platoon sergeants at this same seaside place! Nearly all
who had been through Italy have gone in one way or another, and, unfortunately, the company was very spread with Levádhia still going strong,
and the advance party at Salonika, and various other people detached on
garrison duties. My task finished, I went back to the hotel, taking, I
suppose, at the barrack gate, the last 'Present' from a 2 N.F. soldier.

The biggest ordeal of the day came with the evening – drinks, the last dinner (but no speeches, thank God), more drinks (much more, in fact, and my stomach revolted accordingly!), and finally 'poker dice' with the C.O., Hugh, Dudley, David, Bill, Bob, George. A great strain and a miserable but, I suppose, inevitable way of finishing up one's life in a battalion. When goodbyes come along people always ply you with too many drinks, but the worst of it was being cornered with the regular element, so preventing us having a few last words with the 'likes of ourselves'. God, how thankful I was to finish the handshaking, and all the usual chitchat that goes with it; thankful, indeed, to get into the fresh air and totter alcoholically to bed. Glorious little bed, what a homely and private place you are with your warm blankets and pillow to shroud and protect one from all the superficialities that men display before you. I opened my French windows wide and the cool night air, straight off the channel, poured into my room to alleviate my drink-filled body. It was a happy moment. It was all over at last. The occasion that I had dreaded had come and gone.

On the 26th George and I were up early. We both felt somewhat heavy and slow in our mental reactions – the result of the previous night's drinking, but this wore off as the day proceeded, at least so it was with me. It was a perfect morning and it wasn't long before the night sky had turned through various phases into that beautiful blue. Not a cloud was there to mar it. We breakfasted at 0700 hours, having planned to avoid the mess again, and Cpl. Price did us proud as ever. I wonder how much of my well-being in the Army since 1st January '44 has been due to Price? A great deal, I have no doubt. His cooking, in and out of action, has always been first-class, and must have bolstered the morale of many of us.

We said goodbye and then made ready to set off from the Palleria; many, still in pyjamas, had got up to see us off. John Worthington, Peter Green, Bobby Gore, Peter Gorst, David Dumbreck, all of whom had not got a look-in last night, were there. The kit was loaded, there was a last look round, and then goodbyes and hand-waving from the Utility. We were off at last – finally and irrevocably – we hoped!

It was then about 0730 hours, and as we crossed Khalkis bridge for the last time the sun was well up and it was, I could see, going to be one of those specially beautiful Greek days – days of white and blue. As we climbed the hill we looked down and took our last view of mist-covered Khalkis, the steely placid sea that separates the mainland from the island, the serried ridges that mounted in a crescendo to the glory of Dhirfir, whose steep and southeastern slopes were lit by the rising sun. It was a memorable scene, and one I shall always be glad to have seen. Sandy

Fraser, when he first came over the pass and looked down upon it, said – 'I saw poetry below me', which might sound far-fetched but it just about hits the nail on the head.

So we climbed up the twisting road that might have been a giant's whip lying across the mountain side. All around us were the lovely pines and the fresh green after the snow, looking very beautiful in the early light. We passed the little white church, then a shepherd in his rough cloak watching his sheep and goats. So, topping the ridge, Khalkis and its poetical setting were lost to view for good; and we set along the bumpy road to Thebes.

5.3.46   What a really incredible life this is – I mean that you can never take anything for granted – nothing is certain, always you have to plan, or should plan for contingencies. You would think that life would let off pretty lightly a chap who was going on Release – but no, it makes no difference where you are or what you are doing, even who you are – the 'spoke in the wheel' is always about! So it has been with me these last few days.

I arrived in Athens feeling as fit as a fiddle, almost unassailably fit so it seemed to me, in my stupidity. But my spoke soon put in an appearance in my wheel. It was the morning after Jimmy had come to dinner, and a very quiet and orderly dinner it was too. I was off drink after my 'end of term' experience and consequently felt in no mood for suchlike entertainment. So we sat down and chatted, and all I consumed was two small glasses of vermouth. I felt that Jimmy was probably bored and would have liked a visit to the Frolics, but rather than that I risked his boredom. However, the next morning showed what can happen if you spend an evening too quietly!

It all started in the early hours of the 3rd, which was Sunday. 'It' was an extraordinary pain in my stomach and up at the ribward end. My first thought, of course, was indigestion, and cursing I realised I had no soda mints with me. Then 'it' put the screw on and literally I felt as thought I had been shot through the stomach. Shooting pains kept coming and going as I lay sweating and groaning and wondering what the hell was up. Every move I made caused further pain, and yet the urge, as one lay still, was to move to get away from the pain. George said, 'Shall I get the doctor?' – and, of course, with delayed Release looming up again, I said, 'No, I'm sure it's only indigestion.' Anyway, George went to the M.I. Room and got some sulphur mixture, which I took rapidly, but which had no effect at first. Later in the morning George gave me another dose, after which I fell into a sleep – a blessed sleep, and when I woke up I knew at once that the pain, or most of it, had gone. The pain, the lack of sleep, the sweating, and missing two meals made me feel very weak indeed, but I got up for a few hours later on. Of course, I tried my hardest to think what the cause of it could have been, but really I cannot say. The orange I had after dinner was a bit soft and bruised – could it have been that mixed with vermouth? It may have just been some form of food poisoning. I don't know, but it was most strange that only I was affected. The night of the 3/4 was disturbed and feverish. Disturbed it was by Greek festivities that went on throughout the night. Then, too, I seem to have been left with a 'throat'. Was this a legacy of my stomach, or purely coincidence? Again, hooting taxis began to induce in me a real hatred of Athens. It seemed to cast an ugly spell on me. When I was on LIAP I was ill both going and coming back to Athens, also last February when we were billetted here. It all linked up in my unsettled brain.

Today my aches and pains seem to have gone; my throat is still there and I have no taste for a pipe, but in comparison with yesterday it has gone. The most annoying aspect of this little 'contretemps' is the weakness it has left me. I feel rather as though I have been rinsed out, and a short walk to L.F.G. this morning made me sweat. It really does perplex me as to what I have had, and I wonder if it could be some sort of gastric fever. There is not much time left to get really fit again, for we leave here on the 7th, probably embarking on the 8th. All I ask is to be fit when I arrive home.

Perhaps fate let this incident happen to bring home to me the fact that my Release and reunion with Dulcie does not mean that life from now on will be just one happy series of events. You can't turn life off suddenly like a 'To be continued' film series.

Demobilisation

13.3.46 Over a week since I last wrote, and what a lot of good things have happened since then. No longer does the mad cacophony of Athens reach my ears, no longer is the Acropolis my daily view – indeed, I am sitting down to write this under the shadow of Vesuvius in Lammie Camp, which is situated in the orchards that thrive on the volcanic soil. But I mustn't get ahead of myself, temptation that it is, and accordingly I am flashbacking to a week ago today.

Last Wednesday was our last whole day at the King George, and as such was to be relished, for the 'metro-hotel' atmosphere, a warm centrally-heated stuffy sort of atmosphere, was rapidly depriving me of all energy, and, looking back, was, I am certain, largely responsible for my feeling so ill there. Continuous noise must surely have a very lowering effect, for the nervous system must always be hard at work resisting its ugly invasion. I wonder by how much noise tends to reduce the span of modern man's life? Someone is pretty well bound to have worked it out, but I haven't heard of an anti-noise society. It would never have any success in Athens.

Roy came to see us. He was having his stomach pains again and was seeing the doctor the following day. It seemed almost certain that he would not be able to travel home with us. He seemed very reconciled, but I think worried inwardly. He is very concerned, and quite rightly, to get put right before leaving the Army. We did a little shopping together, but the ant-like pavements and the traffic only served to boil up my hate for the crowded metropolis, and I lost all interest in shopping. I was still far from being A.1, and suffered from headaches and unnatural sweating at the slightest exertion.

In the afternoon we went to Zappion Gardens, that sylvan oasis in a barren city. Here we watched the stately peacocks (I wish Nicolas could

262

have seen them in their royal plumage), and, most interesting of all, what I think was a Bewick's swan, with black and yellow knobless beak. He was very slim and elegant, and somehow out of place in a park pond.

Gill had asked us to dine with him at the Club but we put him off and I said goodbye over the 'phone, asking him to call at 'Benallan' if he was down that way at all. I also said goodbye to Roy, but somehow I feel we shall see each other again. On Thursday I woke feeling very rotten, and packing my kit was an ordeal. I do so wonder what the real cause is of this sort of migraine that had afflicted me, but, at any rate, at 1000 hours we left for the 35 Reception Camp. There we learnt we were to sail for Naples the following day, and after lunch I assisted in collecting money for changing into lire. I collected over 5,000,000 drachmas! By tea-time I was feeling much better for some incredible reason, perhaps the quiet and airiness after the King George. After tea came 'one of those things' – the sailing had been postponed till the 9th! We cursed and moaned, of course, but there it was anyway. I rationalised by saying to myself that I ought to be much better by the 9th.

The next morning found me feeling much more like my old self, and I hoped that at last I had thrown off my 'Athensphobia'. Good news followed after breakfast; we were embarking that day after all. I hurriedly wrote a note to Dulcie giving her the situation, packed my kit and had an early lunch. Then followed one of those seemingly inevitable delays while we waited, all impatiently, in the trucks to take us to the boat. Finally we moved off and passed the Acropolis, and raced down the Leofros Surgron for (I hoped) the last time. At Piraeus we got into landing craft, which took us and our baggage to the *Ocean Vigour*, a converted cargo boat. We just managed to get aboard before a heavy fall of rain.

Our quarters were like ordinary troop decks. The holds had been converted for this purpose, and the three-tier beds gave the place a sort of air-raid-shelter look. I got a top bed for myself in case of a rough passage. Our mess deck was the ordinary troop mess deck, long tables and benches over which hung the stale smell of swill, not a very appetising plan, which was lucky as our food throughout proved to be of the very plain variety – bully, spam, baked beans, bread, margarine, bacon, and tea and suchlike, and only three meals a day, which made us hungry at times. However, one can put up with such inconvenience when one is going home; it's in the reverse direction that it's so painful. We were off Greek soil, so damn the crowded accommodation and poor food, was how we felt; it was a stage nearer dear old Blighty. We were to sail the following morning, so it wasn't long before we settled ourselves down to sleep the night in harbour – hoping like hell that the weather would improve.

The new ship atmosphere provided a fitful but reasonable night's sleep. I dreamt a lot, three times of Dulcie, who seemed to get getting involved in some sort of road accident each time – what the psychological explanation of this was I do not know, except my intense desire to get to her after all this time. The air was not too thick but a light near my bunk that remained on all night was a nuisance. Changing on top of a three-tier bed with the metal deck just above your head needed some skill and a sort of striptease art. We had two blankets provided – smelly ones too – but, using my valise as a base, I made myself warm enough. It was all rather limited and mucky – the more the enjoyment of a double bed at home!

I was up at 6.00 a.m. and got myself some hot water from the galley. It was still dark so I shaved below. After the previous night the deck looked pretty awry with cigarette ends, kit, paper, and what-have-you, all over the place. However, this was all put right in time for the ship's inspection at ten o'clock – thank goodness. It was a beautiful morning, the sun coming up over a mist-covered Athens. The Imittos mountains were flecked with those specks of translucent cloud that moved like so many wreaths from ridge to ridge. Gulls circled everywhere, filling the air with their cries, and making snowflake patterns as they flew around some morsel that had been thrown overboard. Mostly they were herring gulls and black-headed. Then came the inspection and hanging around waiting to sail, watching the tug boats, and, generally speaking, itching to get going. Finally we moved out of the inner harbour, but stopped again outside and sent a man back to hospital – poor chap.

As I stood and gazed upon the barrenness of the grey mountains, that seem so grim and lifeless, so inhospitable, I could not restrain a sigh of relief that I was leaving Greece. Give me the clouds and rains and green fields that have nurtured me all these years. It seemed to me incredible that Athens should have risen up in this rocky wilderness. I thought of the summer sun that would soon be pounding its rays down upon this civic area.

At last, about 11.00 a.m., we steamed away into a glorious smooth blue sea, and we could just discern the Acropolis, and the Hill of Likavitos through the hazy mist. Thus ended fifteen months in the land of Greece. The gulls came with us.

We reached the southern tip of the Peloponnese and turned westward that night. We had a glorious view of the new moon as we steamed between Cape Malea and Matapan and the island of Keritha, the sea smooth and dappled with moonlight, the rocky coast and hills clearly outlined against the light sky. The moon and the stars are lovely to see through the masts and rigging of a ship, which seem to add to their remoteness, making you feel as though you are sailing through space.

The next morning I got up feeling well and happy. It was blowing hard outside when I went for my water but the sea was calm; presumably we were in the Straits. I shaved quickly so as not to miss anything. There were heavy clouds over Sicily and the toe of Italy, but most of the lovely snow-covered slopes of Etna were visible, and a very lovely sight it was in the rising sun. The 'toe' looked very rugged and precipitous and in places the ridges were topped by peculiar minaret-like rock formations. Swirling clouds, however, obscured most of the view. As we progressed north through the Straits Messina came into view and opposite on the mainland, Reggio. The slopes above Messina had a green and wooded appearance, which was attractive, but for all that I was heartily glad I was passing by.

By lunchtime we came into view of the volcanic island of Stromboli, with its castle-like nob on its east side. Stromboli is beautifully symmetrical and I believe this pyramidal shape is usual in volcanoes. We could see one place on the island – I suppose Stromboli itself? Lots of gulls followed us all day, herring and black-headed mostly, and the calls of the former brought into my mind pictures of Seaford Head in the nesting season. It was amazing to see how they stretched their necks and lifted their heads to make these guttural and long sounding calls on the wing. It made them go all out of shape.

So, feeling sunburnt and well, thankful for such a smooth voyage and for the change of air after Athens, I prepared myself for the last night aboard. The next morning, yesterday, we were up about 5.30 a.m., washing, shaving, packing our kit, excited as schoolboys going on holiday. We breakfasted at 0600 hours (very lightly, I might add!) and then began to look around us in the Bay of Naples. There was a lot of early morning mist and cloud, and not much was visible. But we could see Capri and Vesuvius, and some of those large pillared buildings that seem to dominate Naples. Little fishing boats came up to have a look at us, and then a pilot came aboard. Finally, after much waiting and hooting, we were taken into the harbour itself and cunningly moored by some little tugs.

Finally, after ten o'clock, we got the order to disembark, which we did gladly, walking to some vehicles which were to take us to this transit camp. There was the usual wait in the vehicles, while we waited for everyone to disembark. At long last we were off – in convoy – couldn't go independently, that would be too easy. More form filling and hanging around at the Reception Centre for Release, and eventually we were taken to the mess and shown our tent, which I shared with George.

14.3.46   Lamie Camp is situated just outside Naples – off the Naples and Pompeii autostrada – and set amongst the fruit trees which form part of the highly cultivated belt that lies around Vesuvius, the mother of this fertile countryside. The volcano, plumeless since the great eruption of 1944, stands to the southeast of the camp, dominating the whole countryside. The camp has a pleasant set-up, with gift shops, canteens, cinemas, a theatre, even a circus!; nice roads and good feeding arrangements. The officers sleep in tents, but it is quite comfortable as the floors have been concreted and mats put down, and that makes a lot of difference to a tent. The mess is a large nissen hut, divided into an ante room, a bar, and a dining room, all fitted with fire places, and most gaily painted. The windows even have curtains and the tables in the mess are very attractively set with pottery ware that matches the hut! Italian waitresses (highly decorated!) wait upon us at meals, and generally speaking, after the *Ocean Vigour*, it is really first-class.

It is blossom time just now in Naples and I've never seen any Army camp looking so attractive (I know I'm on Release!). All the huts and tents are camouflaged in a sea of pink and white blossom, while all the ground round about is a mass of stitchwort and, I think, mignonette. Each table in the mess is tastefully decorated with blossom and it is really most pleasant to wander about the 'grounds' listening to the birds, of which many frequent the area – ten species so far identified. In the early morning chaffinches sing a very full song, and yesterday I heard a chiffchaff. I am not suggesting that it's a good thing to be staying here, but merely recording the facts, and as delays seem to be inevitable, it's most gratifying to have such well run places. The food is quite excellent, well cooked, well served, and a well-varied menu. There is no train to Milan today, but another goes tomorrow, for which the camp has 220 vacancies. So it's possible we get off tomorrow.

18.3.46   We left Naples at 1920 hours on the 15th, having been taken down to the station in trucks, and, of course, with at least two hours to spare. Naples central station is not exactly a delectable haunt, with its filth, its beggars, its hawkers, its thieves, and its tragic urchins, but somehow two hours went by, and when the train eventually pulled out we all raised a cheer. Naples has something particularly odious about it; its grime and war population seem to typify all the worst by-products of a large port.

At last we were moving on further north and our hearts warmed at the thought of it. Our carriage unfortunately had wooden seats and our lower regions soon became horribly uncomfortable, even a blanket or similar article failing to temper the resistance of the wood to men's bony buttocks. However, it was a case of needs must when the devil drives, and as we had thirty-six hours ahead of us, we had to adapt ourselves as best we could. There was no light in the carriage when we first got into the train, but little street urchins soon produced these very necessary items in exchange for cigarettes. As well as no bulbs we had a fundamental fault with the gadget, but luckily this was fixed up just before the train pulled out. One of our windows was a wooden affair, and only a small part of the glass of the door remained, the rest being wood, so without light it was a pretty dark carriage. There were four of us, and for the first night George and Bunny slept on the floor (how, I do not know!), and Douglas and I slept on the seats. Sleep is an exaggeration; it was a very restless and uncomfortable affair, with much jockeying for a good position, which, in fact, just wasn't there.

Our route took us all over well known ground – Caserta, Capua, over the Volturno, then of course up to Mignano and Cassino. It was incredible to be passing Porchia and Trocchio in a train – on the old track we used to know as 'Speedway' – and, of course, we hung our faces out to catch a glimpse of all these familiar places. We passed in front of Trocchio, in the cutting where they used to put the dead and the prisoners of war, and on over the Rapido to Cassino where we halted. In typical fashion it was pouring hard, but the light of the moon was percolating through the heavy clouds, giving outlines to hills and buildings.

Suddenly as we stood there in that train amid the gaunt ruins of Cassino I remembered that it was two years ago to the very day that the Monastery and the town had been so severely bombed before the New Zealanders' attack. Now as I looked up at Monastery Hill, Hangman's Hill, and Castle Hill, standing up sombrely above the ruined town, the only sounds that echoed the cataclysmic frenzy of that day two years ago were the croaking of the frogs, and the pitter-patter of the rain. Yet even these sounds only served to emphasise the emptiness, the stillness of the scarred and wounded ground upon which thousands of men had given up their lives in one of this last war's most harrowing ordeals. It seemed right that it should have been raining. The clouds, the half darkness, the rain, seemed all in keeping with this now almost haunted place.

The train moved on and we settled ourselves down as best we could for the rest of the night. Two years ago today – I remember it so well – the planes, the guns, the great columns of smoke, the blasted Monastery, the general noise of battle, the speculations, the stark horror of it all – and now tonight a train rumbles through the same valley, over the same ground, taking us home. The contrast was so startling that I couldn't get it out of my mind. It somehow epitomised the sacrifice of the thousands of men who now lie in some military cemetery. They died that night that we might live – easy words but true – and tonight it felt as though we were travelling over the sacred soil of their graves.

We crossed the Po and reached Milan at about 0800 hours yesterday morning; Douglas and I were put into the Excelsior while Bunny and George had to go to the Assembly Centre. After a lovely breakfast, wash and shave, we, too, reported to the Centre so as to get ourselves on the roll for entrainment to Calais. The clerks seemed to think we should get away on Tuesday morning, but as it turned out only George and Bunny are going tomorrow, and Douglas and I presumably will now not leave till the 20th, which is a darn nuisance.

19.3.46   So we are finally set for the last 600 miles to the sea. We leave tomorrow morning on the 0540 train, which gets us to Calais on the evening of the 21st. By catching the early morning train we see Switzerland in daylight, which is most pleasing, and better still perhaps it means we only spend one night on the train. With any luck I should be in England on the 22nd and home on the 23rd. I hardly dare think about such a joyful state of affairs. So remote and impossible has this final reunion always seemed – is it really possible that I have only three more days as a soldier? – how very wonderful. It does not seem certain to which dispersal unit I will go, but Aldershot and Guildford are the most likely, apparently, with the former the best bet.

I feel perhaps that this will be my last entry before I revert once more (and for ever I hope) to citizen rank. I feel also that some fine prose ought to mark the occasion but really all I can sum up is – 'Thank God that's over.' And when these next three days or so are over and I am back with my beloved Dulcie and little Nicolas – there will, indeed, be much cause for eternal gratitude.

26.3.46   And so indeed this last week finished the 'thing'. The speed of events, the increasing excitement, the ensuing reactions, and finally the realisation of a longed-for reunion, have together had a kind of hypnotic effect on the mind. Everything was done that had to be done, and yet I still don't know quite how it all happened. There was no time to chew the cud of the act of the final demobilisation and reunion. There was not time to relish it. The vortex of reality just didn't allow anything like that – there was no standing still to see Hardy Parkhurst become a civilian – in fact, when I put down my heavy kit at Lewes station to hand my ticket to the ticket collector, a howl went up from the back – 'That's a fine place to put luggage!' Those people just didn't realise (and why should they even care) how important a day the 23rd March was to me. They just didn't realise that the fact of my luggage being in Lewes at all was a personal feat that warranted the utmost satisfaction and gratitude. And when I heard from Dulcie that my tin trunk had arrived as well, I really felt as though some guardian angel had been watching over my kit.

Yes, I have been home now for three days, and yet such has been the mental upheaval of this last fortnight that I am not able completely to grasp the fact. Soon though the mental storm will subside, and in the quiet aftermath of all the days and months and years that started on 13th June 1940 and ended on 23rd March 1946, full realisation of the significance of my being home for good will come to me.

Here behind the breakwater of home I hope to be able calmly to re-orientate myself to the new phase ahead. What has always surprised Dulcie and myself is the way that the gladness of reunion obliterated at a stroke all the misery, all the emptiness of separation, and all the uncertainty that has been ours. And during these three days those war years have faded into the remoteness of nothingness. They have never been. They are hardly, if ever, mentioned. Like a nightmare, it has gone – and for us it was a relatively lucky nightmare. We are together. After three years of separation, we have joined hands over the seas.

And that final long train journey from Milan to Calais, how can I sum it up – how can I describe that thirty-six odd hours that changed from minute to minute, from hour to hour? A long train journey like that is very like life really. Inside the coach you have the hourly business of living, of making yourself as comfortable as possible. Your windows give you an ever-changing scene – you see beauty – you see sordidness – you see gaiety – you see misery, but whatever you see, whatever your reactions, you can take unto yourself none of these things for ever. In the reality of life, in its transience, you pass on wondering at the complexity of it all, and yet amazed at the simplicity of the requirements of happiness. All the towns, all the churches, all the cemeteries, all the terraces, fields, bridges, and roads, the factories, the quarries, the railways, reflect in their heterogeneity between place and place, the work of the people, the eternal fight of the people to provide shelter, food and warmth, against the hard, yet fruitful, old world in which we are placed. It is a strange and exhilarating vista, but unsatisfactory in its incompleteness.

28.3.46   By now the journey has faded in its freshness and excited
          atmosphere. It is difficult to instil any life into the dull record
of facts which will inevitably make up the next few pages. The end has
obliterated the means! There is not much desire to look back now, and
perhaps there will be even less later on; so to proceed is the obvious
course.

First, then, the last restless night at the Excelsior – early to bed – the
trains and the lights – the difficulty of getting to sleep – awake before our
call at 0345 hours – kit to the station – finding our carriage and checking
our luggage – and finally settling down in our comfortable seats. I remember as I walked the platform looking up and seeing the full moon against
the shattered framework of the station roof. It was odd suddenly seeing it
there staring down at the train like that. In the fuss and bother of it all, one
had forgotten such serene things as moons.

Finally we moved out – at last – another lap towards home had started.
It was a beautiful day and the Northern Italian countryside looked very
lovely, but best of all I remember the sunrise over Lake Maggiore – a very
beautiful scene indeed.

Our reception at the last transit camp on the Continent – at Calais – was
most efficient. In a matter of minutes our money had been changed (and
how lovely it was to have a solid half crown in one's pocket again!), we
had been shown our sleeping hut, our kit had been lifted for us, and a
wash, a meal, and a 'blue ticket' for the morning boat made us feel fine.

29.3.46   The next day – a week ago today – was a wet and boisterous
          one. The noise of the wind and rain woke me in my hut long
before it was time to get up. Thoughts of cancelled crossings loomed up in
my mind, but, in fact, nothing of that sort did happen. After breakfast we
assembled with our luggage to be transported to the boat. It was still
raining hard and the sea was rough, but we started punctually at 9.30 a.m.
and were soon ploughing through that sea at a tremendous speed. To
conform with British time we had to put our watches back again one hour,
and this made the fourth alteration since leaving Athens. After embarkation was complete and we had got under way, I went up on deck to take
the air. It was glorious to cope with the spray, albeit somewhat cold for
the windward ear. The weather over England was just the same and the
cliffs were partly obscured by mist and rain. We docked at Dover at about
1000 hours G.M.T. and it was a good feeling to get into the shelter of an
English harbour again.

There were the usual priorities for disembarkation, but it all went very
smoothly and it wasn't long before it was the turn of Class A release to

cross the gangway for English soil once more. How lovely it was to have trustworthy porters at hand to deal with all one's kit. The Customs were most benevolent and understanding, and let me through after my declaration of Dulcie's present, without so much as batting an eyelid. That was a great relief and was the topic of conversation as we settled down into our comfortable railway coach. What comfort and cleanliness, and I remember someone asking, 'What on earth do they want to nationalise the railways for?'

It was good to sit in that wet English station, to stare at English advertisements, to see English porters and people again, and to watch English rain masking the window. But we were most amazed when we were all handed a real ham sandwich in a haversack ration. We were off to the demobilisation centre at Aldershot and travelled via Tunbridge Wells, Redhill and Ash. We were all wondering and hoping about getting home that night but as it turned out it was not meant to be.

It was hard to believe that those wet misty woods and meadows were English – but where else would one see such homely hedges, such lovely farmsteads, such sturdy cattle? We were met at Aldershot and taken to Wellington Barracks, our centre. The first thing we found out was that we would be finished on the 23rd after going to Woking for our clothing. Today we were to be 'processed', by which was meant a lot of tearing out of pages of our release books, much stamping, and pamphlet distribution. In a kind of daze you went from table to table; there was a bang and a crash, the tearing of a page, and off you went to the next one. Then we went to get a month's supply of Naafi, and that was that till morning. We were comfortably esconced in a decent room with a fire, and our beds had sheets! Before dinner I rang through to Dulcie, who was in the middle of bathing Nicolas. Tomorrow I should be home! The rain had stopped and in the evening the air was like wine. I gulped it down.

31.3.46   And finally that long-to-be-remembered day – 23rd March – had arrived. It was a beautiful spring day. I woke early and lay for a long time listening to the glorious melody of an Aldershot blackbird. It was a nostalgic and enthralling sound – a slow measured song – mellow but somehow haunting. No better awakening could I have had on my last morning in an Army bed. Soon after 6.00 a.m. I was up, shaved, and my kit packed. Before breakfast I took a short stroll, for the whole world seemed to be glistening in the heavenly rain-washed air. English spring air and absolutely no doubt about it – even in Aldershot! Then came a hurried breakfast, and afterwards out to the lorries that were to take us to Woking.

What a superb preview of the English countryside we had from that lorry. Lovely beech woods, bracken and gorse commons, little fields enclosed by well-trimmed hedges, clean roads, cottages, the whole an embodiment of living freshness that is the very incarnation of England, and all that England means when you have been away from it for any length of time.

After our arrival at the clothing depot, events moved swiftly. We handed in our baggage, had a number allotted to us, were shown into a large waiting room, and finally called forward to fit ourselves out with a suit of clothes, etc. Choosing civilian clothing after six years in the Army was a bit of a business, especially with such a galaxy of stuff to bewilder you, but at last it was all gathered up and packed for us, and off we went – now, at last, civilians – in another lorry to Woking station. And there was a seething mass of similarly demobilised persons all bent on getting home. Fortunately we had a special train and it was good to sit down in it after the morning's rush, and ruminate a little on the fact that we were really going home – no return tickets this time.

A taxi got me from Waterloo to Victoria, where I had about a three-quarters of an hour's wait before I caught the 12.45 to Lewes. But luggage problems and a snack soon made the time go by and before long I was being hurtled past familiar Sussex scenes and the day still as glorious as ever. Then came Cooksbridge and the tunnel that leads into Lewes station. And then – glory be to God, leaning my head of the window, I saw Dulcie and Nicolas waiting for me on the crowded platform. I waved and Dulcie saw me. A Naval Officer assisted me with my kit, and at last we were all together. I can remember Nicolas's rather shy peck of a kiss. A dream-like taxi took us smoothly and serenely along the familiar bottom road to Kingston and 'Benallan'. I was home! And so was all my kit.

The rest of the day was for me spent in a haze of unreality. I remember the joy of having got all my stuff home, of unpacking, of giving Dulcie and Nicolas their presents, of Dulcie's special reunion cake with seven candles – one for each year of our marriage – and of Nicolas blowing them out at tea-time, and perhaps most, of the comfort and seclusion and wonderful sense of home – fires and a beautiful hot bath – clean clothes, primroses and daffodils and aubretia in the garden – and the joy of the perfect, happy, and quiet evening with Dulcie. Yes, I say with all certainty that this day was one of the happiest of my life.